Windsor in the Great War

by

Derek Hunt

and

Dr. Brigitte Mitchell

Windsor in the Great War

First published 2014
by Windsor Local History Group

Copyright © Derek Hunt and Brigitte Mitchell 2014

A catalogue record for this book is available from the British Library.

ISBN 97809550556796

Designed by Nedula Graphics
Typeset by Cidixith

Printed in the United Kingdom

Contents

List of Illustrations

Every effort has been made to credit sources of all illustrations in this book, if there are any errors please contact the authors so corrections can be made to any future editions.

Acknowledgements for Illustrations

The Authors would like to thank the following for permission to reproduce material in their possession as text illustrations:

1. The Royal Collection, Her Majesty the Queen
2. The Windsor and Eton Express
3. The Slough Observer
4. Reserve Collection of the Household Cavalry archive, Combermere Barracks, Windsor
5. Ken Shepherd Archive
6. Berkshire Yeomanry Museum
7. The Royal Windsor Website
8. Windsor & Royal Borough Museum
9. Lynda Cottrill
11. Bill Habgood
12. Beryl Hedges
13. Derek Hunt
14. Sir Peter Luff
15. Brigitte Mitchell
16. Mary Skelly
17. Geoffrey Try

Numbers in brackets after the illustration title refer to the sources listed above.

Front Cover
2nd Life Guards returning from Church Parade before embarkation, August 1914 (4)

Introduction
Peascod Street in 1914 (2)

1914

News of the assassination of Archduke Franz Ferdinand (2)
Life Guards returning from Church Parade 1914 (4)
A Call to Arms (2)
Letter from the King to Mr Knibbs' six sons in the Navy (2)
Lady Jellicoe's appeal (2)
King George V visits his cousin's grave in May 1922, Ypres cemetery

1915

Munition workers wanted (2)
Smith's Lawn Camp Aug 1915 (7)
Roll of Honour (2)
Fred Fuzzens' drawing (5)
Mr Fuzzens (5)

1916

WW1 armoury, state of Bachelors' Acre (7)
Four columns of Roll of Honour (2)
Windsor Empire showing the Battle of the Somme (2)
Advertisement using Zeppelin raids (2)
German prisoners of war (3)

1917

War Loans campaign (3)
Royal Albert Institute showing film: America Prepares for War (2)
Soldiers digging trenches in the Great Park in 1915 (7)

1918

Royal Albert Institute showing Battle of the Ancre and the Advance of
The Tanks (2)
Two posters for War Weapons Week (2)
Potatoes in Berkshire (2)
Victory poster (2)
Cadet Reginald Try (17)

Armistice to Peace

Unveiling of Windsor War Memorial (8)

DORA

The Snake in the Grass, cartoon (3)

The Royal Family at War

Fusiliers at Smith's Lawn Aug 1915 (7)
The anti-aircraft gun at Windsor Castle (1)
Wounded soldiers at Windsor Castle (8)
The Kaiser in Hot Water (3)

The Berkshire Regiments
The Royal Berkshire Regiment on exercise before the war (12)
'A' Squadron Berkshire Yeomanry, with 5 individual photos (8)

Windsor Barracks
Cavalry soldiers leaving Combermere Barracks
Coldstream Guards marching past Victoria Barracks (15)

Letters from the Front
1914
Life Guards riding past Windsor Fire Station, (4)

1915
Christmas truce
Lord Kitchener asks (2)
Windsor Men in India (2)

1916
Chocolate for the troops (2)
Eat less food (2)
'The Morning Toilet' Windsor Lads somewhere in France (2)

1917
A poem written by a soldier (2)
The Navy knows the value of Mackintosh's toffee (2)
Windsor lads on duty in Egypt (2)

1918
'A' Squadron Berkshire Yeomanry, Camel Patrol, Upper Egypt (6)
No more war marmalade (2)

Battle of the Somme
Windsor Empire showing the film Battle of the Somme (2)
Map of Pozieres where Ayres was killed

Windsor Victoria Cross Recipients
Victoria Cross (13)
Harry Greenwood, The Story of Windsor VCs
Oliver Brooks receiving his VC from the King, (National Trust Inventory
Number 1149614)
Advertisement encouraging men to enlist using the Victoria Cross (2)

Belgian Refugees
The Cathedral and Cloth Hall towers in 1918
The Cloth Hall at Ypres today (15)

The Military Service Bill and the Military Tribunal
The King asks you to Enlist (2)
Sunlight Soap, the Cleanest Fighters (2)
Applicants for Exemption (2)
Father's Turn, observer140980000, Cartoon 'Hold the line, Laddie! I'm coming! (3)
Windsor Recruiting Sub-Area, 25 August 1917 (2)

King Edward VII Hospital
King Edward VII Hospital in 1916
Soldiers in hospital uniforms fishing near Windsor, (8)
Wounded soldiers outside Ethel Clinton's house, Glyn Evans

Windsor Boys' School
Unveiling of the Windsor Boys' School Memorial, *The History of Windsor County Boys' School 1908-1929*
Boys' School Memorial, ditto
Cyril Ashman (8)
Herbert Hiley (8)
Leslie Frank Woodland (8)

Eton College
Grenfell War Memorial (13)

The *Windsor Express*
Harold Jefferies (8)
Fred Ayres (2)

The Guildhall
Guildhall during the war (12)
Dinner in the Guildhall with the Mayor after the war (12)

Women at War
International Stores, women taking on men's roles in shops and businesses (2)
5,000 women wanted every day (2)
Women workers' series, Rowntree advertisement (2)
Women Workers' Series (2)
Women's fashion (2)

Charitable Funds
Half a 'mo Kaiser (3)
Warm clothing for the men at the front (2)
Oxley & Son advertise brown paper for wrapping parcels to send to the troops (2)

Entertainment
Windsor Cinema The Brute December 1914 (2)
Windsor Cinema The Italian Navy (2)
Windsor Empire, French Official War Office Film (2)
Royal Albert Institute, Battle of the Ancre and the Tanks 1917 (2)
Windsor Theatre, Aladdin (2)
Windsor Theatre, The Better 'Ole (2)

Trade and Rationing
Creak's Hospital Requisites (2)
Business as usual (3)
Sunlight Soap (2)
In case of Zeppelin raids (2)
Pears' Soap (2)
World's Stores, Jam from Australia (2)
Useful presents for the men (2)
Special Bargains for your boy in Khaki (2)
A Problem of the Day (2)

Public Health and the Workhouse
Windsor Union Workhouse (8)
Bovril advertisement (2)

The Habgood Family
Pte Ernest Habgood in his RBR uniform (11)
Bill Habgood holding his father's medals (15)
George Habgood (11)

Lance Corporal Arthur Frederick Stevens
Arthur Stevens (16)
Field postcard sent by Arthur Stevens (16)
Arthur, far right (16)

Thomas Luff and his brothers
'A' Squadron Advance Guard, Tom Luff next to Cyril Dyson, who is far right (14)
Tom Luff (on the left) at Suvla Bay August 1915 (14)

Private Fred Johnson
Windsor War Memorial before Johnson's name was added (13)
With the addition of Johnson's, name (13)

Private Harry Frederick Sharp
Silk embroidered birthday card(9)
Greetings on the back of the birthday card (9)
Silk embroidered card with RAMC (9)

The Tank on Bachelors' Acre
The tank in 1920 (7)
The tank protected by railings (7)

A Soldier in the Kaiser's Army
Adolf Breitenstein as recruit in 1915 (15)
Adolf as prisoner of war in 1919 (15)

Back Cover
Ernest Habgood's medals, Old Contemptible badge and Royal Berkshire
Regiment badge (15)
Unveiling the Windsor War Memorial (8)

Acknowledgements

We are grateful to the Royal Collection for permission to use extracts from the diaries of King George V and Queen Mary, which are the copyright of Her Majesty Queen Elizabeth II. The Royal Collection also kindly permitted us to reproduce a photograph.

The publishers of the *Windsor, Eton & Slough Express* have been extremely helpful by giving us access to the original bound copies of the newspapers for the period 1914-1919 for our initial research.

We are indebted to the following institutions and organisations, which have been of great assistance, many of them allowing us to reproduce material from their archives:

> Royal Archives, Windsor Castle;
> Windsor & Royal Borough Museum, particularly Louisa Knight;
> Windsor Library;
> Windsor Boys' School;
> Slough Library;
> Reserve Collection of the Household Cavalry archive;
> Berkshire Yeomanry Museum.

Many individuals have· helped us with information and photographs, and we would particularly like to thank:

> Michael Armitage, for information about the Windsor Castle AA gun;
> Lynda Cottrill, for information about Harry Sharp;
> Roger Cullingham, general information and photographs;
> Glyn Evans, photograph of soldiers outside his house;
> Andrew French, photographs of the Berkshire Yeomanry;
> Bill Habgood, information and photographs about the Habgood family;

Rebecca Heaton for graphics;

Lynda King, for Fred Johnson's story;

Elias Kupfermann for resourcing photographs;

John Lloyd and Ted Land, Household Cavalry archive, Combermere Barracks;

Sir Peter Luff MP, the Luff brothers' story;

Stan Price and John David Wise, files on the war dead of Windsor Boys' School;

Mary Skelly, Arthur Stevens' story;

Mark Tegg, the Tegg family story;

Geoffrey Try, Cadet Reginald Try's story;

Tom Wiggins, for information about Eton Excelsior Rowing Club.

We offer our apologies to anyone we may have inadvertently omitted to thank.

We are grateful to our sponsors whose financial backing made the book possible:

Prince Philip Trust Fund,

Louis Baylis (Maidenhead Advertiser) Trust Fund

Royal Albert Institute Trust.

Whilst every effort has been made to trace the copyright holders or the photographers of illustrations used, this has not always proved possible. However, the authors will be glad to rectify in future editions any inadvertent omissions brought to their attention.

We would also like to thank our editorial team, Sue Ashley and Carol Dixon-Smith, and the Windsor Local History Group for publishing our book. Last, but definitely not least, we should like to thank Barbara Hunt and Geoff Goody for their patience and support during the writing of this book.

Foreword

Sir Peter Luff at Suvla Bay

As a Windsorian myself, born in sight of the castle, and whose father's service in the First World War is recorded in these pages, I am very pleased the town's war time history has been recorded in this way.

To browse the pages of this fascinating book is to benefit from years of hard work by Derek Hunt and Dr Brigitte Mitchell. The names it records are of families who have done so much to make Windsor what it is today; of families who have served the town and its community, often for generations. Sadly it also records so many lives cut short, whose own contribution was to fight and die for their country and never to see Windsor again.

I went to Windsor Grammar School, now the Boys' School, where I was in Woodland House, named after one of the school's fallen sons, and whose story is also told here. We need to hear these stories and to know they have been written down and can be remembered by future generations too.

So for many this book will be a very personal one.

When we honour the Windsorians who served and died in the First World War, though, we are not just recalling events that are in themselves hugely tragic and powerful but which also had huge implications for our lives today - and for our futures.

The shape of Europe, the politics of the Middle East, the role of women in society – these and so many other questions, were determined in large part by the events of a hundred years ago.

Derek Hunt and Dr Brigitte Mitchell have done the town a great service and we should be very grateful to them.

Sir Peter Luff, MP for Mid Worcestershire

Preface

This book is concerned with how the First World War, or Great War as it was known at the time, affected the town of Windsor and its inhabitants. It is not intended to be a complete history of the Great War. Campaigns and individual battles are described, although not in any great detail, to support individual stories and letters from men serving at the front. Windsor men fought in campaigns all over the world; from the trenches of France and Flanders to the beaches of Gallipoli, from the deserts of Mesopotamia and Palestine to West Africa and beyond. Local men fought in the air and also at sea, taking part in the Battle of Jutland and the naval action at the Dardanelles. Wherever British servicemen fought for King and Country, Windsor men served alongside them, and over 600 were killed during the War, and many more were injured or permanently maimed.

The names of those who died are recorded on local war memorials, which have been listed as appendices, and brief details are included in the chapters relating to the year they fell. This book is not, however, intended as a full Roll of Honour to Windsor's war dead; further information on this subject can be obtained from the Ken Shepherd Archive, held at the Windsor and Royal Borough Museum. In May 2013, the Royal Borough of Windsor and Maidenhead embarked on a project to research all the servicemen named on war memorials throughout the Royal Borough, and when the project is complete, the information will be recorded on an interactive website.

In addition to stories about, and letters from, servicemen serving abroad, the book tells the story of a town at war. Life continued when the men went off to war, and for many it was very hard. Many food items became scarce because of the difficulties of importing it, and prices of almost all goods increased. Many shops had to close, or limit their opening hours, because their staff had been called up for military service. The Defence of the Realm Act (DORA) imposed restrictions on every area of private life, juvenile crime increased, and there was the ever-present threat of enemy air raids. Despite all these problems, and many more, Windsor people showed they could endure the hardships and support the war effort to ensure victory. A great deal of charitable fund raising took place in Windsor during the war and the town also responded positively to calls to buy War Bonds to finance the purchase of war weapons.

Much of the information used has been obtained from copies of the *Windsor, Eton & Slough Express* (referred to in the book as the *Windsor Express*) covering the years 1914-1919, and microfilm copies of the *Slough, Eton and Windsor Observer* (referred to as *Windsor Observer*) for the years 1914 to 1918. Both newspapers carried a good selection of stories about life on the Home Front in Windsor, as well as letters from Windsor soldiers serving abroad.

Derek Hunt and Brigitte Mitchell
Windsor, July 2014

August – December 1914

Declaration of War

The long, hot summer of 1914 has been described as the 'last Edwardian summer'. It was a time of peace and prosperity, when Britain was a major manufacturing nation and the British Empire, covering a quarter of the Earth's land surface, was at its zenith. Windsor, like elsewhere in the country, enjoyed basking in that last carefree summer and there were no hints in the local paper of dark clouds gathering over Europe. Not even the report of the assassination at Sarajevo gave any clue of tensions in Europe. The *Windsor Express* reported on 3 July 1914:

Windsor, Eton, & Slough Express

FRIDAY, JULY 3rd, 1914.

THE news of the assassination of the Archduke Franz Ferdinand of Austria and his wife, the Duchess of Hohenberg, on Sunday last, in the streets of Sarajevo, the capital of Bosnia, was received in Windsor with profound regret. It was only in November last that they paid a visit to the King and Queen at Windsor Castle, and they made a most favourable impression upon everyone there. The Archduke, who was an excellent shot, joined the King in his shoots over the Windsor Forest coverts, and his wife accompanied the Queen every day to the Royal shooting lodges for luncheon. The Duchess of Hohenberg was a most charming and accomplished woman, and the few present on the Windsor Great Western platform when the Archduke and his wife left Windsor at midnight will not forget the scene. The King and the Prince of Wales, in Court dress, accompanied the visitors to the station after the concert in the Waterloo Chamber by the Halifax Madrigal Society. The Duchess was in evening dress and bejewelled, and looked very handsome. The Archduke was also a fine figure of a man. The King and the Prince of Wales went to railway carriage to take their final adieux, and the ordinary onlooker could not help but notice that it was no mere formal leavetaking. The Archduke and Duchess had greatly enjoyed their visit to Windsor, and everyone at the Castle was really sorry when they were gone. In a few short months they have been overtaken by a terrible death, leaving their three little children orphans. The tragedy of the Habsburg family is overwhelming, and the latest has excited the greatest indignation throughout the world. The sympathies of all go out to the aged Emperor, and the three little ones who have so suddenly been bereft of their beloved parents.

The news of the assassination of the Archduke Franz-Ferdinand of Austria and his wife the Duchess of Hohenberg, on Sunday last, in the streets of Sarajevo the capital of Bosnia, was received in Windsor with profound regret. It was only in November last year they paid a visit to the King and Queen at Windsor Castle, and they made a most favourable impression upon everyone there.[1]

Life continued as normal in the Windsor area. Advertisements for excursions abounded, especially for the bank holiday weekend. The White

1. *The Windsor Express did not give any further details of the assassination as this was covered in the national newspapers.*

Hart Hotel in Windsor organised coach trips, with a 'Special Day to Brighton' costing seven shillings and six pence, and the Great Western Railway advertised weekly excursions to the West Country and Wales.

The Windsor Cinema, in Peascod Street, showed *Lady Audley's Secret* and *An Officer and a Gentleman*. The Theatre Royal had closed for the vacation at the beginning of June, but it promised to re-open in the autumn. Local fetes and carnivals took place, the 23rd annual Rose Show was well attended, and cricket dominated the sporting fixtures. The hot weather prompted Wellman Bros. to advertise refrigerators, ice safes and freezing machines.

The nearest to anything militaristic was a photograph in the *Windsor Express* on 18 July, which showed 18 Windsor men of the 2nd Battalion Royal Berkshire Regiment in India. In September 1914 they were recalled and, after a brief stay in England, landed in France in November.

On 1 August there was a report about 50 Russian teachers visiting Datchet School, but it is not recorded whether they reached back home before war was declared. Many were inevitably caught on the wrong side of the border. Mrs Ryland and her three sons, pupils of Imperial College, were on holiday in Germany and Austria, but nothing had been heard of them since the outbreak of hostilities. Dr Peterson, Medical Officer of Health for East Berkshire along and with hundreds of other tourists, was made prisoner of war. His letter to the Town Clerk of Maidenhead in October 1914 stated that he was well treated, but he asked: 'would you kindly enquire at the Home Office or elsewhere if there is any likelihood of an exchange in the near future?' It must have been successful as he came home in November, but there were continued reports of local people imprisoned in Germany.

In Europe, events had escalated since June. Austria-Hungary held Serbia responsible for the assassination and made demands which Serbia could not accept. War became inevitable when the major European powers took sides in the dispute and began mobilisation. Britain declared war on 4 August 1914 when Germany invaded Belgium en route to France. The *Windsor Express* commented in its editorial on 8 August:

The die has been cast and England is at war with Germany. The conflict has been forced upon this country and France by a policy of aggression, which is perfectly amazing in audacity. The nightmare that has haunted so many of our leading men year by year has become a lurid fact, and in her own defence, England is taking part in the Armageddon. What the end will be no one can forecast. It is a fight for life and everything we hold dear.

The message was foreboding. There was no 'it will be over by Christmas', although this appears to have been the feeling throughout the country. The blame was placed squarely on the shoulders of Germany, and although England was not under any threat, the emphasis was on her defence. It was indeed a fight for 'everything we hold dear'. From the start of the conflict the *Windsor Express* devoted as much space to the war as it affected Windsor and its neighbourhood, as to other local issues.
The declaration of war was reported on 8 August in the same issue:

Great Britain declared war against Germany at 11.00 pm on Tuesday evening 4 August. The Foreign Office issued the following statement on Wednesday morning at 12.15:
Owing to the summary rejection by the German Government of the request made by His Majesty's Government for assurances that the neutrality of Belgium would be respected, His Majesty's Government has declared to the German Government that a state of war exists between Great Britain and Germany as from 11.00 pm on 4 August.

The *Slough, Eton and Windsor Observer* made an 'earnest appeal to all young unmarried men to rally round the Flag'.

Call to Arms

Windsor responded quickly to the call to arms. An Army recruiting office was established at the Guildhall just over a week after the declaration of war, and the local regiments prepared for active service. 'A' Squadron of the Berkshire Yeomanry had mobilised on 5 August, the day after war was declared, and the local newspaper printed the complete muster roll of the 103 officers and men, including five new recruits, under the heading 'The Great War'. Every man had reported for duty in khaki at the Wellington Drill Hall, and they were expected to move at the weekend. 'D' Company of 4th Royal Berkshire Regiment mustered 80 officers and men, and they then marched to the Great Western Railway to catch the 10.20am train for their Headquarters in Reading. The Regiment's 4th Territorial Battalion was established primarily for Home Defence, but more men were needed at the front. When requested to fight overseas, all 1,000 former Berkshire Volunteers of the 4th Battalion volunteered for active service.

Five hundred reservists of the 2nd Battalion Coldstream Guards arrived at Victoria Barracks from Chelsea. Thirty officers were named in the newspaper, but none of the 1,000 men. The regiment was told to be in readiness to leave immediately. On 9 August a special service was held for them at Victoria Barracks, and in the very early hours, a few days later, they left Windsor for France. 'A finer lot of men have never left Victoria Barracks', enthused a reporter. A further 400 officers and men left the Barracks for France on 26 August.

Some 200 men of the 2nd Life Guards Squadron of the Composite Regiment of Household Cavalry left Windsor for the front on 15 August. Many of these men took part in the battle of Mons and the heroic stand of Le Cateau, which halted the German advance.

Numerous articles and advertisements encouraged the young men of Berkshire to join Lord Kitchener's Army. Taxi-cabs and private cars were requested to display recruiting posters, and soon the *Windsor Express* carried its own. The first appeared on 15 August, and the editorial urged men to enlist:

Any young man in Windsor and district who is able-bodied should not hesitate to join the new Regular Army of 100,000 which Lord Kitchener, as Secretary for War, has decided to form. Any able-bodied man between 19 and 30 is eligible and the country needs every one available.

The recruiting office in the Guildhall signed up 25 men for the New Army and nine men for the regulars during the first week. This included men like William Duggan, a youth of no fixed abode who was charged at the Windsor Petty Session with sleeping rough and was released on condition that he joined the Army.

Many would-be recruits were concerned about their jobs once they joined the Colours. To allay fears 108 local firms and businesses, named in the newspaper, including Nevile Reid & Co, Dyson & Son, Oxley & Son, Windsor Gas Co, Caleys Ltd and the White Hart Hotel, gave their assurances to the men that their jobs would be kept open for them when the war was over.

To encourage more recruits, and honour those who had enlisted, the *Windsor Express* printed a form which local people were invited to complete with the name, rank and regiment of local men who had enlisted. It was headed 'Roll of Honour' and the first appeared on 12 September. Initially it was only the names of men who had joined up but later on casualties were to take over. The following week, a half page was devoted to men from Windsor and surrounding neighbourhood. For Windsor, Old Windsor, Eton and Clewer there were 217 names. The list was headed by the Queen's brother Prince Alexander of Teck, a Major in the Life Guards, and included local names like Dyson, Luff and Oxley, all serving in the ranks. One Luff brother, Edmund, returned especially from Canada to join up in Windsor, and there were five sons of Mr and Mrs Turner of Bolton Road, Windsor. (None of these appear on the casualty list for the Great War.) Beside this Roll of Honour there was a small list of recent casualties.

In the last week of September 289 Windsor men were enlisted. Fred Fuzzens and his brothers William and Harry had joined up. William was captured in May 1918 and spent some months as a prisoner of war in Germany, but they all survived the war. There was a somewhat larger list of casualties, but only officers were named. On 3 October 201 Windsor names were on the Roll of Honour.

Mr James Knibbs of Old Windsor received a letter from the King who had 'heard with deepest gratification that you have six gallant sons serving in the Royal Navy'. Sadly, two were killed within one month of each other: H G Knibbs, Chief Stoker died on 23 March 1916 aboard HMS *Brilliant*, and William J Knibbs, Petty Officer Stoker on 5 April 1916 aboard HMS *Victory*.

From October, the form for the Roll of Honour included a request for casualties of local men, and as the casualty lists increased, the numbers of men enlisting decreased.

At the beginning of October there were 134 new recruits listed, but this dwindled to 36 by the start of November and only eight in early December, although after Christmas 27 men enlisted. On 7 November, the *Windsor Express* published a photograph of officers and men of the Berkshire Territorials, Windsor 'E' Company, who had been accepted for foreign service, and on 21 November there was a photograph of 'A' Squadron of the Berkshire Yeomanry, which included local names like Luff and Dyson.

A large poster published on 12 December, listing the names of men who had won the Victoria Cross, aimed to re-ignite the desire to join the Colours with 'there is room for your name on this Roll of Honour. THESE HEROES would never have won the Victoria Cross by staying away from the recruiting office' and 'ENLIST TODAY. The more men we have, the sooner the war will end'. By the end of 1914, over 1,000 of Windsor's young men had marched out of town.

Windsor prepares for war

During an enthusiastic meeting held at the Town Hall on 12 August, the Mayor CouncillorWilliam Carter appealed for volunteers to form a Civic Guard of men over 50 whose duties would be to protect important public works from possible attack. The volunteers met at the Police Station on 20 August, only to be disbanded by request of the Home Secretary, however, the men were invited to join a body of unpaid Special Constables instead and most were happy to comply.

The Mayor also expressed a desire to set up work parties, including Voluntary Aid Committees and Ladies Working Parties. Classes in nursing, sewing and cooking for the sick had already been arranged. Women were looking for new roles. The local suffragettes, as in the rest of the country, suspended their political campaigning and concentrated on encouraging men to join up, often using the notorious white feathers. There was also a Wounded Soldiers' Needlework Guild which met at Clewer Mead, by the kind invitation of Mrs Oppenheim, who also supplied the sewing material. In November, the Guildhall was filled to overflowing at a meeting of a new club for women: The League of Honour.

In early August, the Clewer Horticultural Society issued advice to all allotment holders and owners of vacant land, to immediately sow turnips and other root vegetables, 'in view of the expected extra demand, and the necessity for fresh vegetables in times of war'. Later that month, Clewer Park was placed at the disposal of the Red Cross Society as a convalescent hospital for officers.

During September, the Windsor Post Office was kept open all night for telegraphic work, although nearly a dozen employees had enlisted. Four young men of the Territorials, Yeomanry and Reserves working in the *Windsor Express* office also left for the front.

Windsor had an acute housing shortage, which got worse throughout the war. Councillor W J Dudley made an offer to the Mayor to provide ten free cottages for wives and families of local reservists who had gone to the front; he would even move their goods free of charge.

By the end of September appeals went out to send warm garment to the troops. The Windsor Ladies Working Party sent 118 shirts, 272 pairs of socks and 123 sleeping helmets to the Royal Berkshires.

In October Windsor reduced its street lighting by two-thirds after 8 pm and shopkeepers were asked to close their shops by 7 pm. The Mayor cancelled his annual venison dinner, saying it was hardly the time to hold a banquet, they should wait until peace was declared, and the venison should be used to make soup for the poor.

In November an anti-aircraft gun was set up in Windsor Castle to ward off enemy aerial attacks but Windsor also faced a 'friendly invasion'. Five thousand soldiers of the Surrey Infantry Division and the Southern Division were billeted in the town. The East Surrey Regiment was billeted at Old Windsor, while the Divisional Staff Headquarters was established at the White Hart Hotel. Several warehouses were made available but private residents were expected to house and feed soldiers. Billeting terms for private homes was 9d per night, with breakfast at 7 ½d, and supper at 4 ½d a day, but not everyone was happy as an inhabitant of Denmark Street complained about the way they were treated by the authorities. Others saw the soldiers as an unseemly attraction to young girls: 'They hang around the barrack gates, and run after the soldiers in a way that is most unbecoming', but Windsor had long been a garrison town, and girls had always been 'hanging around the barrack gates'.

Mrs Harvey, the wife of the Vicar of Datchet, was perhaps trying to divert soldiers' minds to other matters, by teaching French to those billeted in Datchet and Windsor. Indeed keeping the troops entertained in Windsor seems to have concerned the town fathers, as well as the local population, and the *Windsor Express* touched on the subject in an editorial dated 21 November. Recreation rooms were opened for the troops in the corn market at the Guildhall, and in church halls. The Royal Albert Institute and political clubs in the town invited the men to become temporary members, but locals were asked not to treat soldiers, whether billeted in town or from the barracks, to drink. A *Windsor Express* editorial on 31 October stated that:

> It is a mistaken generosity on the part of well-meaning people to treat soldiers going to the front. In Windsor, the night before drafts have sailed, the scenes in the streets have not been at all creditable on one or two occasions and the effect on the soldiers is not good.

The Enemy

England suddenly found itself fighting a foe which only 100 years earlier had been an ally in the long struggle against France. The *Windsor Express* reminded its readers in the 'One Hundred Years Ago' column that in August 1814 England had sent soldiers to Belgium to form a garrison in Brussels. Although foes and allies were not mentioned, most people in England still remembered that France was their so-called 'natural enemy' and Germany their 'friend'. Britain and Germany were also linked by their Royal families; King George V and the Kaiser were cousins.

Now German and Austrian merchandise was no longer regarded as acceptable and should therefore not be sold. Shops which still sold German goods were boycotted, even though many shopkeepers could not afford to buy new stock until the old goods, which they had already paid for, had been sold. Everything German was vilified, and first to feel the hostility were German and Austrian 'aliens' living in England.

On 27 August, seven 'aliens' were arrested by the police in Windsor and handed over to the military authorities. The *Windsor Express* noted that 'they were escorted down Peascod Street to the (Police) Station and much excitement and speculation was evinced on all sides as to the nature of the charges'. They were four Austrians and three Germans who had been employed in the town. Oscar Lehmann Schroeder, who had lived at Osborne Road, Windsor for some years was arrested in September, so was a German gardener named Schumann, who had been employed at the Royal gardens for several years. Schumann was later released on parole, but struck off the local parliamentary voters' list.

By September 1,100 civilian aliens and a number of foreign seamen were imprisoned at Frith Hill Camberley, and the local newspaper reported that large crowds flocked there on Sunday to 'have a peep at our enemies'. Windsor Motor Coaches advertised half-day trips to Frith Hill Camp and Aldershot for 3s 6d on Sundays and Wednesdays. Henrietta Schneider of Ascot felt that she had to declare publicly that she was British of British parents, but she still changed her surname.

The headmaster of Eton, The Rev Dr E Lyttelton took it upon himself to demonise the enemy in a series of lectures. He was by all accounts a good speaker, and most of his talks were reported at length in the *Windsor Express*, including the applause and laughter. He talked to different groups, including the Royal Albert Institute, groups of soldiers in both Windsor barracks, and a variety of local societies, mainly on the history of Germany and the causes of the war. Comments such as 'Germany had never been a Christian country, they were taught to believe in brute force and lying' (10 October 1914), or 'The Germans had been taught for more than two generations by their leading writers, that Germany's mission in the world was to destroy Christianity' (23 October 1914) were intended to incite hatred. In December 1914, he published a pamphlet *Britain's Duty Today*, which according to a reporter 'stands out from the war literature by reason of its refreshing vigour and outspokenness'. A Christmas lecture to the troops titled *Christianity versus Heathenism, what the Germans aimed at*, was to spur soldiers on before going to war.

The *Windsor Express* reported after he resigned from Eton in 1916:

> The lectures, sermons and addresses delivered by Dr Lyttelton in this district were always most interesting, and he generally had something arresting to say. He was ever ready to speak at local meetings, and his lectures at the Royal Albert Institute attracted large audiences.

Dr Lyttelton continued his anti-German remarks. In June 1918, writing to *The Times*, he said: 'The prospective scarcity of jam is not pleasant, but how is it that German prisoners are said to be enjoying plenty?'

In late November, the first German prisoners of war arrived at a specially prepared camp in nearby Holyport. Later in the war, small groups of prisoners were taken for walks outside the camp and their route took them past The Eagle public house. It became a routine for the Germans to salute the sign in recognition of the eagle as their national emblem – much to the annoyance of the local population. The prisoners stopped saluting when the name of the public house was changed to The Belgian Arms, the name by which it is still known.

Casualties

The reality of war soon took over from the euphoria. The first death of a Windsor man is recorded in the Ken Shepherd archive as Private Ernest Victor Harper who was killed on 26 August 1914 in France who had been serving with the 1st Bn Royal Berkshire Regiment, stationed at Aldershot when war broke out. It was the first of the Berkshire regiments to be sent to France and was proud to be part of the Old Contemptibles. His death is not reported in the Windsor newspaper, but he was killed during the early days of the Battle of Mons and is buried in the Maroilles Cemetery, France.[2] His comrade Private F Golding of 23 River Street returned wounded from the same engagement and told his story to the *Windsor Express* in its edition of 26 September.

On 5 September the newspaper reported its first war casualty; under the heading:

WINDSOR LIBERAL CANDIDATE KILLED IN ACTION.
BRILLIANT OLD ETONIAN'S CAREER,
We record with the deepest regret the news of the death of Captain Charles Hunter Browning of the Royal Field Artillery, who was killed in action when serving with the British Expeditionary Force at Mons.

Less than three weeks earlier, Browning had said good-bye to his friends in Windsor. The same issue also brought the news that a large number of wounded were brought back from Southampton

2. *All casualties mentioned in this book are on one of the local War Memorials (see appendices) unless otherwise stated.*

to Birmingham.

On 24 October it was stated that 55 Etonians had been killed in the war up to 21 October. The list of names, which was affixed to the Chapel door, included Captain Riversdale Grenfell, brother of Francis Grenfell who had won the Victoria Cross in August.

The death of a member of the Royal Family on 27 October 1914 at Ypres was not reported in the *Windsor Express* until 5 December. Prince Maurice of Battenberg, youngest son of Princess Beatrice, and the only close member of the Royal Family to be killed during the war, was by all accounts buried in a hurry. The Rev E J Kennedy wrote:

> I think Prince Maurice of Battenberg's burial was the shortest Royal interment on record, at which I officiated, and at which Prince Arthur of Connaught was the chief mourner. As the shells were hurling through the air around us, it was deemed wise to curtail the proceedings considerably, besides a retreat was ordered.

Ypres cemetery May 1922,
King George V visits his cousin's grave

1915

The New Year began with the sobering realisation that this war was not going to be 'over by Christmas'. On 2 January the *Windsor Express*, in its first editorial of 1915 stated:

> The Empire is engaged in the biggest war that has ever been waged, and we are fighting for our very existence… Despite the sadness of it all, our Empire was never more united and we are thrilled and heartened by the way in which its sons have rallied to the bugle call…

For the British Expeditionary Force (BEF) and its Allies, 1915 started the way 1914 had finished – occupying a system of trenches which ran from the North Sea to the Swiss border. There had been a brief respite from the fighting on Christmas Day 1914, when an unofficial truce broke out on various parts of the front. Accounts of the Christmas truce did not reach the newspapers until January and several letters were published in the *Windsor Express*. (*See Letters from the Front 1915*) A soldier serving in the Royal Berkshire Regiment described how the Germans had initiated a temporary ceasefire by shouting 'English, Merry Christmas' and received the reply 'Same to you. Want some duff?' Firing ceased and both sides met between the lines and shook hands and exchanged gifts. Other letters had similar experiences to relate, although a Private in the Coldstream Guards had quite a different story to tell and described how his Battalion had fought off an enemy attack on Christmas Eve.

The winter of 1914/15 was one of the wettest in recent years, with flooding of the lower parts of Windsor and Eton, and the wet season produced a great deal of illness. As the weather improved, tourists came back to Windsor. The Whitsun holiday saw thousands of visitors coming by special trains and omnibuses to enjoy the fine weather. Boating on the Thames was particularly popular.

The shortage of farm labourers caused problems during the hay harvest, and many soldiers were given leave to help bring in the hay. However, Datchet farmer John Kinross of Riding Court Farm, managed to fill the gaps caused by twelve of his men who had joined the Colours, with older men.

The lack of horsepower also caused problems. The War Office had bought huge numbers of horses for the front, and when the Windsor Rural District Council wanted to tar the roads in June, they were unable to do so because of difficulties in securing horses. Local motor-car owners were approached 'as to whether in the possibility of an invasion they would place their cars at the disposal of the military authorities, for the rapid transport of troops to any spot where their services might be required'. Appeals were also made, via newspaper notices, for field glasses 'for the use of officers and non-commissioned officers under orders for the front', with the promise that any field glasses engraved with the owners' names would be returned after the war.

RMS Lusitania

The sinking of the *Lusitania* by a German submarine on 7 May 1915 was reported in the *Windsor Express* on the 22nd. It brought its own local tragedy with the loss of local benefactor Mr Edward Gorer of Sutherland Grange, Clewer. He was said to have saved the lives of other passengers on the *Lusitania* at the cost of his own life; the passenger ship sunk with the loss of 1,198 lives. Mr Gorer had been very generous, setting up the Gorer War Fund, which benefitted Clewer people. He also gave freely to many other funds started in connection with the war.

Although there had not been any air raids over Windsor, the Borough police gave notice to inhabitants of what to do in case of hostile air raids, from keeping buckets of water and sand in the upstairs rooms, to staying indoors during a raid. The Notice continued:

In all probability if an air raid is made it will take place at a time when most people are in bed. The only intimation the public are likely to get will be the reports of the anti-aircraft guns or the noise of falling bombs. The public are advised not to go into the street where they might be struck by falling missiles.

The nearest Windsor got to a raid was in October when Zeppelin attacks came closest: guns or bombs exploding on a raid on London were clearly heard at Windsor.

At the Battle of Festubert in May, the British attack could not be continued as the Army had run out of artillery shells. To beat the shortage, the Government passed the Munitions of War Act, which brought private companies supplying the Armed Forces under the tight control of the new Ministry of Munitions, led by David Lloyd George. The Act also opened up employment for women, and in July the Windsor Munitions Bureau, at 10 Clarence Road, opened for enrolment of skilled men and women for munitions work.

MUNITION WORKERS.

WOMEN WORKERS URGENTLY WANTED

For
Government Work in Middlesex.

GOOD WAGES.

No Person already on Government Work will be Engaged.

All Applications should be made to the

Nearest Labour Exchange.

And Reference No. A 2033 should be quoted by all Applicants.

There was just a brief mention in the *Windsor Express* of the Battle of Waterloo, but no celebration of its 100th anniversary on 18 June. Perhaps celebrating a victory over a foe, who was now an ally, assisted by Germany, who was now the foe, was too much to handle, however, school children celebrated the 700th anniversary of Magna Carta. On 26 June the regular feature '100 Years Ago' in the newspaper recorded Wellington's victory.

The Windsor Rose Show and Sweet Pea Display on the slopes of Windsor Castle on 26 June, was 'a great success from every point of view'. The weather was fine and the Band of the 2nd Life Guards provided musical entertainment.

At the end of June, 100 men of the 4th and 9th Battalions of the Royal Berkshire Regiment marched from Slough to Windsor to be entertained to tea by the Mayor at the Guildhall. This was of course a recruiting drive, arranged by the local Recruiting Officer.

The first anniversary of the Declaration of War on 4 August was observed in Windsor, as throughout the country, by religious services, parades and speeches. On 21 August the *Windsor Express* published a full list of local men killed, wounded, missing or taken prisoner during the first year of fighting, but added: 'We do not contend that it is in any way complete'. The list included 251 names for Windsor and District.

Normal life continued. During the summer months fetes, galas and sports meetings took place, and river trips were advertised from Windsor to Marlow, Cliveden or Cookham. A gymkhana was held on 8 September in aid of All Saints' Church, Dedworth, organised by the 2nd Life Guards, and in November the annual exhibition of chrysanthemums, plants, fruit and vegetables took place in the Royal Albert Institute.

In October, Councillor William Carter was elected Mayor of Windsor for the fourth year – he remained Mayor until 1919 and was knighted for his work during the war. In addition to being Mayor, Councillor Carter was also the Chief Magistrate and held many fund-raising positions.

In December, the Imperial Services College in Windsor received a very generous gift of £10,000 from Patrick Y Alexander, the famous pioneer of aeronautics, who had previously given the College an Aero Laboratory. P Y Alexander spent the rest of his life teaching aeronautics at the College and died penniless, having given away all his wealth.

The last editorial of the year in the *Windsor Express*, on 25 December had a melancholic tone:

> The joy-bells are muffled again this Christmas! From near and far come tidings of war and desolation. Our homes may be decked with holly and mistletoe but our thoughts will be of those we shall never see again or with those who are fighting for us in East and West. It is impossible for us to

enter the Christmastide with the customary feelings, and the angelic message seems strange what time the deadly devices of mankind breathe forth death and slaughter…

Soldiers in Windsor were uppermost in the thoughts of the *Windsor Express*. The 1914 Christmas and New Year celebrations in both barracks and King Edward VII hospital were reported in detail. 1,550 men of the Coldstream Guards 'participated in the luxuries, which were provided on a very generous scale' at Victoria Barracks, while at Combermere Barracks the Reserve Squadron of the 2nd Life Guards 'enjoyed the tasty extras which were provided for their benefit'.

Thousands of troops were quartered in Windsor waiting to go to the front. There could have been all sorts of trouble in the town, but the *Windsor Express* praised the excellent conduct of the soldiers. It stressed that Windsor owed much to the troops, as they helped many of the shopkeepers 'to tide over a bad time'.

In late spring canvas encampments were set up, and a huge encampment in Windsor Great Park received 20,000 troops in

April, while there was another large camp at Cranbourne.

The YMCA had been raising money to provide a building where soldiers could relax away from barracks, and in January 1915 the YMCA Hut was opened on Bachelors' Acre. It was a large wooden structure, erected on the grass plot by the side of the pathway across the Acre, with the intention that it would be removed after the war. The Hut could seat 350 and was 'fitted up very comfortably, and novels, magazines, games and writing materials were provided.' On 12 February the first of a series of concerts was held there. The YMCA also organised regular talks for soldiers, and at Christmas there was a candle lighting contest and carol concert.

Concern was expressed about the lack of facilities for soldiers billeted in the town to have a hot bath. Some households were not allowing soldiers to use their bathrooms, and there were no public baths in Windsor. This does not seem to have been resolved despite several letters on the subject in the local press.

In early May, the 4th BattalionThe Queen's Royal West Surrey Regiment left Windsor. They had been billeted in the town since November 1914 and a large number of townspeople turned out at 5 am to wish them God-speed. By the end of the month other regiments had followed them; the East Surrey Regiment, the Army Service Corps, Royal Engineers, Royal Army Medical Corps and other Divisional Troops, all of whom had stayed in Windsor and Eton for the previous seven months. The *Windsor Express* reported: 'their conduct has been most exemplary, and they have been a credit to the gallant regiments to which they belong.'

The 4th Battalion Coldstream Guards left for 'an unknown destination' in July. 'A splendid farewell concert was given on Wednesday in the new dining room at the Victoria Barracks prior to their leaving Windsor'.

In the autumn the billeting of troops in the town was again discussed by the Town Council, as the encampments were closed for the winter. The soldiers did appreciate Windsor's hospitality, as one private of the East Surrey Reserves wrote to the *Windsor Express*: 'I am sure that I voice the sentiments of all the troops when I say that we shall take away with us very pleasant memories of Windsor'.

In December, the children of soldiers and sailors, whose homes were in the Windsor district, were given a Christmas party in the Riding School at Windsor Castle. Queen Mary sent a number of toys while Princess Alexander of Teck distributed many of the toys and assisted in serving the tea. The winter brought news from the trenches that soldiers were constantly wet through. The Mayor organised parcels with shirts, woollen wraps and so forth, to be sent out from Windsor to the Berkshire Territorials in France.

Rolls of Honour

At the beginning of the year the *Windsor Express* published the names of all local men who had enlisted since the beginning of

A black soldier joins the Coldstream Guards

In March 1915 Private[1] James Slim was interviewed by a *Windsor Express* reporter, who commented on his good looks and military bearing. Slim was born in Jamaica in 1892. He went into the shipping business after school, and was in France when war broke out. He immediately joined the French Foreign Legion and soon found himself fighting in the trenches where he was shot in the wrist. After spending some time in hospital he decided to join a British regiment and thus became the first black soldier in the Coldstream Guards in the war – 'so far as the Regimental records go'. Slim seems to have survived as he does not appear on the casualty lists of the First World War.

the war, and this was designed to encourage enlistment. *The Times* published an article praising the men of Windsor and Eton, who 'are doing their part well. Perhaps, after all, there is no recruiting appeal as good as a living soldier', referring to the crack regiments stationed in the Windsor barracks.

The first Roll of Honour of the year, and the fifteenth list since the beginning of the war, contained 24 Windsor and Eton volunteers. Numbers remained in the twenties most weeks, but on the 23rd January the *Windsor Express* recorded 52 names. They included Frederick Plumridge of Alma Road, who had joined the Royal Berkshire Regiment, fought in France, and was killed on 25 January 1915, only days after his name appeared on the Roll of Honour. He is buried at Fauquissart Military Cemetery in France.

Although recruiting figures nationwide had steadily decreased since August 1914, in April 1915 the Government decided against conscription. In May the local numbers were as low as five a week, while casualty lists grew. In July there was a brief turn around, with 60 men enlisting, and at the end of the month the *Windsor Express* reported that the largest number of recruits since November 1914,

1. The rank of Private in all Guards Regiments was replaced by Guardsman in 1919 in recognition of their service during the war. Before then, Guardsman was used as a generic term for a non-commissioned soldier in one of the Guards Regiments

had presented themselves at the Windsor Recruiting Office.

By October 1915, over 800 Windsor had men joined up. The Theatre Royal was praised in an article on 27 November for being the most 'patriotic theatre staff'; eighteen men who worked there, plus fourteen old members of staff had enlisted.

One name familiar to Windsor was on the casualty list on 9 October 1915. Lancelot Daniel Edward Gooch, Midshipman on HMS *Implacable* had died in hospital in Malta after being wounded during the Dardanelles landing. He was the great-grandson of Sir Daniel Gooch of Clewer Park, who had brought the railway to Windsor.

The staffs at Windsor Castle and the Royal Farms were reported to have been depleted, but there were still not enough men to fight in the war so compulsory National Service became inevitable.

Boy soldier killed

One of the names on the Roll of Honour on 17 July 1915, listed under Missing, (he was actually killed at Festubert on 15 May) was Old Windsor resident Private William Frederick Branscombe of the Royal Berkshire Regiment. The tragedy is that he was only 16 years old. Full time soldiers had to be eighteen, and combatant soldiers serving overseas nineteen, but few checks were made when young men enlisted. Private Branscombe was not the only under-age soldier fighting in the trenches or killed in action, and he is remembered on the Le Touret Memorial. Two other members of his family were killed in action, James Branscombe on 2 January 1917 in Greece and Harry Branscombe on 25 July 1917 in the Somme area, both served in the Royal Berkshire Regiment.

Old soldier

At the other end of the scale, Francis Henry Goodchild, aged sixty-seven, joined the Middlesex Regiment claiming to be thirty-eight. His story came to light when he was charged with stealing a barrow, belonging to Antonio Sacco of 21 River Street, as a drunken prank. Goodchild was a well known character in Windsor, a hawker of fly-papers who would 'kick up a row' with his shouts of 'Catch-'em-aliveo'. When he appeared before the Windsor Magistrates, the Mayor discovered that Goodchild had previously served with the Royal Artillery in India, and had campaign medals for all the wars in which he had fought including the Afghan War and the Sudan War. The Magistrates acquitted him, telling him to go back to his regiment, and do as well as he had done in the past. The Goodchilds, an old and sometimes notorious Windsor family, nevertheless lost two of their sons in France; they had both joined the Royal Berkshire Regiment.

Windsor families with several boys at the front

Windsor widow, Mrs S White of Peascod Place, Sun Passage was mentioned in the *Windsor Express* on 13 March. She had five sons on active service, three in the Royal Berkshire Regiment, one in the Royal Field Artillery and one in the Royal Welsh Fusiliers. Not one of them is on the local casualty lists. Their names appeared on the Roll of Honour of 26 March, which included 28 Windsor names.

Mrs Tame of Sun Passage, a widow, lost three of her sons, two on the same day. Cpl William G Tame, 2nd Battalion Royal Berkshire Regiment, was killed in action on 9 May 1915. L/Cpl Alfred Tame of the same regiment, was killed on the same day during a disastrous attack on German positions near Fromelles. They are commemorated on the Ploegsteert Memorial. Another brother John Tame was killed on 16 June 1917 and his name is recorded on the Tyne Cot Memorial.

On 26 June the local newspaper reported: 'Windsor mothers

have never begrudged giving their sons to the war'. Mrs Sumner, of 23 South Place, had four sons, in the Army and Navy, and a son-in-law in the Life Guards. Frederick was serving on HMS *Superb* in the North Sea, Alfred George on HMS *Cornwallis* was in the Dardanelles, and Frank and Henry were in the Army Service Corps. They all appeared on the Roll of Honour on 26 June. Trooper George Morris, her son-in-law, had been wounded at Ypres and was in Wandsworth Hospital.

Mr and Mrs Kidd of Oxford Road had five sons and a son-in-law in the Army. Lance/Corporal W E Kidd, of the Oxford and Bucks Light Infantry, had been killed near Ypres in October 1914. Another son, F G Kidd of the Royal Engineers, was killed in Greece in October 1918.

Mrs Beasley of 74 Gardeners Cottages had three sons and sixteen nephews all on active service in the Army. Mrs Hills, of 95 St Leonard's Road, had eleven members of her family serving in the Forces: two sons, one son-in-law and eight nephews.

In December, several families with a number of their men-folk serving at the front were mentioned in one article. Mrs Taylor's husband and two sons were fighting in France, a third was missing in Turkey, and a son-in-law was in the Coldstream Guards. Mrs Bosher of Arthur Road had three sons and a grandson serving. Mrs Miles living in Goswell Road had four sons, two grandsons, a nephew and two sons-in-law in the Forces. Finally, Mrs Mott of Gardeners Cottages had two sons and four nephews at the front.

Gallipoli

In September, reports of casualties were coming in from Gallipoli. The Berkshire Yeomanry had been sent there from Egypt and among the names on the Rolls of Honour under Missing and Dead were the following: Sgt Len Hawes, the Windsor and Eton footballer, Cpl Lancelot Reginald Davenport of York Road, Trooper Herbert H Hiley, L/Cpl Harold Jefferies, Trooper F Pearce of The Tapestries, Old Windsor, and Trooper Henry D Ashman. A letter to Ashman's parents about his heroic death is in the Windsor Museum. On 25 September the *Windsor Express* published a list of the casualties of the Berks and Bucks Yeomanry regiments. It included the name of Major Edward Sinclair Gooch, Berkshire Yeomanry, whose parents lived in Bracknell. He was a distant relative of Daniel Gooch.

The First Gas Attacks

The first use of poison gas by the German Army on the Western Front was on 22 April 1915 at Ypres. One of the first victims was a Windsor lad, Ernest S Weeks, of St Mark's Place, who had gone to Canada to work on the Canadian Pacific Railway. At the outbreak of war he joined the Gordon Highlanders Canadian Contingent and took part in the Second Battle of Ypres. He died of suffocation on 27 April.

What was not reported in the *Windsor Express* until November 1915 was the gas attack on 25 May. Windsor soldier Fred Fuzzens was gassed and in 1982 he recalled the incident in an interview:

> I was gassed and ordered to the nearest FDS (Field Dressing Station) by our section officer. I did not go as the chap on the Kings Own end said 'Keep us in contact with the Artillery Fuzz we need them badly'. And that's what I did although I felt rotten. When the German infantry attacked the Artillery smashed it and drove them back. I honestly thought that I would be put on a charge for refusing an order from an officer. But months afterwards our officer came to me and said 'Fuzzens do you remember when you were gassed?' I said 'Yes Sir I thought I would have been charged for refusing an order'. 'Well' he said 'You will be pleased to know that you have been awarded the

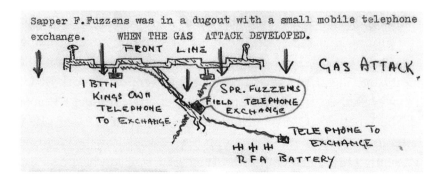

Sapper F. Fuzzens was in a dugout with a small mobile telephone exchange. WHEN THE GAS ATTACK DEVELOPED.

MM for staying at your post.'

The citation for Fred's Military Medal reads:

No 24549 Sapper F Fuzzens, 4th Division Signal Coy RE displayed great courage and devotion to duty throughout the Second Battle of Ypres especially at Au-Bon-Gite, when although badly gassed, he refused to leave his post. It was due to his splendid devotion to duty that the infantry was kept in touch with the artillery throughout.

Fred Fuzzens received a bar to his Military Medal in 1916, and was Mentioned in Despatches in April and October 1917 for 'displaying great courage and devotion in repairing telephone lines under very heavy shell fire'. He had attended the National

School and was a member of the Holy Trinity Church Lads' Brigade. He had been in the Berkshires some six years before joining the Royal Engineers. After the war he went into local politics and became Windsor's first Labour councillor and Mayor in 1947.

Eggs for the soldiers

Civilians were asked to collect eggs for wounded soldiers in English hospitals and at the front. Queen Alexandra became the patron of the collection and eight million eggs had been collected between November 1914 and August 1915. One little girl attending Englefield Green School always wrote her name on the eggs she collected. One day she received a letter from A McMillan, a soldier in the 9th Argyll and Sutherland Highlanders, the recipient of one of her eggs. He told her how he had been gassed twice: 'It is an awful thing this gas which the enemy are using; it takes the breath completely away from you, and leaves you absolutely helpless… However, I am progressing fine (with the aid of your fresh eggs) and hope to be out of bed soon'.

1916

The first editorial in the *Windsor Express* of 1916 looked back on a year 'of toil, bloodshed and suffering', and forward: 'we trust that before the close of 1916 the goal will have been attained'. Christmas 1915 had passed off very quietly with unusually warm weather. Celebrations at Victoria Barracks were muted. There were no decorations, but a 'scrumptious Christmas dinner' was served to the 5th Bn Coldstream Guards. There was an abundance of evergreen at Combermere Barracks, and Christmas fare was provided. The ceremony of the 'hanging of the brick' in the NCOs Mess was performed as usual.

The Post Office admitted that letters and parcels had been less numerous as in previous years, yet temporary workers, including women, had been employed to deal with the absence of some two-thirds of the skilled male staff. They also announced restricted services: from 16 January, there would be only two deliveries per day and letter-box collections were reduced to seven daily.

In February the *Windsor Express* announced that due to the wartime shortage of paper the newspaper would be reduced from eight to six pages in normal weeks. In order to carry as much news as possible there were separate Windsor and Slough editions. Another consequence of the paper shortage was that many schools considered returning to the use of slates, despite the health risks involved.

A heavy fall of snow in late February caused chaos. There was no one to clear the streets as all the available men were in the forces or working, but 'by the kindness of the Commanding Officer of the Coldstream Guards, fifty men of the famous regiment were permitted to undertake the clearing of the streets on Saturday'. [1] At the end of March the worst blizzard reported for many years raged

1. *Windsor Express 4 March 1916*

throughout the country, accompanied by sleet, rain and severe winds. Trees were up-rooted, and the ancient elm avenue running parallel with Datchet Reach was almost wholly demolished.

Easter was celebrated without Hot Cross Buns on Good Friday due to the shortage of materials and bakers. The concluding comment of the editorial on the matter of Hot Cross Buns was: 'We never remember to have read that such an event has occurred before in our history: but this war has been responsible for a great many unheard-of occurrences'.

Meanwhile, the state of Bachelors' Acre was causing concern. It had been used by the Garrison Artillery and it was high time to put it 'in such condition as the school-children would be able to play

on it, as was originally intended'. The War Office was approached, and the Town Council accepted an offer of £100 from them in June for damage done to the Acre and for help towards repairs. At the end of August the Acre had been restored: 'it now forms an admirable drill and playground for the school children, and when the YMCA Hut is removed at the end of the war, it will once more form a splendid open space in the centre of town'. [2]

Reports of the 'Easter Rising', in Ireland, revealed a Windsor connection. Sir Roger Casement, who was arrested in connection with the abortive attempt to land arms in Ireland from Germany, had been a regular visitor to Windsor, frequently dining at the home of a German count in Alma Road. Those who had met him said that he was a most well-informed man and a delightful conversationalist.

2. *Windsor Express 16 September 1916*

St George's Day was celebrated with displays of bunting on High Street and Peascod Street and flags of all the Allied nations and British Colonies outside the Great Western Station. Queen Mary, with Princess Mary and Prince Albert, drove through the town in 'semi-state, amid a remarkable demonstration of loyalty by the inhabitants'. [3]

In May, two companies of the Baden Powell Girl Guides were formed in Windsor. Mr W B Mason of Meadowcroft in Bolton Avenue kindly lent the house to them for their headquarters. The president was Mrs Payne Cooke.

An ambulance train constructed at the Swindon Works of the Great Western Railway at a cost of £30,000, and destined for the French Government, was on show for one day at the Great Western Station in Windsor. One shilling was charged for inspecting the train, the money going to charity. All who saw it were 'surprised at the splendid equipment'. The Princesses Alexander of Teck, May of Teck and Josephine of Belgium were among the visitors, but heavy rain kept many away.

At the end of May, Union Flags were flying from all the buildings for Empire Day celebrations. There was a grand parade in the Home Park, school children sang Rule Britannia and the National Anthem before being given a half-day holiday. The Whitsun Bank Holiday was postponed by the Government to 8 August, as there was an urgent need for an increased supply of war materials (for the forthcoming Somme offensive), but a Military Tournament by the 2nd Life Guards went ahead on Whit-Monday on the Dolphin Ground in Slough. The Windsor and Eton Rose and Horticultural Society celebrated its 25th anniversary on 24 June on the slopes of Windsor Castle, although 'the weather was almost as bad as it could be'. The band of the 2nd Life Guards were playing in the afternoon, which 'did a great deal towards cheering everyone up during the storm'.

There was concern about the shortage of labour on farms; 250,000 agricultural men had been called up but only 50,000 women had replaced them, many as part timers. An urgent appeal

3. *Windsor Express 29 April 1916*

went out for more women to work on the land, and for farmers to accept female labour.

Lord Kitchener's death on HMS *Hampshire* on 5 June was remembered in a sermon at St George's Chapel, where he had a stall plate as a Knight of the Most Noble Order of the Garter. The *Windsor Express* noted in its editorial on 10 June: 'Lord Kitchener has died in the service of his country, and the British Empire has sustained one of the heaviest blows that it has been called upon to bear since the outbreak of war'. Many Windsor men had joined 'Kitchener's' Army' at the beginning of the war, and on this last trip Lord Kitchener had been on his way to Russia to meet Czar Nicholas II to discuss the flow of supplies between the two allies. He knew this war was going to last for some time yet.

On 8 July the newspaper looked at the great Somme battle that had started on 1 July with a great deal of optimism:

> The general offensive against the Germans appears to have commenced in earnest, and all the world is looking on at the terrible struggle with breathless interest. Following the blows on the Russian and Austrian Fronts, the British and French troops leapt from their trenches on Saturday morning, after a week of terrific bombardment of the enemy lines, and they have now advanced some miles, over a twenty mile front, with gratifying results. Some ten thousand prisoners have passed into the hands of the Allies, and the Germans have sustained many casualties. Vigorous counter-attacks to regain the lost ground have been made, and the Allies' progress day by day is necessarily slow. Our men have fought like heroes, and have paid the price…

The following week the Government cancelled the August Bank Holiday, and postponed all military and other sports, because of 'the urgent military requirements of the moment'. The mood was sombre after the casualty lists were published. The editorial of the *Windsor Express* for 15 July concluded:

> There is much sorrow in the land, but the mothers of England who have lost their sons may console themselves in

the thought that they have died the noblest death a man can die, and that their names will shine out for ever in the annals of our great Empire!

In July, the Mayor invited 260 badly wounded men from Queen Mary's Hospital, Roehampton near Wimbledon, to visit Windsor. Among them was Private Wilks a local man who had been a prisoner of war, but sent home because he was unfit to fight again. He told the Mayor that he had been treated very well by the Germans, but had always appreciated the parcels sent to POWs through the Mayor's initiative. A large number of residents gave the wounded soldiers a good send-off.

On 4 August, the second anniversary of the Declaration of War, a special service took place in St George's Chapel. The choirs of churches of all denominations had been invited to enhance the singing, and there were also the band of the Life Guards and the drums and fifes of the Coldstream Guards. After the service, a public meeting was held on the green outside the Chapel, where a huge crowd was assembled.

The editorial on 19 August looked forward with confidence to an end of the war:

> After two years' struggle each day now brings good news. On every front the ring is drawn implacably tighter, the stranglehold becomes firmer and more obvious, and the grip which means victory for us, and doom for the enemy, closer and more deadly.

The list of 250 local men who died for their country during the first two years of the war, covered more than two columns of the same edition.

On 23 August, the 99th Essex County Battalion, raised in Essex County, Ontario and trained in Windsor, Canada, deposited their beautiful silken Colours for safe-keeping in the Parish Church for the duration of the war. They had been made by the ladies of Windsor, Ontario. The colour party of the regiment, which was stationed in Shorncliffe prior to going abroad, arrived in Windsor by train, and were cheered by large crowds of spectators as they marched up towards the Guildhall.

SURREY & MIDDLESEX JOURNAL; ASCOT & DISTRICT ADVERTISER.—SEPTEMBER 19, 1914. 5

WINDSOR, ETON, SLOUGH AND DISTRICT
ROLL OF HONOUR
Of those Serving their Country in His Majesty's Forces.

FIRST LIST OF NAMES.

WINDSOR.

Prince Alexander of Teck, Major, 2nd Life Guards.
Barry, E. C., Lieut., Berks Yeomanry.
Browning, C. H., Capt., Royal Field Artillery.
Fairbank, H. W., Lieut., Royal Field Artillery.
Foster, E. B. C., Lieut., Berks Yeomanry.
Gedge, D. R., Lieut., 4th Batt. Royal Berks Regt.
Grainger, H., Lieut., 5th Dragoon Guards.
Hillsborough, Lord, Rt., Lieut., Berks Yeomanry.
Lewis, C. A. L., Capt., 4th Batt. Royal Berks Regt.
Mason, W. E., Lieut., 2nd Border Regt.
Shipley, R. B., Capt. in H.M. Army, Col. commanding Queen Victoria's Rifles (9th County of London Regt.).
Skevington, Mr. J. O., F.R.C.S., Red Cross Society.

Ayres, F., Pte., 4th Batt. Royal Berks Regt.
Attride, T. T., Pte., 4th Batt. Royal Berks Regt.
Attride, G., Pte., 4th Batt. Royal Berks Regt.
Aitken, J. H., Pte., London Scottish.
Balchin, Percy, Pte., Lord Kitchener's Army.
Balchin, Francis, Pte., West Surrey Regt.
Balchin, W. H., Pte., Royal Fusiliers.
Balchin, A., Pte., 4th Batt. Royal Berks Regt.
Balchin, Walter, Pte., 4th Batt. Royal Berks Regt.
Balchin, Frank, Pte., 4th Batt. Royal Berks Regt.
Balchin, William, Pte., 4th Batt. Royal Berks Regt.
Baverstock, H., Pte., 5th Batt. Royal Berks Regt.
Barlow, John, Pte., 4th Batt. Royal Berks Regt.
Barrow, A., Pte., 4th Batt. Bedford Regt.
Barlow, C., Pte., 4th Batt. Royal Berks Regt.
Barry, W., Tr., Berks Yeomanry.
Beard, W., Sailor, H.M.S. *Dominion*.
Beard, A., Sailor, H.M.S. *Birmingham*.
Best, H. C., L.-Corpl., Berks Yeomanry (signaller).
Beesley, E. R., Sergt., 4th Batt. Royal Berks Regt.
Betteridge, A., Pte., 4th Batt. Royal Berks Regt.
Blackford, William, Pte., 2nd Batt. Norfolk Regt.
Blane, L. F., Pte., 4th Batt. Royal Berks Regt.
Blane, A., Tr., Berks Yeomanry.
Bower, G., Q.-M. Sergt., Army Service Corps (Taplow Coy.).
Basher, Alfred, Pte., King's Royal Rifles.
Booth, M. S., 3rd Batt. Coldstream Guards.
Boucher, H. G., Sergt., 4th Batt. Royal Berks Regt.
Bewcott, E. T., Pte., 4th Batt. Royal Berks Regt.
Borlase, H., Pte., 4th Batt. Royal Berks Regt.
Bowcett, E., Pte., D. Coy. 4th R.B. Terr. Midland Brigade.
Brant, B. G. L., Pte., 4th Batt. Royal Berks Regt.
Brodie, N. D., Canadian Forces.
Brown, W. J., Gunner, Royal Horse Artillery.
Brown, W. F., Pte., Royal West Kent Regt.
Buckell, Leonard, Pte., G Co., Rifle Brigade.
Bullen, R., Pte., 4th Batt. Royal Berks Regt.
Cave, Reg., Driver, Berks Yeomanry.
Cawley, C. A., L.-Corpl., 4th Batt. Royal Berks Regt.
Cardrick, A. W., Pte., 4th Batt. Royal Berks Regt.
Carey, M., Pte., 4th Batt. Royal Berks Regt.
Caron, W., Pte., 7th Batt. Bedfordshire Regt.
Cooter, F. E., Pte., 4th Batt. Royal Berks Regt.
Clark, Henry, Drummer, 2nd Grenadier Guards.
Climo, G., Pte., 4th Batt. Royal Berks Regt.
Chandler, W. B., Pte., 4th Batt. Royal Berks Regt.
Charlish, E., L.-Corpl., Berks Yeomanry.
Cocking, J. H., L.-Corpl., 4th Batt. Royal Berks Regt.
Coe, W., Pte., 4th Batt. Royal Berks Regt.
Coe, William, Pte., 4th Batt. Royal Berks Regt.
Cox, S. G., Sergt., Royal Flying Corps.
Cooper, F. W., Pte., 4th Batt. Royal Berks Regt.
Cox, L.-Corpl., 4th Batt. Royal Berks Regt.
Cousins, S., Pte., 4th Batt. Royal Berks Regt.
Cox, T. J., Pte., 4th Batt. Royal Berks Regt.
Cooper, G. J., Pte., 17th Lancers.
Crump, Edwin, Pte., Army Service Corps.
Darby, J. S., Corpl., 4th Batt. Royal Berks Regt.
Darby, T. C., Pte., 4th Batt. Royal Berks Regt.
Dainty, A. J., Pte., Honourable Artillery Company.
Davenport, R. C., L.-Corpl., Berks Yeomanry.
Disbury, Pte., Royal Army Medical Corps.
Dempster, W. F. H., Coy.-Sergt.-Major, Army Gymnastic Staff.
Dempster, W. B., Almeric Paget Massage Corps.
Denham, T., Pte., 4th Batt. Royal Berks Regt.
Dickinson, R., Tr., Berks Yeomanry.
Dobson, E. J., L.-Corpl., 3rd Batt. Royal Berks Regt.
Dolby, W. H., Pte., 4th Batt. Royal Berks Regt.
Doe, C. E., Seaman, H.M.S. *Irresistible*.
Downes, A., Sapper, Royal Engineers.
Dyson, J. G., L.-Corpl., 4th Batt. Royal Berks Regt.
Dyson, C. D., Tr., Berks Yeomanry.
Elkins, C. V., Pte., 4th Batt. Royal Berks Regt.
Ewen, A. F., Col., 4th Batt. Royal Berks Regt.
Evans, F., Pte., 4th Batt. Royal Berks Regt.
Falkner, James, Pte., 3rd Batt. Royal Berks Regt.
Ferris, A., Pte., Bedfordshire Regt.
Fry, Pte., Royal Army Medical Corps.
Fowler, James, Tr., 19th Hussars.
Foreman, P., Pte., 4th Batt. Royal Berks Regt.
Foreman, A., Pte., 4th Batt. Royal Berks Regt.
Franklin, J. E., Gunner, Royal Horse Artillery.
Garwood, A. L., Gunner, Royal Field Artillery.
Garwood, H., Drummer, 1st Batt. Coldstream Guards.
Gaze, E., Able Seaman, H.M.S. *Hindustan*.
Gaze, A., Able Seaman, H.M.S. *Centurion*.
Garlick, G., Pte., 4th Batt. Royal Berks Regt.
Gale, E., Tr., Berks Yeomanry.
Garner, G. W., H.M.S. *Hermione*.
Giles, F. C., L.-Corpl., 4th Batt. Royal Berks Regt.
Geary, H. J., Pte., 4th Batt. Royal Berks Regt.
Goddard, J., Lieut., Honourable Artillery Company.
Goldswain, A. E., Corpl., 4th Batt. Royal Berks Regt.
Gray, H. B., Pte., 28th Brigade Royal Field Artillery.
Gray, Pte., Royal Army Medical Corps.
Gray, A., Pte., 4th Batt. Royal Berks Regt.
Hanney, Cr.-Sergt.-Instr., 4th Batt. Royal Berks Regt.
Haines, H., S.Q.-S.-M., Berks Yeomanry.
Halliday, C., Sergt., Berks Yeomanry.
Harmse, A. W. J., Rifleman, 12th Batt. London Rifles.
Harnack, C., Tr., Berks Yeomanry.
Hatty, C., Pte., National Reserve.
Hatty, Fred, Transport Motor Driver, Hants Yeomanry.
Haverley, W. R., Pte., 7th Batt. Hants Regt.
Haverley, W. J., Pte., 1st Batt. Royal Berks Regt.
Haverley, F. R., Gunner, H.M.S. *Invincible*.
Hawtree, J. G., Pte., Army Service Corps.
Hatton, S., L.-Sergt., 4th Batt. Royal Berks Regt.
Hearn, T. A., Pte., 1st Batt. Royal Berks Regt.
Headland, J. G., Pte., 4th Batt. Royal Berks Regt.
Hennass, W. J., Tr., Berks Yeomanry.
Hester, James, Pte., 4th Batt. Royal Berks Regt.
Hester, George, Pte., 4th Batt. Royal Berks Regt.
Herne, F. P., L.-Corpl., Berks Yeomanry.
Higgs, A. W., Pte., 4th Batt. Royal Berks Regt.
Hill, T. J., Pte., 3rd Batt. Royal Berks Regt.
Hicks, H. G., Corpl., Berks Yeomanry.
Hiley, H. H., Tr., Berks Yeomanry.
Holloway, H. S., Pte., National Reserve.
Hobbs, E., Pte., 4th Batt. Royal Berks Regt.
Harley, A. W., Pte., 4th Batt. Royal Berks Regt.
Humphrey, George, Corpl., 1st Batt. Coldstream Guards.

WINDSOR (continued).

Hutchinson, J. W., Cr.-Sergt., 4th Batt. Royal Berks Regt.
Hutchinson, G. H., Sergt., 4th Batt. Royal Berks Regt.
Hunt, S., Pte., 11th London Regt.
James, C. W., Gunner, 7th London Brigade Royal Field Artillery.
James, R., Gunner, 7th London Brigade Royal Field Artillery.
James, J., S.-S.-M., Berks Yeomanry.
Jefferies, H. G., L.-Corpl., Berks Yeomanry.
Jannaway, A. E., L.-Corpl., 4th Batt. Royal Berks Regt.
Jannaway, A., Pte., 4th Batt. Royal Berks Regt.
Johnson, R., Pte., 4th Batt. Royal Berks Regt.
Kanna, S., Pte., 4th Batt. Royal Berks Regt.
Kidd, W. E., L.-Corpl., 2nd Batt. Oxon. and Bucks L.I.
Knapp, W., Pte., 4th Batt. Royal Berks Regt.
Kirk, H. E., Tr., Berks Yeomanry.
Lambert, W. G., Pte., 5th Batt. King's Royal Rifles.
Lambert, A. J., Pte., 4th Batt. Royal Berks Regt.
Langham, T., Pte., 4th Batt. Royal Berks Regt.
Lingwood, J. H., Pte., Honourable Artillery Company.
Ling, A. R., Pte., 4th Batt. Royal Berks Regt.
Long, D., Pte., 4th Batt. Royal Berks Regt.
Lovell, E. F. B., Pte., 4th Batt. Royal Berks Regt.
Lott, T., Tr., Berks Yeomanry.
Luff, H., Tr., Berks Yeomanry.
MacGill, Patrick, Pte., Irish Rifles.
Marshall, E., Shoeing-Smith, 18th Hussars.
Martin, W., Tr., Berkshire Yeomanry.
Mason, P. J., L.-Corpl., Royal Engineers (Signal Section).
Mattingley, F., Sergt., 4th Batt. Royal Berks Regt.
May, W., Pte., 4th Batt. Royal Berks Regt.
Miles, D., L.-Corpl., 2nd Batt. Royal Berks Regt.
Miles, David, Corpl., National Reserve.
Miles, T. J., National Reserve.
Miles, W. T. G., Pte., 4th Batt. Royal Berks Regt.
Melvin, R. G., Pte., 1st Batt. Coldstream Guards.
Morgan, H., Pte., 3rd Batt. Royal Berks Regt.
Moody, G., Pte., 4th Batt. Royal Berks Regt.
Mumford, J. A., Pte., 4th Batt. Royal Berks Regt.
Mumford, H. W., Pte., 4th Batt. Royal Berks Regt.
Naylor, F., Pte., National Reserve.
Nicholls, G. C., Drummer, 2nd Batt. Border Regt.
Noyes, Arthur, Tr., 3rd Hussars.
Noyes, Harry, Corpl., 1st Batt. Royal Berks Regt.
Newport, J., Pte., 1st Batt. Royal Berks Regt.
O'Connor, T. J., Pte., 1st Batt. Coldstream Guards.
Oxley, G. H., Pte., 5th Batt. Gloucester Regt.
Ottrey, J., Corpl., Berks Yeomanry.
Palin, A. P., Pte., Yorks and Lancs Regt.
Peirce, Alfred, Sergt., 18th Hussars.
Palmer, J., Sergt., 3rd Batt. Royal Berks Regt.
Price, E., Pte., 2nd Batt. Grenadier Guards.
Pottow, V., Tr., Berks Yeomanry.
Ray, P. T., Pte., Royal Engineers.
Rainer, T. F., Pte., 4th Batt. Royal Berks Regt.
Randall, G., Q.-M.-S., Berks Yeomanry.
Radnor, H., S.-Q.-S.-M., Berks Yeomanry.
Raymont, H., Pte., Royal Army Medical Corps.
Rickard, Ernest, Bugler, 2nd Batt. Oxon. and Bucks L.I.
Rowland, E., Pte., 4th Batt. Royal Berks Regt.
Rowland, E. J., Pte., National Reserve.
Russell, W. H., Able Seaman, H.M.S. *Lion*.
Russell, W. W., Able Seaman, H.M.S. *Thistle*.
Rooke, G., Gunner, Royal Field Artillery.
Roberts, J., Corpl., Berks Yeomanry.
Shardlow, H. W., Coy.-Sergt.-Major, 5th Batt. Oxon. and Bucks L.I.
Short, G. W., Musician, 2nd Dragoon Guards.
Scott, T., L.-Corpl., 4th Batt. Royal Berks Regt.
Skittles, E., Pte., 4th Batt. Royal Berks Regt.
Smith, John, Pte., Royal Engineers.
Spencer, A. J. H., L.-Sergt., 4th Batt. Royal Berks Regt.
Sparks, A., Pte., 4th Batt. Royal Berks Regt.
Smithers, G., Pte., 4th Batt. Royal Berks Regt.
Spencer, E. G., Pte., 4th Batt. Royal Berks Regt.
Smith, T., Gunner, Royal Field Artillery.
Streamer, F. C., Driver, 5th Division Field Ambulance Army Service Corps.
Streamer, Harry, Driver, Army Service Corps.
Sumner, Fred., Leading Stoker, H.M.S. *Superb*.
Sumner, Alfred, Stoker, Chatham.
Swain, A., Pte., 4th Batt. Royal Berks Regt.
Thompson, Alfred, Pte., 4th Batt. Royal Berks Regt.
Taylor, Sidney, Driver, Army Service Corps (Taplow Coy.).
Thompson, A. W., Pte., 4th Batt. Royal Berks Regt.
Taylor, Charles, S.P.O., H.M.S. *Agamemnon*.
Taylor, H., Pte., 5th Batt. Royal Berks Regt.
Tracy, H., Pte., 2nd Batt. Grenadier Guards.
Tracy, James, Gunner, Royal Field Artillery.
Tracy, Wilfred, Royal Field Artillery.
Tracy, Donald, Stoker, H.M.S. *Lord Nelson*.
Turnbull, James, Pte., National Reserve.
Tustin, William, Driver, Royal Field Artillery.
Tustin, James, Driver, Royal Field Artillery.
Turner, J. F., Tr., 2nd Dragoon Guards.
Turner, H. J., Tr., 2nd Dragoon Guards.
Turner, W. A., Pte., 1st Batt. Royal Berks Regt.
Turner, P., Pte., 1st King's Own R.L.R.
Turner, A., Corpl.-Drummer, 3rd Batt. Coldstream Guards.
Udell, E. E., Pte., 4th Batt. Royal Berks Regt.
Upton, R., Pte., 4th Batt. Royal Berks Regt.
Warskett, M. S., Pte., 4th Batt. Royal Berks Regt.
Ward, A., Pte., 4th Batt. Royal Berks Regt.
Wells, G. H., Pte., 4th Batt. Royal Berks Regt.
White, A., Rifleman, Rifle Brigade.
White, F. E., Corpl., 9th Hants Cyclist Batt.
Whitman, T. H., Pte., National Reserve.
Whitman, L. W., Pte., Royal Berks Regt.
Williamson, Charles, Pte., 3rd Batt. Royal Berks Regt.
Williams, G. T., Pte., 4th Batt. Royal Berks Regt.
Wilson, R. G., Pte., 4th Batt. Royal Berks Regt.
Willis, Thomas, Able Seaman, H.M.S. *St. Vincent*.
Woodson, A. J., Pte., 3rd Batt. Welsh Regt.
Woolton, H., Pte., 4th Batt. Royal Berks Regt.
Woodland, L. F., Tr., Berks Yeomanry.
Yarlett, Sidney, A.B., H.M.S. *Cyclops*.

ETON.

Attlee, Mr. W., M.D., Red Cross Society.
Martyn, Mr. H. L., M.B., F.R.C.S., Civil Surgeon, Royal Army Medical Corps.

Ashman, H. D., Tr., Berks Yeomanry.
Barrett, R. A., Driver, Army Service Corps.
Batt, G. W., Corpl., Royal Field Artillery.
Batt, Harry, Pte., 8th Batt. Devon Regt.
Batt, Cecil, Pte., 7th Batt. Suffolk Regt.
Batt, Charlie, Pte., 7th Batt. Suffolk Regt.
Blackford, Edward, 1st Batt. Royal Berks Regt.
Brown, Alfred, 2nd Batt. Grenadier Guards.
Clements, C. G., Pte., Oxon and Bucks L.I.
Climo, Tom, Sergt.-Farrier, Army Service Corps (Taplow Coy.).
Climo, Albert, Sergt.-Farrier, Army Service Corps (Taplow Coy.).
Husted, Driver, Army Service Corps.
Huston, T., Seaman, H.M.S. *Fearless*.
Ironmonger, Alfred, Lc.-Corpl., 2nd Batt. Royal Berks Regt.
Lee, A., Corpl., Army Service Corps.
Newell, Fred, Driver, Royal Field Artillery.
Smith, Tom, Pte., 2nd Dragoon Guards.

DATCHET.

Beavers, J. G., L.-Corpl., Mechanical Transport, Army Service Corps.
Knowles, W., Pte., Worcestershire Regt.

SLOUGH.

Barrett, H. L. C., Capt., Bucks Batt. O. and B. L.I.
Buckmaster, R. A., Lieut., Bucks Batt. O. and B. L.I.
Goddard-Jackson, G., Lieut., Bucks Batt. O. and B. L.I.
Rendell, H. T., Lieut., Army Service Corps.

Andrews, W. A., Bugler, Bucks Batt. O. and B. L.I.
Andrews, G. G. F., Tr., Berks Yeomanry.
Barclay, E., Corpl., Bucks Batt. O. and B. L.I.
Barrett, E. J., Corpl., Bucks Batt. O. and B. L.I.
Blading, F., Pte., Bucks Batt. O. and B. L.I.
Bailey, P. L., Pte., Bucks Batt. O. and B. L.I.
Baldwin, F. J., Pte., Bucks Batt. O. and B. L.I.
Bannister, W. C., Pte., Bucks Batt. O. and B. L.I.
Berry, H. J., Corpl., Royal Engineers.
Berry, E. G., Sapper, Royal Engineers.
Berry, S. E. G., Sapper, Royal Engineers.
Berry, T. S., Bugler, Royal Engineers.
Bensley, Frank, L.-Corpl., Oxon. and Bucks L.I.
Bresham, A., Pte., Bucks Batt. O. and B. L.I.
Blackman, G., Pte., Bucks Batt. O. and B. L.I.
Bradley, J. E., Corpl., Bucks Batt. O. and B. L.I.
Brown, F., Pte., Bucks Batt. O. and B. L.I.
Buck, C. E. S., Pte., 4th Batt. Bucks and Oxon. L.I.
Caley, H. O., Pte., R.B.R.
Cannon, A. A., Pte., Bucks Batt. O. and B. L.I.
Chowne, A., Pte., Bucks Batt. O. and B. L.I.
Chown, C. A., Pte., Bucks Batt. O. and B. L.I.
Chown, R., Pte., Bucks Batt. O. and B. L.I.
Clark, W., Pte., Bucks Batt. O. and B. L.I.
Clements, C. W., Pte., Bucks Batt. O. and B. L.I.
Chandler, W. B., Pte., 4th Royal Berks Territorials, Midland Brigade.
Coward, E. W., Pte., Bucks Batt. O. and B. L.I.
Devonshire, J., Pte., Bucks Batt. O. and B. L.I.
Drewitt, A. W., Pte., Bucks Batt. O. and B. L.I.
Ellwood, E., Pte., Bucks Batt. O. and B. L.I.
Ferris, J., Sergt., Bucks Batt. O. and B. L.I.
Field, W. F. C., Cr.-Sergt., Bucks Batt. O. and B. L.I.
Fox, B. E., Pte., 1st Gloucester Regt.
Fox, W. H. J., Pte., Bucks Batt. O. and B. L.I.
Fox, H. E., Ldg. Tel., H.M.S. *Cressy*.
Francks, F., Pte., Bucks Batt. O. and B. L.I.
Fuzzard, W. G., Pte., Bucks Batt. O. and B. L.I.
Franklin, J. W., Pte., Bucks Batt. O. and B. L.I.
Garetty, V. B., Pte., Bucks Batt. O. and B. L.I.
Gladwell, C. W., Q.-M.-Sergt., Army Service Corps (Taplow Coy.).
Gould, C. T., Pte., Bucks Batt. O. and B. L.I.
Gostick, I. W., Pte., Bucks Batt. O. and B. L.I.
Goulding, C. H. A., Pte., Bucks Batt. O. and B. L.I.
Goddard, E. C., Pte., Bucks Batt. O. and B. L.I.
Groves, G. H., Pte., Bucks Batt. O. and B. L.I.
Groves, E. W., Pte., Bucks Batt. O. and B. L.I.
Green, G. H., Pte., Bucks Batt. O. and B. L.I.
Halliday, G. S., Driver, Army Service Corps (Taplow Coy.).
Hankins, E. A., L.-Sergt., 1st Batt. Scots Guards.
Harris, Robert, Sapper, Royal Engineers.
Hazell, F., Pte., Bucks Batt. O. and B. L.I.
Hawthorn, H., Bugler, Bucks Batt. O. and B. L.I.
Hawthorn, A. W., Pte., Bucks Batt. O. and B. L.I.
Hedgcock, S., Pte., Artists' Rifles.
Hacker, A. T., Royal Fusiliers.
Hester, G. J., Lord Kitchener's Army.
Higgins, E. E., L.-Corpl., Bucks Batt. O. and B. L.I.
Hill, W. W., Pte., Bucks Batt. O. and B. L.I.
Hockley, G. W., Pte., Bucks Batt. O. and B. L.I.
Jones, J. W., Pte., Bucks Batt. O. and B. L.I.
Kemp, W. H., Pte., Bucks Batt. O. and B. L.I.
Keen, F. H., Pte., Bucks Batt. O. and B. L.I.
Langford, H., L.-Corpl., Bucks Batt. O. and B. L.I.
Ladd, J., Pte., Bucks Batt. O. and B. L.I.
Lacey, G. J., Pte., Bucks Batt. O. and B. L.I.
Liddiard, W., Pte., Bucks Batt. O. and B. L.I.
Lovejoy, Tr., 1st Dragoon Guards.
McGowan, H., Cr.-Sergt., Bucks Batt. O. and B. L.I.
Mayne, W. T., Sergt., Bucks Batt. O. and B. L.I.
Mayo, T., Pte., Bucks Batt. O. and B. L.I.
Mitchell, W. F., Pte., Oxon and Bucks L.I.
Mitchell, A., Drummer, 3rd Batt. Border Regt.
Mills, H., Pte., Bucks Batt. O. and B. L.I.
Merriman, A., Pte., Bucks Batt. O. and B. L.I.
Morgan, J. J., Sergt., Bucks Batt. O. and B. L.I.
Montague, T., Pte., Bucks Batt. O. and B. L.I.
Morgan, C. R., Pte., Bucks Batt. O. and B. L.I.
Morris, H. E., Pte., Bucks Batt. O. and B. L.I.
Morton, A. V., Pte., Bucks Batt. U. and B. L.I.
Newport, Pte., Bucks Batt. O. and B. L.I.
Owen, C. F., Pte., Bucks Batt. O. and B. L.I.
Passingham, Albert, Signaller, 1st Batt. Royal Berks Regt.
Phillips, G. F., Sergt., Bucks Batt. O. and B. L.I.
Pallett, R. E., Pte., Bucks Batt. O. and B. L.I.
Payne, G., Pte., Bucks Batt. O. and B. L.I.
Pearson, E. A., Pte., Bucks Batt. O. and B. L.I.
Pitt, J., Pte., Bucks Batt. O. and B. L.I.
Porterfield, V., Pte., Bucks Batt. O. and B. L.I.
Powell, J., Pte., Bucks Batt. O. and B. L.I.
Pritchard, E. J., Pte., Bucks Batt. O. and B. L.I.
Ravenscroft, S. J., Pte., Bucks Batt. O. and B. L.I.
Renn, W. F., Pte., Bucks Batt. O. and B. L.I.
Reynolds, W. J., L.-Corpl., 1st Batt. Irish Guards.
Rogan, J., Sergt., Bucks Batt. O. and B. L.I.
Roberts, F. H., Sergt., Bucks Batt. O. and B. L.I.
Smith, R., Pte., Bucks Batt. O. and B. L.I.
Stevens, G. W. F., Corpl., Bucks Batt. O. and B. L.I.
Stevens, J. H., Pte., Bucks Batt. O. and B. L.I.
Summers, E. E., Pte., Bucks Batt. O. and B. L.I.
Tack, H., Pte., Canadian Forces.
Thomas, A., Regt.-Sergt.-Major, School of Instruction, Chelsea.
Tomsett, W., Pte., Bucks Batt. O. and B. L.I.
Trimby, C. W., Pte., Bucks Batt. O. and B. L.I.
West, Arthur, Pte., Bucks Batt. O. and B. L.I.
Wilson, C. S., Sergt., Bucks Batt. O. and B. L.I.
Willis, H., Pte., Bucks Batt. O. and B. L.I.
Wiggins, A. J., Pte., Bucks Batt. O. and B. L.I.
Willis, Frederick, Pte., Oxon and Bucks L.I.
Wright, J. R., Pte., Bucks Batt. O. and B. L.I.

STOKE, FARNHAM and DISTRICT.

Bowen, Lieut., H.M.S. *Implacable*.
Decies, Lord, D.S.O., Lieut.-Col., Irish Rifles.
Howard-Vyse, R., Brigade Major, 5th Cavalry Brigade.
Walmsley, G., Lieut., Rifle Brigade.
Walmsley, A., Lieut., Welsh Fusiliers.
Bisset, A. W. L., R.N., H.M.S. *George V.*

CLEWER and DEDWORTH.

Adey, Edward, Pte., 12th Lancers.
Cardrick, Alfred, Pte., 4th Batt. Royal Berks Regt.
Dawson, O. F., Pte., Windsor Coy. Berks Territorials.
Etherington, Frederick, Pte., 1st Batt. Royal Berks Regt.
Fletcher, A. P., Pte., London Irish Rifles.
Pelley, W. E., Warrant Officer, Royal Marine Artillery (H.M.S. *Ocean*).
Ranscombe, William, Pte., Royal Berks Regt.
Sampson, William, Pte., Army Ordnance Corps.
Tilbury, W. D., Bugler, 1st Batt. Scots Guards.
Tilbury, E. W., Corpl., 2nd Batt. Scots Guards.
Webb, Arthur, Pte., Royal Engineers.

OLD WINDSOR.

Beasley, Dick, Stoker, H.M.S. *Hermes*.
Bilbo, C., Bombdr., Royal Field Artillery.
Carter, W., Pte., Territorial Batt. Warwickshire Regt.
Carter, George, Pte., 13th Hussars.
Farrow, M. M., Pte., 1st Batt. Royal Berks Regt.
Marshall, J. R., Seaman Gunner, H.M.S. *Nubian*.

ASCOT, SUNNINGHILL, SUNNINGDALE & WINKFIELD.

Bowden-Smith, P. E., Lieut., 19th Hussars.
Bulteel, Mark, Lieut., 2nd Batt. Royal Scots.
Bulteel, John Crocker, Lieut., Royal Bucks Hussars.
Bulteel, T. C., Midshipman, H.M.S. [illegible].
Clarke, C. L. G., Lieut., Royal Bucks Hussars.
Cruichley, Victor A. C., Sub-Lieut., H.M.S. *Centurion*.
Dawnay, Alan, Lieut., 2nd Batt. Coldstream Guards.
Eden, E., Capt., Black Watch.
Elliott, A. G., Midshipman, H.M.S. [illegible].
Ferguson, Adam, Lieut., H.M.S. [illegible].
Ferguson, Stuart, Lieut., Royal Field Artillery.
Ferguson, Robert, Lieut., Irish Guards.
Montagu, G., Lieut., Royal Field Artillery.
Palliser, Arthur F. E., Lieut., H.M.S. *Albemarle*.
Tollie, Oscar, Lieut., H.M.S. *Aboukir*.
Tollie, Lieut., Northumberland Fusiliers.
Wedmacott, C. B., Lieut.-Col., Worcester Regt.

Allington, Arthur, Gunnery Instructor, Royal Navy.
Bartholomew, Tom, Pte., 5th Batt. Royal Berks Regt.
Barfield, M. C., Mess Room Steward, H.M.S. *Royal Arthur*.
Benstead, Archibald, Pte., National Reserve.
Bellworthy, F. W., Pte., National Reserve.
Bish, W. G., Army Service Corps.
Blanchard, Stanley, Pte., 5th Batt. Royal Berks Regt.
Bowyer, R. M., Pte., 4th Batt. Royal Berks Regt.
Brant, E. H., Pte., 1st Batt. Royal Berks Regt.
Brind, Herbert, Pte., Rifle Brigade.
Buckle, Charles, Corpl., Royal Field Artillery.
Carter, William, Pte., 1st Batt. Middlesex Regt.
Camm, Arthur, Pte., Royal Fusiliers.
Cole, V., Pte., Royal Field Artillery.
Dyble, Robert, Pte., Royal Field Artillery.
Ewart, Archibald J., Stoker, H.M.S. *Royal Arthur*.
Ferne, A. G., Pte., 4th Batt. Royal Berks Regt.
Ferns, J. W., H.M. Submarine C 35.
Fletcher, Arthur, A.B., H.M.S. *King Alfred*.
Fletcher, George, A.M., H.M.S. *St. Vincent*.
George, W. P., Gunner, Royal Field Artillery.
Gough, C. F., Pte., Army Service Corps.
Goddard, Arthur, Pte., Army Service Corps.
Groves, E. E., Pte., Royal Marine Artillery.
Haskell, Hugh, Pte., Royal Field Artillery.
Havell, W. L., Pte., Royal Marine Artillery.
Hillier, Robert, Pte., National Reserve.
Kettle, W. H., Pte., Army Service Corps.
Kettle, George, Pte., King's Royal Rifles.
Lambourne, G. G., Pte., 4th Batt. Royal Berks Regt.
Lee, A. E., Pte., City of London Fusiliers.
Leverett, Arthur, Pte., Royal Fusiliers.
Lovegrove, William, Pte., 2nd Batt. Oxon. and Bucks L.I.
McGregor, Duncan, Pte., Royal Engineers.
McSween, Roderick, Pioneer, 2nd Suffolk Regt.
Martin, E. H., Pte., Worcestershire Regt.
Maycock, A., Pte., National Reserve.
Mumford, W. W., Sergt., 12th Lancers.
Parker, T. F., Driver, Army Service Corps.
Palmer, Arthur C., Pte., 4th Batt. Royal Berks Regt.
Perkins, Ernest, Pte., 4th Batt. Royal Berks Regt.
Ponsford, George, Pte., 4th Batt. Royal Berks Regt.
Ponsford, A. J., Pte., Coldstream Guards.
Ponsford, A. H., Pte., Royal Engineers.
Ponsford, E. R., Pte., 2nd Batt. Coldstream Guards.
Rogers, W. J., Pte., 4th Batt. Royal Berks Regt.
Roots, Walter, Pte., Grenadier Guards.
Robinson, H. H., Pte., National Reserve.
Sarney, A. E., A.B., H.M.S. *Suffolk*.
Sarney, F. H., Pte., Grenadier Guards.
Searle, Raymond, Pte., 11th Batt. Royal Fusiliers.
Squires, John, Pte., Royal Field Artillery.
Stephens, George, Pte., National Reserve.
Symes, Frederick, A.B., H.M.S. *King George V.*
Tickner, W. E. A., Pte., Royal West Surrey Regt.
Talbot, W. E., Pte., 4th Batt. The Buffs.
Taylor, W., Corpl., National Reserve.
Walls, L. H., Pte., 5th Batt. Royal Berks Regt.
Walls, C. J., Pte., 1st Batt. Royal Berks Regt.
Warner, William, Pte., 4th Batt. Royal Berks Regt.
Warner, E., Pte., Royal Berks Regt.
Wake, William, Ex-Signaller, R.N., Army Motor Service.

COLNBROOK and LANGLEY.

Adams, Alfred, Pte., Oxon and Bucks L.I.
Alford, E., H.M.S. *Owl*.
Blackwell, William, Pte., Wiltshire Regt.
Brislowe, John, Pte., Oxon and Bucks L.I.
Clarke, James, National Reserve.
Dowling, John, 1st Royal Welch Fusiliers.
Earl, F., Pte., Wiltshire Regt.
Gomm, Nelson, 10th Hussars.
Gomm, Sidney, Pte., Royal Fusiliers.
Humphreys, Thomas, Pte., 1st Royal Welch Fusiliers.
Joys, E., H.M.S. *Implacable*.
Leader, Fred., Driver, Royal Field Artillery.
Leggott, G., Pte., Wiltshire Regt.
Major, C., Pte., Wiltshire Regt.
Newell, H. G., Army Service Corps.
Odell, J. W., Tr., 1st Life Guards.
Sanders, Fred., Pte., 1st Batt. The Buffs.
Shepherd, M., H.M.S. *Swiftsure*.
Walker, James, Royal Field Artillery.

The above list comprises only those names received up to Wednesday.

Further lists will appear in our forthcoming issues.

We ask our readers to send us in further names or corrections of any inaccuracies.

A form for filling in will be found printed on page 7.

THE GOVERNOR of WINDSOR CASTLE

Major-General Carteret-Carey, M.V.O., Governor of the Military Knights of Windsor, has been appointed by the King to represent the Governor and Lieutenant-Governor during the war, or such time as his Majesty may determine; and to exercise all jurisdiction and authority over the Castle and its approaches, and over the military and police, and all persons resident, or entering within the precincts now exercised by the Governor or Lieutenant-Governor.

LOCAL FOOTBALL.

NO SENIOR COMPETITIONS.

A meeting of the Great Western Suburban League was held on Wednesday evening, when Mr. A. O. Collard, the president, occupied the chair. It was decided to suspend the competition for 1914-15, and the subscriptions of clubs be payable to meet current expenses, but for 1915-16 no subscription [illegible] charged old clubs, only that in the event [illegible] a deficit at the end of that time, a levy [illegible] made upon the clubs in membership. Clubs withdrawing from the English and Amateur Cups will be able to compete next season without further subscription.

The meagre attendances at the various professional matches show that the country is in no mood for football at the present time, although it is pleasing to note many instances of men in khaki watching a match prior to their departure for the front.

Apart from the most serious reason that makes the winter pastime practically impossible now, the almost compulsory lapse of a few months will do the game an immense amount of good upon the resumption. Worn competitions will come out as new, opponents will appear fresh as [illegible] Military opponents will everywhere [illegible] sought after and welcomed on the field [illegible] play as never before, and officials who [illegible] guided the fortunes of clubs for many [illegible] will take up their duties again with renewed vigour, all the better for the rest, or [illegible] experiences with the Red, White and Blue.

The Windsor, Slough and District [illegible] League have decided to pass over [illegible] present season. We believe the [illegible] school competition will go on as usual [illegible] this is as well, for the boys of the day must be kept fit and well, so that they [illegible] be ready to help the nation in [illegible] of life when [illegible]

The summer of 1916 saw a spate of bicycle thefts in Windsor. Padlocks and chains were to be employed in future, but in August the Mayor's bicycle was stolen from outside the Guildhall, where he usually left it when he attended meetings. During the next council meeting the Mayor was presented with a new bicycle by his colleagues. 'The gift was a very acceptable one, as his Worship depended greatly on his iron horse to carry out his multifarious engagements'. Councillor Carter was a much-loved character and was often mentioned in letters from the front; Private Jack Angell wrote: 'I am glad the Mayor has been presented with a new 'horse' and I hope he is well'.

The annual sports day of the 1st Life Guards, went ahead at Smith's Lawn at the end of August despite the bad weather. The King and Queen with Princess Mary, the Grand Duchess George of Russia, and Prince Andrew of Greece arrived at 4pm, by which time the rain had stopped. There were games such as bolster fighting on a greased pole across a lake, or Victoria Cross racing which involved riding through raking fire of dummy ammunition.

The official War Office film, *The Battle of the Somme* was shown to the King at Windsor Castle on 2 September. Afterwards the King said: 'The public should see these pictures that they may have some idea of what the Army is doing and what war means'. In fact this film broke all records and remains the most watched film in the history of the British film industry.

The Mayor arranged another visit for 500 wounded soldiers to Windsor in early September. Their Majesties were at the Castle and the soldiers met them on the East Terrace. A further 500 wounded soldiers visited Windsor Castle two weeks later; the Royal party asked the men with artificial limbs how they were getting on with them. They all replied that they were 'getting along very well indeed. Another visit of six thousand wounded soldiers to Windsor Great Park for a giant tea party took place in October. Luckily the weather was fine and the day was said to have been a great success.

On 29 September, the band of the famous French *Garde Republicaine* visited Windsor and received a cordial reception. They marched from the Great Western Railway station to Windsor Castle and played in the quadrangle, after watching the ceremony of guard mounting. Afterwards they were entertained to lunch at Victoria Barracks.

In October Councillor William Carter was elected Mayor of the Royal Borough of Windsor for the fifth time. This was a record in the long history of the town, but there was no Mayoral Banquet for his inauguration in November, owing to the war.

The dark nights without streetlights, in addition to gales of wind and rain, made it very unpleasant for people who had to go out in the evening. The unlit streets created their own casualties; one woman knocked out several teeth running into a lamp-post in early November. White bands were painted around lamp-posts and trees in the borough, but this did not seem sufficient. People with torches had to take care not to flash them skywards, as they would have got into trouble with the police under the Defence of the Realm Act (DORA).

There were no bonfires or fireworks displays that November, for fear of attracting Zeppelins. In any case, DORA regulations had prohibited any kind of fireworks. The Windsor, Eton and District Chrysanthemum and Horticultural Society held their show as usual, at the Royal Albert Institute. It was their twenty-fifth annual exhibition and the committee was much praised for holding their show in war-time. 'It was in every way most successful'. Proceeds went to the Mayor's Fund for Prisoners of War.

The Windsor and Eton

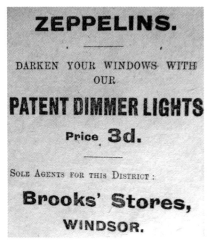

Permanent Building Society (established 1866) celebrated its fiftieth anniversary in November at the Royal Albert Institute. The *Windsor Express* reported on statements made by the older members present.

On 5 December, Herbert Asquith resigned as Prime Minister, and was replaced by David Lloyd George, the Secretary of State for War, who was a frequent visitor to Windsor to see the King.

At Christmas, the King made a gift of coal to anyone living in Windsor who was over sixty years old. Those not on the list, were asked to contact the Vicar of Windsor, Rev E M Blackie. A simple Christmas was advocated by the newspapers but 'in these hard times, we must all try to help one another, and by purchasing goods in the town, we shall be helping our friends and neighbours through a time of stress and anxiety'. People were also asked not to travel for pleasure 'simply travel for the sake of travelling is to act in a way which is detrimental to the interests of the country'. The sombre mood of the nation was reflected in the *Windsor Express* editorial of 23 December:

> It will be a saddened Christmas again this year. The shadow of the Great War is over the land, and in thousands of homes husbands, sons and brothers will be missing from the festive board. Never in our history has the Empire had to mourn the loss of so many gallant sons. There will, in consequence, be less gaiety and less entertainment this year…The children will, of course, expect as good a time as we can give them. They know nothing – and rightly so – of the horrors of war…

Shops were closed for an extra day over Christmas that year, which was the Wednesday after Boxing Day, giving staff four clear day's holiday. The extra day was to compensate for the lost August Bank Holiday.

Some 400 children, between the ages of three and twelve, whose fathers were serving in the Army were entertained and given tea in the Riding School, Royal Mews on 26 December. Mrs Carteret Carey, wife of the Deputy Governor of Windsor Castle, had arranged a large Christmas tree from Windsor Great Park, and the Queen and Princess Mary had provided 200 gifts for the tree.

HEROIC ACTION BY A CLEWER MAN [4]

News has come to hand of the gallantry of a young man from Clewer, which was the means of saving the lives of many of his comrades, but at the expense of over a hundred wounds for the man concerned. The soldier in question is Lance-Corporal J H Smith, of the Middlesex Regiment, whose mother lives at 'Fernlea', Surly Hall Road, Clewer, and he has previously been awarded the Military Medal for bravery in action, so that what he will receive for this last act of gallantry remains to be seen. Lance-Corporal Smith was in a bomb shed when he saw a fuse ignited, and at once attempted to throw himself on the bomb to save his comrades in the shed. The bomb went off before he got to it, but he received the charge instead of his comrades, and the rest of the stores were saved. It is a fortunate thing for him that things happened as they did, for he would probably have been blown to pieces had he acted a minute earlier. As it was, he was not wounded so very severely, for though he received over a hundred bits of shell in him, not a wound was of a serious nature... Lance-Corporal Smith was formerly apprenticed at Mr C C Harrison's of Peascod Street, and he was a very well-known local footballer.

Roll of Honour

The first Roll of Honour of 1916, and the 59th since the start of the war, listed just nineteen men from Windsor who had volunteered. It included four members of the Birrell family, two of whom were killed. Private A A Birrell served with the Alberta Canadian Infantry, but was said to be prisoner of war in 1916. He died on 1 January 1919 and is buried in Windsor Cemetery. Private W E Birrell serving with the Royal Fusiliers was killed in October 1918 and is buried in Rouen. It also included men who were sick, for example Cpl Reg Cave, Berkshire Yeomanry, who was in hospital at Alexandria with scarlet fever.

Each week more names appeared under killed, wounded, in

4. *Windsor Express 12 August 1916*

hospital, missing or taken prisoner, even shell shocked, than under volunteered, and casualty lists increased alarmingly in July, as the cost of the Somme offensive became only too evident. The casualty list for the first week in July had twenty-eight names on it, but ninety the following week. Many of these have no known grave.

Schools published their own Rolls of Honour. The Royal Free School recorded 400 names of past pupils and masters in January, twenty-four of whom had been killed and twenty-nine wounded. Clewer St Stephen Boys' School published a list of old boys and staff on 1 April, eighteen men had been killed in action or had died from wounds, two were prisoners of war, and 226 were on active service, including five Quarterman boys who had enlisted together in January. On 29 April the school added another 79 names to the list of those on active service. St Edward RC School, a small school attached to the church presented their Roll of Honour in June; forty-two were serving, five had been killed in action and five were wounded.

Mr G Bates, 98 Grove Road, lost his son, Leading Seaman Bernard Emile Bates, aged 31, on 5 June 1916 when HMS *Hampshire* struck a mine. Mr Bates had only just received a telegram from his son, telling him that both he and his brother George, who was serving on the *Emperor of India*, were safe after a battle. Leading Seaman Bates had fourteen years' service in the Navy and had just passed his examination as a First Class Petty Officer. He has no known grave but is remembered on the Portsmouth Naval Memorial.

The suicide of a soldier from Windsor was reported on 13 May. Driver Frederick T Pomfret aged 40, of the Royal Engineers, was probably suffering from shell shock when he took his own life in Aldershot on 8 May. He left a widow and six children living in Oxford Road. He is buried in Clewer Cemetery.

A list of drummer boys serving in the 2nd Bn Grenadier Guards was published in the *Windsor Express* on 15 July. Of a total of twenty-nine boys who went out with the regiment in 1914, only eight were still remaining, ten had been killed, nine were wounded and two were prisoners of war. Drummer boys were enlisted from the age of 14 but should not have been in the trenches.

Pte George Ernest White, eldest son of Mr E G White, of 249 St Leonard's Road, was an 'Old National' boy. After leaving school, he was in service with Miss Riley, of Osborne Terrace, and later with Lady Tress Barry. In 1912, he emigrated to Canada, but came over with one of the earlier Expeditionary Forces, and had been in France only two months when he was killed on 3 August, aged 26. He is buried at Brandhoek Military Cemetery, Belgium but is not on any local war memorial.

On 12 August, the casualty list had 63 names on it, including three for shell-shock. Two Windsor heroes were specially mentioned; L/Cpl J H Smith, and 2nd Lt L E Parson, Royal Berkshire Regiment, whose parents lived in Thames Street, who was awarded the Military Cross.

Mystery death of a soldier in the Coldstream Guards.

Private Robert Sargeant aged 29, 5th Bn Coldstream Guards, who had fought at Mons, was killed by falling 27ft from the window of his cubicle at Victoria Barracks and breaking his neck. The small window was 3ft 8in above his bed and shut, and he would have had to make an effort to get up to the window and go out head first. The medical officer thought that he might have been dreaming that he was in France and not realising where he was, got out of the window. An inquest recorded that Sargeant died from a broken neck caused by a fall from the window but that there was no evidence as to what caused him to fall.

Aliens in Windsor

In February, notice was given that aliens of all nationalities residing in Windsor, except the Belgian refugees, must register at the Police Station on or before 14 February. Inn-keepers and lodging house-keepers were told that they must keep a register of all aliens over the age of 14 who were staying with them.

A strange case came before the Magistrates in May. Arthur Bruckner aged 36, who had enlisted in the Berkshire Yeomanry in July 1915, was charged with being an enemy subject, to wit, a German and had failed to comply with the Alien Registration Order 1914. Although he had been born in Australia, his parents were German and he had contact with a German brother, sister and a wife. He admitted to having lied about being a British subject, but he wanted to serve in the British Army and in order to do so, he had to lie. The magistrates sent him to prison for six months with hard labour.

Another alien, Marie Louise le Bihan, employed by Caleys Ltd, had also offended against the Alien Registration Order. As she had limited English and did not understand the need to register as an alien, the Bench dismissed the summons against her, but fined Caleys £1 1s for employing her without making sure she was registered.

In June, lodging house keeper Charlotte Hobbs of Sheet Street was summoned for failing to get signed statements from her guests or keep a register of them, and for failing to inform the authorities about who was staying with her. She was fined 9s.

A man giving the name of Morris Leeche aged 65, described as a Russian Pole of no fixed abode, was charged with being an alien and unlawfully failing to furnish the Registration Officer in Windsor with the particulars of his arrival on 5 September. He was also charged with a similar offence carried out on March 10. He was sent to prison for two weeks on each charge, making one month in all.

German prisoners of war were also causing problems. In late September five of them escaped from a camp near Aldershot. Three days later three men were recaptured in Ascot, which created a great deal of excitement in the town. The prisoners had walked at night and hidden themselves during the day, and had not the faintest idea of where they were. The other two were caught near Winkfield the following day, hungry and tired.

In early December, there was another breakout from the prisoner of war camp at nearby Holyport. Lt Anton Cmentek, 15th Reserve Infantry Regiment and Lt Otto Thelen, German Flying Corps escaped by hiding in bundles of waste paper:

… It was the rule to collect the waste paper about the grounds, which was tied into bundles and wheeled in barrows by German orderlies to some stores outside the grounds… It would appear the two officers had been bound around with waste paper, and to get air used a stick of elder wood from which they had removed the pith. The stick just emerged from the paper and nothing unusual was noticed. The men had also provided themselves with blankets to rest their heads on. It is thought that they lay in the waste paper for some time. After they had been deposited in the stores they seemed to have freed themselves, put off their uniforms, and donned mufti. [4]

SOME OF OUR PRISONERS.

The Germans have boasted of the capture of prisoners in the Great Offensive. Our men captured prisoners too. Here is a sample group.

According to the newspaper they were recaptured in Old Windsor at midnight on 7 December:

Police Constable Crook, of the Berks Police, saw the two men coming along the road from the direction of Datchet. They were well dressed in civilian clothes, and the constable's suspicions were aroused. He stopped them and asked them who they were. One replied that he was Swiss and the other said he was an Englishman and came from Kent… The policeman was not satisfied with their story, as although they spoke English well, it was with a German accent. When asked their names one replied 'Nelson'. The constable took the men to Clewer Police Station, and here they were questioned by Superintendent Jannaway. They then admitted that they had escaped from the Detention

4. *Windsor Express 16 December 1916*

Camp at Holyport... The prisoners were searched, and on them were found a map of London, a compass, chocolate, and money. Each man had 5s in English money, and one had an Italian document on him...

The future of the aeroplane

On 25 November a long article in the *Windsor Express* by Windsor resident F J Camm, (brother of Sydney Camm who designed the Hawker Hurricane used during the Second World War), predicted that aircraft would play an important part in shaping the future. 'The war has done more for private aviation than private experiment could have accomplished'. He foresaw the building of aerodromes as 'business minds' will explore it as a 'new means of transit'.

1917

The New Year has dawned on a sorrow-stricken world, and 1917 will undoubtedly be a very critical year for our Empire… Let 1917 be for every Briton a year of abstinence, economy and self-sacrifice – a year of achievement which will ensure victory and a lasting peace.

These were the sombre notes of the first editorial of the *Windsor Express* in January 1917.

Christmas had passed with the customary celebrations, if somewhat muted. Combermere Barracks held their New Year Concert and punch bowl at the NCO's Mess. At Victoria Barracks the wives and families of the Coldstream Guards were entertained in the spacious dining hall.

At the Windsor Town Council meeting in January one of the main subjects that came up for consideration was the question of allotments for local people as 'the best solution to the food supply problem at the present crisis'. Following an advertisement in the paper fifty men had applied for land. An Allotments Committee was set up and anyone who had land for cultivation was invited to get in touch. The Council was further empowered to 'enter upon unoccupied land for the purpose of allotting plots to cultivators for the production of food'. [1] It was also decided to allow the keeping of pigs. Seed potatoes were soon made available. Fifty-one plots out of sixty-four had been taken up by the end of the month.

Also launched in January was the War Loans Campaign at a public meeting at the Guildhall, though it was not as well attended as it should have been. On 10 January readers of the *Windsor Express* were warned:

Less than a week now remains during which applications can

1. *Windsor Express 13 January 1917*

be sent in for the War Loans. The smaller subscriptions are wanted just as much as the larger... It must be clearly borne in mind, too, that if there is an inadequate response to the Victory War Loan, money will be taken from people compulsorily.

In the end it was a gigantic success, as vast sums were invested during the last few days.

The huge explosion at the TNT factory in the East End of London on 19 January was heard in Windsor, 'it made the windows at the Castle rattle'. Seventy-three people lost their lives in the explosion, and 900 nearby houses were destroyed.

The Windsor Fire Brigade was fifty years old in February. There was a formal gathering at the Town Hall, attended by Mr F B Buckland, one of the few surviving member of the original Brigade, but proper jubilee celebrations were put off till after the war. Fourteen of its members had joined the forces, thus the strength of the Brigade was much diminished.

The winter of 1917 was the severest one of the war. At the beginning of February heavy snowfalls covered the Thames Valley and sharp frost transformed lakes into skating rinks. March was the coldest for twenty-five years, and it was noted that snow had fallen on twenty-one days since the New Year. Conditions on the Western Front were, however, much worse, in some areas the frost and snow lasted well into April. A film at the Royal Albert Institute on 5 March showed America preparing for war. (The USA declared war on

Germany in April, but there was little mention of this in the *Windsor Express*.)

With spring bringing better weather, wounded soldiers were again invited to visit the Royal Apartments at Windsor Castle, after which they were served tea in the Servants' Hall.

The clocks went forward on Easter Sunday, 8 April, as daylight saving was implemented for the second year. Car owners were once more asked to place their vehicles at the disposal of the Berkshire Territorial Force in case of military emergency or for helping with the Red Cross. An editorial on 21 April looked forward with optimism to an end of the war by September.

St George's Day was celebrated in Windsor with a market selling fruit, flowers, dairy produce and other articles. Young ladies sold flags in the streets and Queen Mary drove through the town, which was gaily bedecked with flags of Britain and all our Allies, even the Stars and Stripes were in evidence. There were large crowds to watch the Royal procession and the bells of the church were ringing. The fine weather added to a joyous occasion.

The food shortage was a major topic of debate during 1917, not just the disruption of supplies from abroad caused by the submarine menace. There had been fifty-five vessels lost in a single week in April, and farm-workers had been called up in such numbers that it seriously affected the production of food. Women volunteers could not replace the shortfall. The Army Council decided that the number of men to be taken from agriculture was not to exceed the 30,000 already taken, and soldiers on leave, or those stationed in the UK should be made available for farm work. Meanwhile allotments were seen to be part of the answer. Schoolboys were encouraged to work the land in their spare time. The Board of Agriculture recommended that house sparrows should be culled, as they ate enormous amounts of grain in the autumn.

In May, three acres of Crown Land near Bourne Lane was secured for allotments providing a further 30-40 plots. All allotment holders were urged to spray their potatoes against disease in July, to combat the shortage of potatoes; machinery and chemicals were provided by the Board of Agriculture at the cost price of 4d per pole.

The Windsor Rose Show was cancelled, instead the Committee decided to join with the Chrysanthemum Society and the Windsor Town Council Allotments Committee to work towards the production of vegetables under the banner of Windsor, Eton and District Horticultural Society.

Empire Day was celebrated in Windsor with a parade, followed by displays in the Home Park by the Navy League Boys, Windsor Holy Trinity and Parish Church Cadets, Boy Scouts, Wolf Cubs, Girl Guides and the Cadets of Windsor County Boys' School.

During the Whitsun Bank Holiday weekend, Windsor was busy with visitors enjoying the fine weather. River boats were in great demand and boat owners had a busy time. In June a party of wounded soldiers from King Edward VII Hospital were treated to a river trip to Bourne End and back, with 'a bountiful tea'.

In June the Mayor welcomed soldiers of the American Army on a visit to Windsor and Eton. There were no flag waving crowds, as few knew an hour beforehand that the men were coming. Another foreign group to visit Windsor was a party of Norwegian sailors sight-seeing before returning home. Meanwhile, the Canadian Forestry Corps settled into a camp in the Great Park. The Colours of the 122nd Overseas Battalion of the Canadian Expeditionary Force were deposited in St George's Chapel in July.

Record rainfall was recorded for July, it 'fell with pitiless persistency' the *Windsor Express* reported. Much damage was done to corn, and reports came in of potato disease in Maidenhead. The rain also fell on the Western Front, turning the battle for Passchendaele into a sea of mud.

On Saturday 4 August, the war had lasted three years, and there were no signs of peace being declared. Hope was expressed that 'when America puts her full strength forth the end will be in sight'. At Windsor there was a special service at the Parish Church and a public meeting on Castle Hill. The Stars and Stripes were flown next to the Union Flag at Windsor Castle.

About 80 wounded South African soldiers came to Windsor from Richmond Park, where they were staying. They marched to the Castle headed by four pipers of the Scots Guards, with the Union and Rhodesian flags flying.

In September, two more prisoners escaped form the prisoners' camp in Holyport; airmen Lts von Scholtz and Flink, aimed to steal an aeroplane and fly back to Germany. They managed to get to Beckenham in Kent, before being recaptured. Also in September the home of the late Sir Francis Tress Barry, MP for Windsor 1890-1906, on St Leonard's Hill, was sold by Lady Tress Barry.

The autumn saw a number of military sport days and a Great Autumn Show of vegetables and fruit at the Royal Albert Institute, in conjunction with the Windsor and District Horticultural Society. Princess Alice opened the show; she was surprised at what working men had accomplished in such a short season, considering that most allotments had been grass land at the beginning of the year. In October an Allotment Holders' Association was formed for Windsor and District for the mutual benefit to all concerned. One object of the Association was to obtain more land for allotments. In November, sixty-one acres of grass land at Spital was identified as suitable for allotments. The Association numbered 100 members by the end of the year.

Councillor William Carter was formally re-elected Mayor of Windsor, making it five years in succession. The council expressed the wish that he would be the Mayor who announced that peace was declared.

On the night of 19/20 October, thirteen of the latest design German airships followed their usual bombing route from across the North Sea, and after bombing London, a storm blew several of them off course and at least one flew over Windsor. Air raid warning had been given and blackout restrictions were in force; the Zeppelins passed silently over Windsor causing panic amongst the local population.

Next day, Saturday 20 October was called Our Day. Flags were sold in the streets and there were stalls for the sale of various items outside the Guildhall. The amount raised for the British Red Cross was £460.

An appeal went out in October from the Berkshire War Pensions Committee for light part-time work for wounded and disabled soldiers who were no longer able to take up their old employment.

Moonlight bombing raids on London by German planes caused concern in Windsor in October, as many Londoners were coming out to the country. Windsor had never been so full; there was not a single house to let, and many had taken in lodgers. In addition, the shortage of housing for working people was a subject for debate throughout the year. The council promised to build new houses once the war was over, but the urgent need for homes became apparent in a letter to the *Windsor Express* by a soldier on leave, who had no luck trying to re-house his family. 'Now my wife and children are faced with the prospect of being put into the street in a fortnight's time, unless a seeming miracle should happen'.

There was further distress in Windsor for the poor. Many could not adequately feed themselves and their families, so a communal kitchen was set up by the War Savings Committee. The Council made a loan of £25, which was repaid in December, when the kitchen was fully running and self-supporting. The kitchen was next to the National School with an entrance in a narrow passage near the Almshouses. During the week ending 8 December 80 gallons of soup were handed out. 'It is a great improvement on the old Soup Kitchen and has undoubtedly come to stay'.[2] The Queen paid a visit to the kitchen in September, even helping to serve the dinners.

In December a meeting was held at the Gladstone Hall to establish a branch of the Workers' Union at Windsor, in conjunction with the Windsor and District Trades and Labour Council. Woman were urged join the Workers' Union so that their interests might be looked after once the war was over. Miss Manicom, the women's organiser, said they had long wanted to form a Worker's Union in Windsor, but Windsor was one of those places, which was particularly hard to tackle. 'One reason was because a great many of the people had been brought up to bow and scrape to those above them...'

A tragic accident happened at Victoria Barracks in December, when a young soldier, Private George F Gates of the Coldstream Guards was killed by a shot from a Lewis gun while attending

2. *Windsor Express 8 December 1917*

an instruction class. He was buried at Windsor Cemetery with military honours.

Boys and Bombs

On a Thursday morning in September 1917 just after 9.30am, the residents of Eton were startled by hearing a loud report that was caused by the explosion of a bomb in one of the small houses in King Stable Street. Some three weeks earlier a fourteen-year-old lad named Charles Bampton, son of Mr and Mrs C A Bampton, 4 King Stable Street, picked up a practise bomb on the Brocas and took it home. His father, realising the dangerous nature of the find, took the bomb from the lad and hid it in the scullery roof. The boy managed to discover the hiding place and took the bomb into the front room of the house, where he endeavoured to unscrew it, with the intention of emptying it. Hearing a hissing noise he immediately dropped it on a table, ducked his head and rushed for the door, which he just managed to open when the bomb exploded. All the panes of glass in the front window were smashed, as were a quantity of plates, cups and saucers… and a number of holes pierced in the ceiling. The boy had a miraculous escape and sustained no injury whatever. His mother, with the baby, had only left the room a moment or two previously and thus had a fortunate escape. [3]

A few weeks later some boys searching for bombs in the trenches in the Great Park, not far from the Long Walk, found two in a pond and others in the trenches. They threw one of the bombs on the ground, and it exploded. A little girl, Winifred May Streamer, was in the Park with her older brother, also looking at the trenches. Unfortunately a piece of shrapnel struck the girl on the cheek, and the other boys run off in the direction of Old Windsor. The girl was taken to hospital by a passing Army Chaplain. Warning signs were then placed pointing out the danger of handling anything found on the ground there.

Trenches had been dug in the Great Park during 1915 to give raw recruits a taste of the fighting to come, by 1917 they were little used, but no one had thought of removing any live ammunition.

3. *Windsor Express 15 September 1917*

Roll of Honour

The first few months of 1917 were relatively quiet, with fewer names on the weekly Roll of Honour. L/Cpl C J Goodchild of 2 Manor Terrace, Clewer Green who was serving with the Royal Berkshire Regiment died of wounds on 24 November 1916. He was mentioned in January. Also in January, Windsor lad Frederick Somner aged 17, received a commendation for commendable service. He was the third son of Mr and Mrs John Somner of 23 Russell Street, and serving in the Navy as a signaller, a skill he learned while in the Windsor Parish Church Company of the Church Lads' Brigade. His brother Ernest was killed in October 1914 and another brother John was wounded in October 1916.

Another family honoured in the *Windsor Express* in February

63

was the Gray family of Goswell Cottages. Mr and Mrs George Gray had three sons fighting, a fourth serving in the Training Reserve and a son-in-law just returned from active service. Mr Gray was himself an old pensioner of over 37 years service.

Windsor baker, Edward Hicks of Oxford Road, was proud to claim six sons in the Army, three in the Royal Engineers, two in the Transport Corps and one in the Berkshire Yeomanry. They all came back home.

A second tragedy hit the Groves family of Hundred Steps Lodge. Private Frederick Groves, Royal Scots Regiment was killed on 4 May and is buried in Faubourg D'Amiens Cemetery, Arras. His older brother was killed in December 1914. (*See Letters from the Front 1914*)

On 9 April the Battle of Arras had started and the casualty list contained more names than in recent weeks. Sixteen casualties, including eight deaths were recorded on 21 April and seventeen casualties with nine deaths the following week. Among those listed were Sergeant F C Giles, Royal Berkshire Regiment, a former Windsor National School boy who lived in King's Road, killed on 16 April, and Second Lt David V Humphreys, Argyll and Sutherland Highlanders, killed in action on 24 April. Humphreys' Commanding Officer wrote:

> …The task set to the Regiment was one of the hardest in the war: the taking of a barbed wire trench followed by a village, and the ground ahead. Your son was one of the first of the assaulting waves, and like many of his poor comrades was killed cutting the wire. [4]

Both are remembered on the Thiepval Memorial, as they have no known grave.

The next wave of casualties came with the third Battle of Ypres, (Passchendaele) during the summer and autumn months of 1917. Several Windsor men are buried at Mendingham Military Cemetery in Belgium. Here are just three: Private W G Green, husband of Annie Green of Arthur Road serving with the Royal Berks Regiment, was killed on 19 August, and Bombardier J B

4. *Windsor Express 12 May 1917*

Tracy of the Royal Flying Corps died on 7 September after he was wounded by a shell; his wife lived at 285 St Leonard's Road. Gunner Arthur Edward Draycott of 16 Russell Street, serving with the Royal Field Artillery was gassed on 24 November and died two days later. His younger brother, Private F E Draycott, Worcester Regiment was killed on 26 May 1918.

Many others were buried in the Tyne Cot Cemetery, the largest British cemetery in Belgium. Private Sidney Ernest Webb, Royal Berkshire Regiment, killed in Flanders on 12 December, and Sapper George Polden Ledgley, Royal Engineers, killed on 25 October aged 29 are both remembered on the Tyne Cot Memorial. George Ledgley had been the only surviving son of Mr and Mrs Ledgley, of 40 Albany Road, Windsor, their younger son was killed in action in August 1916, and Mrs Webb of 19 Ray Avenue Clewer had three sons and three sons-in-law in the forces.

There were also local casualties at sea. Edward Parsonage of 67 Bourne Avenue was drowned in the sinking by a U-boat of HMS *Recruit* on 9 August. He was 25 years of age and educated at the Windsor National School. He is remembered on the Chatham Naval Memorial, but not on any Windsor Memorial. His brother Albert was killed on 21 August 1915 in Gallipoli.

The Windsor and District Liberal Club unveiled a plaque inscribed with 116 names of club member who had joined the Forces. Of these 19 were killed and 20 wounded.

The Tegg family

George William Tegg, a farm labourer and his wife Sarah moved from Waltham St Lawrence to Windsor during the 1880s. They had six children, four boys and two girls. At the outbreak of war they lived in a cottage on St Leonard's Hill.

Of their four boys James Frederick, born in 1881 had married Helen Cousins and they had two children, Georgina Helen and James Frederick junior. James joined the Hampshire Regiment and died in Iran on 15 November 1918, just days after the armistice. He is buried in Tehran Cemetery in Iran.

Charles Edwin, born 1884, had joined the Royal Berkshire Regiment, and was sent to Salonika where he died on 22 October

1917. He is buried in Karasouli Military Cemetery in Greece.

Arthur, born 1888, still lived with his parents when he joined the Royal Berkshire Regiment. He died of wounds on 29 March 1918 and is buried in Doullens Cemetery in France. All three are on the Clewer War Memorial.

Only William George born 1877 survived the war, he may not have served, as there is no war record for him.

James Frederick junior's grandson, Mark Tegg still lives in Windsor.

Blood transfusion at the front

A Windsor man and old Clewer St Stephen boy who lived at 11 Alma Road, was praised for bravery of a different kind. Trooper Albert Stannett of the 2nd Life Guards was wounded by a shell in September 1917, and while in hospital in France he volunteered to give blood so that another man might be saved. Driver Alick Shearer, severely wounded, was losing blood from a main artery. Stannett, after offering to help, was placed on the operating table beside him and a great quantity of blood was transfused. Unfortunately, his brave action proved of no avail as Shearer died, and Stannett took a long time to recover, because of the loss of blood.

At the end of the month a letter was published from Helen Shearer, the mother of the soldier who had died. It was addressed to the wife of Trooper Albert Stannett, praising her husband's brave action:

> … Two days ago I received the sad news from a chaplain that my dear son, Driver Alick Shearer, RFA, had been very severely wounded, penetrating the main artery of the left thigh. His condition was so weak that the doctors, as a last resort, resolved to try transfusion. A comrade volunteered that blood should be taken from his veins to supply what the doctors required in their endeavours to save my dear son's life. The soldier's name given to me by the chaplain is trooper Albert Stannett… Sad to say, his generous sacrifice was of no avail, as I received another letter yesterday saying that my son Alick had passed away on the 23rd August… I shall be greatly indebted to you if you would kindly send me Trooper Stannett's present address so that I can write to him, and send him a mother's gracious thanks for his heroic sacrifice. Hoping this letter will be the means of me getting in communication with such a brave soldier.

1918

There were no joy bells to speed the parting of 1917, and only sombre notes ushered in 1918.

Christmas and the New Year were celebrated at both barracks with concerts and dances. On Christmas Eve, members of the Life Guards band went round Windsor to visit several officers' homes and that of the Mayor of Windsor, and serenaded them according to an old custom called 'the peregrination of Christmas waits'.

The first Sunday of the year was a memorable one throughout the Empire. In all churches and other places of worship the King's Proclamation was read, and special prayers were said. The congregations in the Windsor churches were exceptionally large.

The Royal Albert Institute was feeling the strains of the war. Over one hundred of its members were doing war work or fighting at the front, and the loss of their subscriptions was severely felt. Members were encouraged to nominate friends and relatives as possible new members, however, there did not seem much hope of clearing their deficit until after the war. Only their entertainment programme was successful.

Royal Albert Institute, Windsor.

SPECIAL CINEMA WEEK,
MONDAY, JANUARY 29th, & DURING THE WEEK.

When Mr. G. E. BENNETT presents the following programme of Special Attractions:

BATTLE OF THE ANCRE
And THE ADVANCE of
" THE TANKS "
(Official War Office Film).

THE ROMANCE OF

DAVID LLOYD GEORGE,
EXCLUSIVELY BOOKED FOR THIS SPECIAL WEEK.
A Cartoon Film of Britain's Great Statesman, founded on sittings specially given to Mr. Ernest H. Mills.

CANADA'S FIGHTING FORCES, Royal Naval Air Service Section.

Three Performances Daily: 3, 6 & 8 p.m.

PRICES OF ADMISSION :—Balcony (reserved and numbered), 2s. 2d. ; Body of Hall, 1s. 2d. and 7d. All prices include Tax.

Reserved Seats may be booked in advance (till one hour before each performance), of Messrs. Oxley and Son, 4, High-street, Windsor (Phone, Windsor 46).

In February the *Windsor Express* reported: 'By the new Reform Act eight million more voters were added to the Parliamentary Register'. This meant that every man who was a householder and, for the first time, women who were over 30 and householders or householders' wives would have a vote. 'The introduction of the female vote is a great stride', enthused the editor.

In March, the Prince of Wales accepted the office of High Steward of Windsor, a position vacant since the death of Prince Christian in October 1917.

The German Spring Offensive, Operation 'Michael', was received with a mixture of gloom and defiance. The editorial on 30 March read: 'The peril is great, and the situation is grave, but if we only stick it we shall come eventually to victory'. Even Queen Mary, who did not usually comment on the progress of the war, wrote in her diary that the news from France was not very good. The German Spring Offensive led to a new crisis; the Army needed more men. A further editorial in the *Windsor Express* on 20 April sounded more defiant:

> We have our backs to the wall and we mean to fight it out to the last man and the last shilling. We have had a rather bad week, and serious inroads have been made into our lines in Flanders. The battle has been raging fiercely and the German troops have gained fresh territory… When we think of what our gallant soldiers are enduring, our inconveniences and troubles are most insignificant.

In April the Royal Albert Institute held a War Exhibition, combined with a sale of a number of trophies and relics from the battlefields. There was also a display of artistic work done by British, French and Belgian soldiers in the trenches, in internment camps and in hospitals. The proceeds of the sales of artwork went to the men and their families.

Also in April, King George V and Queen Mary presented their State portraits to the Mayor and Corporation on behalf of the people of Windsor; the portraits were hung in the Windsor Guildhall.

St George's Day was observed at Windsor as it had been throughout the war. The King sent the Mayor a cheque for £100 for local charities and the Queen drove through the town that was decorated with flags. Fancy goods were sold in the market place and one lady selling flags got up at 6am to catch the munitions workers going away by train. Five hundred and five pounds was raised on the day.

Over 100 officers and men from an American air squadron were invited to Windsor Castle in early May. They were shown round St George's Chapel, the Albert Memorial Chapel, and some parts of the Castle. The officers were presented to the King, and all the airmen were entertained to tea in the Grand Hall. The visit finished about six o'clock.

The Spring Bank Holiday at the end of May was blessed with good weather. Windsor was visited by thousands of holiday-makers and the river was alive with crafts throughout the day. Some bad conduct of the 'hooligan variety' with bad language was reported, but most people seemed to enjoy themselves.

The National War Aims Committee of the Ministry of Information found a way to entertain the people of Windsor with a giant outdoor cinema show. A large screen covered the south side of the Guildhall, a projector with a dynamo was placed on a motor lorry, and projected pictures and information of what 'our fighting forces are doing' onto the screen. The large crowd that gathered was said to be 'much interested and amused'.

At the end of May, news from the front was still 'very critical'. The editorial of The *Windsor Express* on 1 June read:

> The German forces have begun another great offensive movement, and are now holding positions which have been in the Allies possession since September 1914... for the sake of future generations we must fight on.

A week later the editor wrote: 'The sky is very overcast just now, and the times are very anxious', but 'the Allies have faith in ultimate victory'. This was the second phase of the 'Kaiserschlacht', Germany's last offensive, which soon was to run out of steam.

The Windsor Rose Show was abandoned again and funds were given instead to encourage food production.

War Weapons Week was planned for 8 -13 July. The aim was for Windsor and Eton to raise £20,000. The editorial of the *Windsor Express* on 6 July encouraged the readers:

Wokingham had raised that sum, so it should be an easy matter for Windsor and Eton to provide that sum... We have yet to win the war, and in order to do this we must plank down our money; every cent that we can spare, and we must remember that we are not asked to give the money. All we are required to do is to invest it in National War Bonds and War Saving Certificates and the country will pay 10s interest yearly for every £10 invested...

They wanted to raise enough money to buy a large gun, which would be named after Windsor, a sea-plane named after Eton, and perhaps even an aeroplane named after Clewer. The Mayor had managed to get a German Howitzer gun, which was on display on Castle Hill. In the event Windsor managed to raise a staggering £75,000.

Also in July, the Government announced it needed fruit stones and hard nut shells for a special war purpose, and householders were urgently requested to form 'Stone and Shell Clubs'. There was no clue what the special war purpose was, but it was said to be vital for the safety of our soldiers at the front. However, on 31 August, a newspaper report revealed that they were vital in the manufacture of anti-gas masks. A number of Windsor grocers' shops then collected them on behalf of the Government. Paper, too, was in short supply and a special collection of paper started on Monday, 15 July.

On 4 August, the anniversary of the start of the war was marked as a Day of Remembrance in every town throughout the Empire. Later that month, a British airship flew over Windsor on two separate occasions, 'the occupants of the gondola were plainly visible'. [1]

The United Kingdom was preparing for a general election in November. The number of voters in the Windsor district contained twice as many names as formerly, and of course for the first time included women.

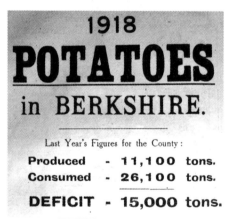

1918
POTATOES
in BERKSHIRE.

Last Year's Figures for the County:

Produced - **11,100** tons.
Consumed - **26,100** tons.

DEFICIT - **15,000 tons.**

LORD RHONDDA & MR. PROTHERO appeal to every man in the County who has a Farm, a Garden or an Allotment to plant more Potatoes and

MAKE THE COUNTY
SELF SUPPORTING.

The harvest was the best in recent years, and was being got in under practically ideal conditions. At Eton, German prisoners of war were helping with harvesting and threshing wheat grown on the playing fields.

Jam was scarce due to the shortage of sugar, and most supplies went to soldiers at the front, but many people went to pick blackberries and came back loaded. A number of local people were able to get extra sugar

1. *Windsor Express 17 August 1918*

for jam making

In September the news from the front was much better. 'Everything, in fact, is going well for us', the editor of the *Windsor Express* wrote, but he pessimistically added 'it may take a year or two before the war is ended'.

A national railway strike by the locomotive engineers and firemen, which took place in October was condemned by all. It closed among others the Great Western line from Windsor. The editor of the *Windsor Express* commented:

> To have done this when the gravest interests of the nation are at stake is both un-English and unpatriotic... The strikers are playing the German's game, and it does seem remarkable that when everything is going on so well on all our Fronts we should have this selfish and short-sighted strike.

It seems incredible, that DORA, which banned flying kites and lighting bonfires, was unable to prevent a strike like this, which could have had devastating consequences. In fact, the end of September saw a major turning point in the war. The new offensive against the Hindenburg Line marked 'the beginning of the end'.

A new store opened in Windsor on 12 October 1918, when W J Daniel & Co, general drapers of Ealing, acquired the site in Peascod Street, where they still continue their business.

'Peace Talks' was the great news proclaimed by both local papers on 19 October, but the following week the main topic was the ongoing influenza epidemic. Most of Windsor's schools were closed.

Another flag day called

COMRADES
of the Great War
(Windsor & District Branch)

VICTORY.

If YOU consider it your duty to make a VICTORY OFFERING to the men who have secured VICTORY: may we remind you that the above organization is in urgent need of funds to open premises in Windsor for ex-Soldiers and Sailors of all rank,

OBJECTS :

ASSISTANCE BUREAUX.—To assist comrades and other dependents in the way of pensions, employment, &c., &c.
RECREATION & SPORTS.—To arrange weekly programmes, including Whist Drives, Discussions and Concerts, etc., etc.; also to organize all kinds of sports.
MUSEUM. — To preserve personal trophies presented by ex-sailors and soldiers.

The Boys at the Front have not let you down—God alone knows what that has meant sometimes—so do not let them down now, but send us a donation, large or small, and help us to keep our Comradeship for ever.

Local Hon. Secretary : A. L. SHARPE,
46, Alma-road, Windsor.

The Boys will soon be home so let us be prepared for them.

'Our Day' to raise money for the British Red Cross was held on the last Saturday in October. A very respectable £540 was collected by selling a variety of articles, flags and emblems at stalls around the Guildhall.

Samuel Maun, the Stationmaster of the Great Western Railway in Windsor, was one of the first to receive the news that the war had ended. On the morning of 11 November, Princess Alice, Countess of Athlone, told Maun that an armistice had been signed earlier that morning but he had to keep the news secret until it was officially announced at 11.00am.

The glorious news that an armistice had been signed with Germany on 11 November was reported in the local newspapers on 16 November. Windsor fittingly celebrated the great day and an editorial in the *Windsor Express* described 'scenes of joyousness such as have not been witnessed in the Royal Borough for a decade'. A further article in the same edition cautioned that: 'we must never forget, in the midst of all our joy, to be thankful to the men who have fought and bled and died for us.' The Coldstream Guards and Windsor Firemen, headed by the band of the 2nd Life Guards paraded through the town at midday, and there was a torchlight procession in the evening. Churches were crowded to overflowing during services of thanksgiving, Princess Alice, Countess of Athlone attended the Parish Church.

Recruiting was stopped and all call up notices cancelled. Many of the restrictions on ringing of bells and chiming of clocks were cancelled, and the bells of the Parish Church and the Curfew Tower, Windsor Castle rang out for the first time in many years, lighting laws were also lifted. The Military Tribunal was suspended and all cases cancelled.

Roll of Honour 1918

Men who were killed during the third Battle of Ypres were still recorded on the Roll of Honour in early 1918, like L/Cpl William Thomas Thorn of the Oxford and Bucks Light Infantry, whose home was at 11 St Mark's Place. He was killed on 16 October, and is on the Tyne Cot Memorial but not on any Windsor memorial.

Gas and shell-shock were cited more frequently as causes of

death; Private Herbert Frederick Biggs , 2nd Royal Berks Regiment, died in King Edward VII Hospital on 18 February aged 21, as the result of gas poisoning and shell shock. He had been wounded twice but was badly gassed at Cambrai on his third time at the front. He used to live at 15 Gardener Cottages and was buried at Clewer Churchyard.

The early months of 1918 were relatively quiet and few casualties were reported, but with the German Spring Offensive in full swing, the numbers on the Roll of Honour started to increase. Ten local men were killed in March, three of them on the 28th: Captain John S Darby aged 27, Royal Berkshire Regiment whose parents live at 2 Lynton Villas, New Road, is buried at Villers-Bretonneux Cemetery. Private Alfred Swain, Northumberland Fusiliers, was just 20, and is remembered on the Pozieres Memorial. His parents, who had three sons fighting in the war, lived at 73 Victoria Cottages. Private J Lessimore of Clewer had joined the Scottish Rifles, and is remembered on the Arras Memorial but not on any local war memorial.

One of the first American casualties of the war had a Windsor connection. Private Montagu Horsley, born in the USA, had worked as a printer at Messrs Oxley and Son in 1915. He tried to join the British Army but was turned down as an American national. Soon after America entered the war he volunteered into their Army and went to France in January 1918, but he was one of the first Americans to fall in action.

A number of awards were also recorded in early 1918; two Windsor brothers, Sergeant Major George H Skinner, Royal Berks Regiment and Private H G Skinner ASC won the Military Medal in April. They had both attended the Windsor National School. Another brother, Bert, was serving in Italy. Company Sergeant Major A W Wellbelove, an old Clewer St Stephen boy who had joined the Mechanical Transport, Army Service Corps, eldest son of Mr and Mrs Wellbelove, Curfew Tower, Windsor Castle, was awarded the Military Medal for devotion to duty. His younger brother Bombardier John Victor Wellbelove, Royal Field Artillery, died in action on 21 June at the age of 26. His Captain wrote:

'He, together with the other men this morning, were cleaning up the guns, when a few shells fell nearby, and whilst running down the road another shell fell amongst them, killing your son and five others instantaneously. I am very sorry to lose him, as he was a good, keen boy, and very popular in the Battery'.

He is buried at Crucifix Corner Cemetery, Villers-Bretonneux.

Much has been published about those who gave their lives at the front, but less about those who had given their health. Private Ben Cutts serving with the Machine Gun Corps, of The Tapestries Old Windsor, was gassed and severely burned in April 1918. He spent six weeks in hospital in France, and after two further months in Birkenhead Hospital was said to be making slow but satisfactory progress.

Second Lt Jack Sanders, eldest son of the late Mr Frederick Sanders, coal merchant at Windsor, died of wounds on 6 August and is buried at Gezaincourt Communal Cemetery. He had served for many years in the Berkshire Yeomanry, and after returning from South Africa on the outbreak of war he joined the 2nd King Edward's Horse, and in April 1915 went to France. During the German retreat on the Somme, February-March 1917, he was awarded the Military Medal. In August 1917 he took up a commission, and was gazetted to the Royal Fusiliers.

One of the many victims of influenza was Private E J Kidd, of 70 Oxford Road, Windsor, a Driver in the Royal Engineers. He died in hospital in Salonika in October, aged 22, but is not on a local war memorial

Private W J Squelch, eldest son of Mr and Mrs Squelch, 10 Rays Avenue, Surly Hall Road, Clewer, serving with the Wiltshire Regiment, died of pneumonia following influenza, on 1 November in Stevens Hospital, Dublin, aged 18.

Finally, two Windsor men who served through most of the war and were killed just before the armistice:

Corporal William Richard Butler, Machine Gun Corps, eldest son of Mrs Butler, 9 Adelaide Square, died on 23 October 1918, aged 21. He had been employed in the Lord Chamberlain's Department, Windsor Castle. He joined the Berkshire Yeomanry in 1915 and saw service in Egypt, Palestine and France. The King and Queen were informed of his death and sent his mother a message expressing their Majesties' deep sympathy at her loss. Cpl Butler is remembered on the Tyne Cot Memorial.

Private John Harry Nash, Devonshire Regiment, son of Mr H Nash, 1 Cleveland Villas, Springfield Road, was killed in action in France on 4 October, aged 24. He had been in the Army since 3 September, 1914. He was sent to France in July 1915; in the following autumn was in the severe fighting in Loos and came though unharmed. Owing to exposure he was in hospital for about five months, and was sent home to England for a period of convalescence. On recovering his health, he acted as a physical instructor to recruits. In January 1918 he joined the British Force in Italy and saw fighting in the mountains. He was transferred to France in September, and seventeen days later was killed in action. He was an old Clewer St Stephen boy and played for his school in the McCloskie Shield competition. He is buried at Beaurevoir Communal Cemetery but his name is not recorded on any local war memorial.

Newsagent's Roll of Honour

Mr W Bye, newsagent of Peascod Street, had a Roll of Honour displayed in his shop, of boys who had joined up who were formerly employed by him. The list contained 101 names, the last being that of Mr Bye's eldest son, who had just joined the Royal Warwickshire Regiment on reaching the age of 18, and he was responsible for drawing up the Roll and illuminating it. Of the 101, ten had been killed, three had gained the DCM, one had a bar added to it, and one received the Military Medal.

Caleys

Captain Hugh William Caley died on 16 September 1918 aged 32. He was the only son of Mr and Mrs Hugh A Caley, of Thornbury House, Osborne Road, owners of the department store in Windsor High Street He was educated at Clifton College, University College School, and Pembroke College, Cambridge, taking his BA degree in 1908. He became a chartered accountant in 1911, and was in Brussels and Paris some few years for his firm. At the outbreak of war he was financial controller of a firm of motor engineers, near Paris, and became manager when it was taken over by the French Government as a munitions factory. He gave up this work in May 1916, and applied for a commission in the Army through his old Corps, the Cambridge University OTC, and being appointed to the Army Service Corps was, in July, sent to France as Railway Transport Officer.

Caley was later transferred to the Investigation Department at the Headquarters of this branch, where he quickly became adjutant. In July 1918 he was sent home for an operation, which was successful, but just before his discharge he was found to be suffering from nephritis, which took a very rapid course, and he died at Queen Alexandra Military Hospital, Milbank, on Monday, 16 September. He left a young widow, as he married Suzanne, daughter of the late Paul Dufresne of Versailles, in October 1917. The funeral service was held at Windsor Parish Church, where the whole of Messrs Caleys' staff assembled. He is buried at Windsor Cemetery. Hugh was destined to take over the store after the war, and his death led to the sale of Caleys to Selfridges after 100 years as a family business. The store was closed by John Lewis the then owner, in 2006.

A keen airman who never got his wings

Cadet Reginald Aden Robert Try, Royal Flying Corps, as told by his son.

My father was born on 9 April 1900. He was eager to 'do his bit' for the war, but it was not until September 1917 that he was old enough to realise his dream of joining the Royal Flying Corps. He told me: 'I applied for a Flying Officer Commission in the Royal Flying Corps at the age of 17 years and 5 months. I was interviewed at Whitehall, London and I was accepted'. But first he had to report to the Royal Berkshire Regiment in Reading for some basic drill. This is the regiment to which he would have been RTU'd (Returned to Unit) if he had failed.

He passed all the very difficult exams, first in Hastings, then at No 5 School of Aeronautics in Oxford, where he chose to become a Single Fighter Pilot. 'There were 15 of us to be fitted out with flying officer uniforms of the Royal Air Force in Oxford', he said. The RFC and RNAS had recently been amalgamated into the RAF.

In April 1918 King George V reviewed his group of newly qualified airmen in Hastings. Further gunnery training at Uxbridge was next, and in October he was ready and raring to go to France to gain his wings.

Too soon for young Reginald Try, Armistice Day came and he celebrated with his pals in Ealing. A few days later they were informed that they would be demobbed at once, as the Royal Air Force was going to be disbanded! He complained: 'We should have been given a chance to gain our wings'. He returned home to Windsor disappointed and deflated, but soon set himself up in business. He bought a military ambulance, turned it into a charabanc, and started Windsorian Coaches.

Geoffrey Try

Armistice to Peace

A 'better Britain' was the theme of the *Windsor Express* editorial on 23 November 1918. It was taken from the King's speech given to both Houses of Parliament after the armistice. 'We have to create a better Britain, to bestow more care on the health and wellbeing of the people, and to ameliorate further the conditions of labour', said George V. 'These words ought to be framed and hung up in every Council Chamber in the Kingdom', enthused the editor. While Windsor's Town Council discussed the problem of housing of the working classes, the subject of a befitting war memorial for Windsor was also under discussion. The Mayor suggested that re-building the Windsor Bridge, which was inadequate and out of date, would be a splendid memorial for Windsor men who had fallen, but there should also be a smaller memorial in the town. Other proposals included adopting a housing scheme and a free library, building a public hall, setting up a memorial club with sleeping accommodation, and new iron gates and railings in front of the Parish Church. At High Wycombe over £7000 had already been subscribed towards a War Memorial Hospital; Windsor felt sure it could match that figure and a fund was set up.

The Mayor, Councillor William Carter, was elected for the seventh time in the Council Chamber of the Guildhall in November, and a General Election took place on 14 December. Two candidates stood for Windsor: C S Edgerly (Labour) and Ernest Gardner (Unionist Coalition). For the first time women over 30 had the right to vote, as well as all men over 21. According to the editor of the *Windsor Express* 'women realised to the full their new position in the State, for they have out-polled the male voters in many places'. The Coalition won a landslide victory and Lloyd George remained in office, however, the Labour party increased its share of the vote and gained important seats, but not in Windsor.

A week before Christmas 1918, the gates on Castle Hill and the Hundred Steps were opened to the public for the first time since 1914. Two German guns were on display on Castle Hill in December before they were taken on tour throughout the country.

A new education Act raised the school leaving age from 12 to 14, and promised to provide nursery schools, medical inspections for all children and technical education.

1919

The year's first editorial in the *Windsor Express* stated:

> The year before us is full of tremendous possibilities. It should be an epoch-making year, in fact it is bound to be. The meeting of the Peace Conference will make it forever memorable in the annals of time.

Hoping to attract many visitors to Windsor, the State Apartments in the Castle were re-opened on 4 January, after five years closure, and bringing much needed income to 'replenish the funds of local charities and institutions, which are badly in need of money'. [1]

The King set up a fund to raise three million pounds in gratitude to the disabled officers and men of the three forces. The aim was to help find a new place in civilian life for them, and for the widows and children of those who had given their lives for their country. 'A state pension must be hard and fast', said the King. At the time 900 applications for assistance were received each week and 4,000 grants had been made.

A Victory Week in Windsor from 13 to 18 January raised £110,622 18s for War Bonds and War Savings Certificates. The total amount subscribed throughout the war was £824,363 'which is simply splendid, the collection of this colossal sum is undoubtedly one of the wonders of the war', enthused the editor of the *Windsor Express*.

During the spring and summer of 1919 Windsor started to look at itself. The town was dirty and run down, there were complaints about a dusty Peascod Street, run down Thames Side, the eyesore River Street, but the hottest debate was the urgent need for

1. Windsor Express 11 January 1919

81

new housing. Nothing much happened in Windsor during the following months, while Slough decided to build 330 houses on Nash's Field.

The 2nd Battalion Coldstream Guard returned to Windsor from Cologne on 1 March. The men were welcomed by the Mayor, and a thanksgiving service was held at Holy Trinity Church.

Lectures in the YMCA Hut during March, on the havoc of War and on 'Our Campaign in East Africa' were well attended, but it was announced that the Hut on the Acre would soon be closed. This may have been because the town council had accepted the gift of a tank in recognition of its great effort in War Savings, and it was to be placed on the Acre.

Food coupons were abolished in April, and the Windsor and District branch of the National Federation of Discharged Soldiers held its first meeting in the Guildhall, presided over by Cllr T E Luff. Princess Alice, Countess of Athlone opened a Windsor Comrades Club in William Street. Thanks to the fine weather everyone could get out, and Windsor was visited by thousands of holiday-makers. It was the happiest Easter tide for five years pronounced the *Windsor Express*. An Airship that flew over Windsor displaying the flag of the new Royal Air Force before the King, drew huge crowds.

In May the 2nd Life Guards held their service of thanksgiving at Holy Trinity Church, and on St George's Day Queen Mary drove through Windsor as before, but this time she also visited the more humble parts of the town, finishing back at the Guildhall. The sum of £420 was raised for local charities.

The Windsor Kitchen, which had been successful throughout the war, and even made a profit, had to close in May, as did the Eton War Hospital Supply Depot at Savile House, which had opened in October 1916. The Colours of the Canadian Expeditionary Force, deposited in St George's Chapel in July 1917, were handed back.

Royal Ascot was one of the most brilliant on record, wrote the *Windsor Express*. There was a royal procession on each of the days, instead of only on two days as in pre-war times. The weather was splendid and 'this year's gathering will always be remembered as Victory Ascot'. The King of Spain also attended.

The Rose Show and Sweet Pea Exhibition, which also saw a welcome revival after two years absence, was held on the slopes of Windsor Castle, and reported a record attendance. An Eton, Slough and Windsor branch of the Workers' Educational Association (WEA) was also established, and this is still going strong today.

Peace Day finally came in July. A grand peace celebration subscription list soon filled up, but the subscription list for the Windsor War Memorial was not doing so well.

The Festival of Peace

'Throughout Great and Greater Britain rejoicing took place on Saturday in celebration of peace. Reports from all parts of the world show that the day was observed with the same patriotic fervour even in the remotest parts of the Empire', reported the *Windsor Express.*

On Saturday, 19 July Windsor's Festival of Peace started at 11am with a parade consisting of members from all branches of the services, which went from Bachelors' Acre through the town and across the river into Eton, then back via Peascod Street. The band of the 2nd Life Guards and Comrades of the Great War played during the parade. At 2.30pm athletic and military sports took place at the Imperial Service College; attractions included the Musical Ride of the 2nd Life Guards, tent pegging and jumping. At 2.30pm there were water sports and a regatta on the Thames, arranged by the Eton Excelsior Rowing Club and Windsor Swimming Clubs. A grand carnival procession started from William Street at 7.30pm followed by a torchlight procession at 10.00pm, organised by the local fire brigade, with 200 torches carried by men in uniform. When the procession had passed, 1,000 schoolboys came through Eton School Yard carrying torches. Princess Alice and the Earl of Athlone were amongst those watching as the children passed the chapel steps. By this time rain had started to fall, but it did not dampen the spirit of the day, or the evening dance in Alexandra Gardens.

Old Windsor

Old WIndsor celebrated in the grounds of Beaumont College, the proceedings started at 2.00pm in the Tapestry Hall with a short service, concluding with the National Anthem. A procession led by Major A Innes Keys and patrol leader Newman bearing the Union Jack wound its way to Beaumont. There were several bands, including one from the American Forces, followed by demobilised and serving soldiers. A laurel wreath in memory of the fallen soldiers was laid at the village shrine of St Luke's. The afternoon was spent with sports and feasting, then afternoon tea was followed in the evening by dancing on the lawn for 350 people. Four thousand children enjoyed their own Peace Day celebration in the Home Park.

Rolls of Honour

Rolls of Honour of men killed during the last weeks of fighting continued to be published after the Armistice, but also increasingly of the flu epidemic. The toll of Spanish Flu victims was particularly high in November, for both soldiers and civilians.

The story of Clewer boy, W G Harris, who joined the RAMC in November 1914 at the age of 14, was published in the *Windsor Express* in November. He claimed to be 17 when he joined up, served in Salonika, latterly with the Royal Berks Regiment, where he recently celebrated his 18th birthday.

War Memorials

The Windsor County Boys' School was the first to unveil its War Memorial on Saturday 28 June 1919. It included the names of fifteen old boys who lost their lives and a sixteenth was added in 1921.

Windsor

The Windsor War Memorial subscription list closed at the end of November 1919. It had aimed at £10,000, but only raised £2,229, enough for a memorial, which was finally unveiled and dedicated by Princess Alice Countess of Athlone and Lady Mary Cambridge on Sunday, 7 November 1920 in the Windsor Parish Church. The ceremony was performed by the Rev E M Blackie, Chaplain to the King and the Vicar of Windsor, the Windsor Territorials forming a guard of honour. Also present were the Mayor and Corporation, the Borough Police, and Windsor Boy Scouts. The band of the

1st Life Guards played and a trumpeter sounded Last Post and Reveille, which was followed by the National Anthem. Relatives of the fallen then came forward to place flowers at the foot of the memorial which had 200 names inscribed, though several more were to be added later.

Clewer

At the end of May 1919 the *Windsor Express* reported that the Clewer War Memorial subscription list was closed with over £460 raised, though collections and subscriptions may have continued, however, as the memorial was not unveiled until 1923. On Saturday 7 July, the Earl of Athlone inaugurated the memorial, an obelisk fountain in Cornish granite, which cost £800. The names of 180 local men are inscribed around the base. The service was conducted by the Rector of Clewer the Rev ATC Cowley and the vicar of St Stephen's, the Rev W Boys. Buglers of the Grenadier Guards sounded Last Post and Reveille.

The Imperial Service College War Memorial

The Imperial Service College has thirty-four names on its Roll of Honour, of boys who had attended the school in Windsor between 1905 and 1915. They came from all over the United Kingdom, but only two can be identified as having a Windsor connection; both were in Camperdown House.

Cpl Lancelot Reginald Davenport, Berkshire Yeomanry, was killed in Gallipoli on 21 August 1915 and is commemorated on the Helles Memorial. His parents lived in Fernbank House, York Road, Windsor.

Pte John Grant Anderson was the son of Lt Colonel J G Anderson, a Military Knight living at 14 Castle Yard. He went to Canada but came back with the Royal Canadian Regiment. He was killed in Belgium on 13 October 1915, and laid to rest at Kemmel Chateau Military Cemetery. Both men can be found on the Windsor War Memorial.

An Unusual Memorial

All Saints' Church Dedworth has a war memorial dedicated to just one man, and not even a Windsor man. Belford Alexander Wallis Wilson from Hampshire, who had been a tea planter in Ceylon, and fought in the Boer War, volunteered again for military service in 1914, and saw action in Gallipoli. Commissioned in the Hampshire Regiment in 1916, he was wounded on the Somme and gained the Military Cross and Bar. He was killed during the Passchendaele offensive on 26 September 1917 in his 43rd year. It is not clear why he is commemorated in Windsor, no connection has been established.

Eton Excelsior Rowing Club

The club has its own memorial dedicated to nine of its members who were killed in the Great War. Many of them were Windsor men.

L/Cpl Robert Edward White, Royal Berkshire Regiment, lived in Bolton Crescent, killed 22 August 1917 aged 27, and is commemorated on the Tyne Cot Memorial.

Trooper Herbert Henry Hiley, Berkshire Yeomanry, killed 21 August 1915 at Gallipoli, is commemorated on the Helles Memorial. He is also mentioned in the Windsor Boys' School chapter.

2nd Lt Walter Le Grove, London Regiment, grew up in Bournemouth, killed on 25 April 1918 and is commemorated on the Pozieres Memorial.

Trooper Alfred Blane from Windsor, Berkshire Yeomanry,

seriously wounded during the same action in which Trooper Hiley was killed, died of his wounds on 24 September 1915 and is commemorated on the Alexandria War Memorial.

Pte Stanley W J Bennett from Staines, Royal Berkshire Regiment, died 31 August 1917, and is buried in Cologne.

Pte Christian Frederick Charles Harnack of 33 Frances Road, Machine Gun Corps, killed 30 August 1918, buried in Aubigny Cemetery in France. He is also mentioned in the Windsor Boys' School chapter.

Pte Leslie Baynes Starling, from Farnham in Surrey, London Regiment (London Scottish), died 29 August 1918 aged 18, buried in Queant Road Cemetery, Buissy.

2nd Lt Walter Scott Mertz, from Porthcawl in Glamorgan, Royal Engineers, died 28 July 1916, buried in Newton Nottage Churchyard, Glamorgan.

Nothing further is known of C S Jackson. The Commonwealth War Graves Commission list four casualties under this name, but none of them has a local connection.

Defence of the Realm Act (DORA)

The Defence of the Realm Act (DORA) was passed, without parliamentary debate, on 8 August 1914. It allowed the Government to take whatever actions it deemed necessary for securing the public safety and the defence of the realm, and gave it wide-ranging powers for the duration of the war. This included censorship on newspapers as well as letters sent home from the front. Reports on troop movements were forbidden, but also flying a kite, igniting a bonfire, buying binoculars, feeding bread to wild animals, discussing naval and military matters and shooting homing pigeons; they all became criminal offences. The Act was amended several times during the course of the war, and anyone who breached the regulations with intent to assist the enemy could face the death penalty. DORA ushered in a variety of authoritarian social controls such as licensing laws to curb drunkenness. Licensing hours throughout the country were restricted, and in November 1914, public houses in Windsor and district were closed an hour earlier, at 10pm on weekday and 9pm on Sunday. More draconian opening times were introduced in 1916, (which lasted until

THE SNAKE IN THE GRASS.

Notwithstanding the fact that all domestic controversy has been stopped by mutual consent, the teetotal fanatics are using the war as an engine of their propaganda for destroying the Liberty of the citizen.

1988). Beer was watered down to reduce drunkeness, and a No Treating Order stipulated that drinkers in public houses could not buy alcoholic drinks for others. There was little resistance to the new regulations, however a cartoon in the *Windsor Observer* on 7 November 1918 titled The Snake in the Grass claimed that 'teetotal fanatics are using the war as an engine of their propaganda for destroying the Liberty of the citizen'.

Other restrictions included the Lighting Orders, which came in soon after the first Zeppelin raids. They were the same as the 'black-outs' of World War II, but were not always as well observed. Several local businesses, including Caleys, were prosecuted and fined for showing too much light in the evening. These lighting regulations, and others on compulsory red rear lights, and on how much or how little light should be shown on a motorcar or bicycle led to many new criminal convictions.

In early April 1916, an order banned the ringing of church bells or chiming of public clocks during hours of darkness, but with the arrival of spring bells for Sunday service could be heard again. No one was to display or make signals of any nature, which could be mistaken 'for any signal authorised to be used in the case of an attack by the enemy'.

A Daylight Saving Bill was introduced in May 1916, which moved clocks forward an hour on 21 May, then back again on 1 October. The early closing of shops was finally tackled by DORA in October, after much argument, and Regulation 10B was passed on 27 October 1916. Every shop had to be closed no later than 8pm on Friday, 9pm on Saturday and 7pm on every other day. Alice Page of 'The Sports Arcade' in Peascod Street was the first person to be summoned, on 3 November, for trading after 8pm. As there was some uncertainty about whether she was entitled to remain open after 8pm, the magistrate decided to adjourn the case, 'with liberty to restore'.

In 1917 DORA introduced a Food Controller, who appealed to the public to voluntarily limit its weekly purchases of bread to 4lb, meat to 2½lb and sugar to ¾lb per person. Compulsory rationing was not seen as the right solution, as it was perceived not to be working in Germany, and the cost of printing millions of tickets was deemed too high. Food shortages were only too apparent. Darville & Son of 93 Peascod Street, informed their customers that they were unable to fulfil orders for sugar in full, but were doing their best with the supplies allotted to them.

A Prevention of Corruption Order was introduced in 1917, which made it an offence for shop assistants to accept gifts or tips as an inducement to get favourable service. Sugar was rationed in January 1918, followed by meat in April and butter in July. General rationing, with ration books did not come into force until October 1918, by which time the war was almost over.

The Lighting, Heating and Power Order of 2 April 1917 made it an offence for restaurants to serve hot meals after 9.30pm or before 5am. Kitty Boxall, 93 St Leonard's Road, was the first person in Windsor to fall foul of the order. She was found to be serving eggs on toast to soldiers after 10pm on 6 April, and was reported to the police. The magistrate told her that she could not serve a cooked meal after 9.30, even if she had cooked it at 9.00, but he dismissed the case upon a fine of 5s, as the defendant may not have been fully aware of the new orders.

Another order, which came into force on 12 April 1918, prohibited larger shops from selling sweets, to protect small shopkeepers, costermongers and hawkers who relied mainly on this trade.

Britain imported much of its food and merchant ships bringing supplies were sunk in great numbers by German submarines. To protect home-grown foodstuff, it was made illegal in May 1918 to damage growing crops on farms, or trespass on allotments. Offenders could be liable to a fine of £100, or six months imprisonment.

There even was a Venereal Disease Order. Mary Crockford was charged with an offence against this order in June 1918, but the case was not proven and the prisoner was discharged. The newspaper did not give any details of the offence.

DORA was not completely laid to rest at the end of the war; it continued to restrict people's lives, although most of the regulations were scrapped. The licensing Acts were not finally abolished until 2005.

The Royal Family at War

King George V had been monarch for just over four years when Europe was plunged into chaos following the assassination of Archduke Franz Ferdinand in June 1914. During the next four years the King, with the support of his family, worked tirelessly for the nation. Though not a charismatic leader, he was the respected figurehead. With Queen Mary he visited munitions factories and hospitals, toured the country and entertained wounded soldiers at Windsor Castle. The King inspected troops at Aldershot, reviewed the fleet at Scapa Flow and made several visits to the Western Front. This chapter is concerned, mainly, with Royal visits in and around Windsor and events connected with the town.

The King and Queen kept diaries, extracts of which are reproduced by kind permission of Her Majesty The Queen. In his diary entry for 31 July 1914, after Austria declared war on Serbia, King George recorded:

Had a very busy & anxious time of it, telegrams from the FO coming in all day long. Everything alas, looks very bad, both Russia and Germany mobilising, almost impossible to prevent a general European War. [1]

Once Britain declared war on Germany on 4 August 1914, anyone considered German was treated with suspicion. King George V, despite his German ancestry, was above suspicion but Admiral Prince Louis of Battenberg was forced from his position as First Sea Lord. The Kaiser, cousin to the King, became a figure of hate. As early as September 1914, letters appeared in the *Windsor Express* questioning whether the Order of the Garter banners of the German Emperor and his family should be displayed in St

1. *GV/PRIV/GVD/1914-1918, Diary entry from the personal diary of King George V, held in the Royal Archives, Windsor Castle*

George's Chapel. On a personal level, King George was fond of the Kaiser although he held him responsible for starting the war, but he considered that pre-war family arrangements should remain in place. Eventually, the King yielded to public opinion over the banners.

On 10 May 1915, King George V signed an order dispensing with the statutes appointing eight members of the German and Austrian royal families as Knights of the Garter. A few days later the King signed a warrant authorising the removal of their banners from St George's Chapel, although their stall plates remained in place. The eight names, in order of seniority of appointment to the Order of the Garter, were:

Francis Joseph, Emperor of Austria
William II, Emperor of Germany
Ernest, Duke of Cumberland
Albert William Henry, Prince of Prussia
Ernest, Grand Duke of Hesse
Frederick William, Crown Prince of Germany
Leopold, Duke of Albany and of Saxe-Coburg and Gotha
William II, King of Wurttemberg

There was no mention of these developments in the King's daily diary, although the *Windsor Express* noted:

The removal of the Kaiser's banner and that of the Austrian Emperor and six others from the choir of St George's Chapel has given the greatest satisfaction. The German Emperor and the Emperor of Austria have been adjudged unworthy of the most famous Order of Chivalry in the world...[2]

A further eleven new Knights of the Garter were created during the war; among them were Albert, King of the Belgians, Prince Albert, later King George VI, and Earl Kitchener, the Secretary of State for War.

In December 1914 it was reported that the King had sent sums of money to many local charities and institutions, including £175 to King Edward VII Hospital, £50 to the Royal Albert Institute

2. *Windsor Express 22 May 1915*

and £60 to the Mayor's Poor Box. Also in December every soldier and sailor had received a Christmas card with greetings from the King and Queen, while Princess Mary helped to organise a fund to ensure that each soldier serving on the Western Front received a small brass tin containing cigarettes, tobacco or chocolate. Throughout the war the King took a personal interest in the men serving in his Forces.

Shortly after the start of the war, Queen Alexandra made an appeal through the local newspaper [3] for donations with which to provide for the wives and families of soldiers and sailors, 'thus relieving the breadwinners during their separation, and the hardships they may have to undergo, of all anxiety as to the care of their families and relatives, and the keeping of their homes intact.' Princess Alexander, with the Duchess of Albany attended a concert at the Guildhall in February 1915 for troops billeted in the Borough.

Princess Christian continued to help raise funds for the hospital named after her and in April 1915 a Princess Christian Hospital Train was completed. It was inspected by the King and Queen at the Great Western Railway Station before being handed over to the War Office. The train had provision for 174 beds and 400 sitting patients and accommodation for doctors and nurses. The *Windsor Express* noted that the train 'owes its existence entirely to the initiative and labour of Princess Christian, by whom the funds were raised.'

On 20 July 1915 the King visited the Canadian Red Cross Hospital at Cliveden and wrote in his diary that 'it is run entirely by Canadian doctors and nurses, there are 600 sick and wounded there now and it will be increased to a 1,000.[4] The Queen was also impressed. In her diary entry for the same day, she recorded, '…we talked to nearly all the men… then went to the Astors' to tea.'[5] Another visit was made on 23 August 1917, and the King noted in his diary:

3. *Windsor Express 15 August 1914*
4. *GV/PRIV/GVD/1914-1918*
5. *QM/PRIV/QMD/1915,1917 Diary entry from the personal diary of Queen Mary, held in the Royal Archives, Windsor Castle*

In the afternoon May & I motored over to Cliveden & visited the Duchess of Connaught's Canadian Red Cross Hospital

where we saw 1,000 sick & wounded who are there now, a splendid hospital.[6]

The King and Queen made several visits to the Canadian Forestry Corps Camp at Smith's Lawn and watched the troops playing baseball matches.

The King himself set a good example to the rest of the country by his restraint and thrift. During his Easter stay at Windsor Castle in April 1915 he commanded that no alcohol would be consumed in any of the Royal households until the war was over. The King noted in his diary on 6 April 1915:

This morning we have all become teetotallers until the end of the war. I have done it as an example, as there is a lot of drinking going on in the country. I hate doing it, but hope it will do good.[7]

The decision was well received throughout the country, although perhaps less so by guests to dinner at Windsor Castle. The following month, it was announced that all celebrations of the King's birthday in June, would be dispensed with for the rest

6. GV/PRIV/GVD/1914-1918
7. GV/PRIV/GVD/1914-1918

of the war with the sole exception of the flying of flags.

From the beginning of the war it was recognised that Windsor Castle would be a likely target for Zeppelin air raids. The Admiralty agreed to send an anti-aircraft gun to protect the Castle and this

was put into position on the East Terrace in early November 1914. Six months later, in June 1915, the Acting Governor of Windsor Castle issued regulations for notifying local residents of air raids. A siren, sounded from the vicinity of the Magazine Tower would warn of hostile aircraft. One blast of the siren of about a minute's duration would signify that hostile aircraft were attacking London and two blasts, with an interval of ten seconds would signify that hostile aircraft are approaching Windsor. The King paid £572 a year to the Metropolitan Police, for the protection of Windsor Castle and the Royal Family.

The Royal Family returned to Windsor during the summer of 1915, staying from 14 July to 14 September. Contemporary newspaper reports noted that the Court's stay at Windsor had been the longest since the reign of Queen Victoria and that the King and Queen were very much attached to Windsor.

While the King was visiting troops and making VC presentations, the Queen visited a great many hospitals, nursing homes and hostels for Belgian refugees.

The Royal Family spent Easter 1916 at Windsor, arriving from Buckingham Palace on 20 April and staying until 15 May. During their stay, the King and Queen visited a munitions works at Slough, while Princess Alexander of Teck and Princess May of Teck inspected a new ambulance train, built for the French Government, which was on view at the Great Western Station in Windsor. The *Windsor Express* noted:

> The stay of the King and Queen at Windsor Castle has been extended, and it is gratifying to know that their Majesties have benefitted by their rest at Windsor … We learn, however, that several war economies have been effected even at Windsor Castle, and that there is still a total absence of alcoholic liquor at the Royal tables. The grey horses are being used more now that motor cars are taboo owing to national economies in petrol, and it is a very pleasing sight to see members of the Royal Family driving in an open carriage drawn by greys.[8]

Later that year, the King gave orders that every unmarried man of military age at Windsor Castle and other Royal households, no matter what the nature of his employment, was to report to the local recruiting office. From the beginning of the war, the King had set an example where military service was concerned, and when war was declared had allowed as many men as could be spared to enlist.

The King and Queen saw the film *The Battle of the Somme*, at Windsor Castle in September before it was shown in cinemas in Windsor. After seeing it, the King expressed his approval of the film and remarked: 'The public should see these pictures that they may have some idea of what the Army is doing, and what war means.'

At least eleven Victoria Crosses were presented at Windsor Castle. One VC presentation which would have given the King particular pleasure was to Lt W L Robinson, Royal Flying Corps, on 8 September 1916. The King had noted in his diary on 3

8. *Windsor Express 13 May 1918*

September 1916, while staying at Windsor:

> Last night 13 Zeppelins made a raid on East Coast, 5 came over Norfolk & destroyed some of my cottages in Dersingham.[9]

Lt Robinson was awarded the VC for shooting down a Zeppelin on the night of 2-3 September, the first time a German airship had been shot down over England. He should have arrived at Windsor by train from Paddington, with a number of other officers who were to be decorated by the King, but decided to travel by car. His car broke down at Runnymede, making him late for the presentation, but on his arrival he was welcomed warmly by the King, who asked him for an account of how he brought down the Zeppelin. By the time Robinson left the Castle, a large crowd had gathered outside, and he was enthusiastically greeted by the people.

Wounded soldiers from Queen Mary's Convalescent Hospital, Roehampton, as well as King Edward VII Hospital, Windsor, made frequent visits to Windsor Castle. When members of the Royal Family were in residence they spoke to the wounded men and showed great interest in their welfare. In September 1916, the King and Queen, accompanied by Princess Mary and Prince Henry, went on to the East Terrace to speak to over 500 wounded service men.

From Christmas 1915 onwards, residents of the Parish of New Windsor (and also Clewer in 1918) who were over 60 years of age, and had lived in Windsor for at least one year, were eligible to receive a gift of one and a half hundredweight of coal from the King. Application for the gift had to be made to the Rev E M

9. *GV/PRIV/GVD/1914-1918*

Blackie, Vicar of Windsor.

In December 1916, 400 local children aged between three and twelve, whose fathers were serving in the Royal Berkshire Regiment and children whose fathers were serving in the Army and employed on the Castle Estate, were entertained to tea at the Royal Riding School at the Castle. A large Christmas tree was sent over from Windsor Great Park, and the Queen and Princess Mary presented presents to the children.

King George and Queen Mary, accompanied by Princess Mary and Prince Henry, arrived at Windsor Castle from Buckingham Palace on 5 April 1917, and stayed until 8 May. The day after their arrival the USA declared war on Germany. During their stay in Windsor, the King and Queen made two visits to the Canadian Base Forestry Corps camp at Smith's Lawn, Windsor Great Park. After inspecting the camp, they witnessed the Canadians cutting down trees, which supplied the Army at the front with pit-props and railway sleepers. On St George's Day 1917 the Queen recorded the occasion in her diary:

> Drove with the children in a Landau with 4 horses round Windsor town as St George's day was being celebrated – a good many people were about and I stopped at the Town Hall where flowers etc were being sold and left some money with Mrs Carey for flowers for the Hospital.[10]

With the food shortages beginning to be felt all over the country, the King realised that there was an urgent need for economy in food. It was officially announced in April 1917 that the Royal Family had adopted the recommended scale of self-rationing and that there were five potato-less days and one meatless day each week at Windsor Castle. The *Windsor Express* had previously noted that 'King George and Queen Mary have set all an example of plain living and self-sacrifice since the beginning of the war.'

Despite the tireless work of the King and Queen, there were still doubts, albeit held by a small minority, about the loyalties of the Royal Family. The problem was the Germanic family names. The King decided, as a first step, in June 1917, that British princes

10. *QM/PRIV/QMD/1915,1917*

bearing German titles should immediately relinquish them, and adopt British surnames. The *Windsor Express* commented:

> The King's action is a wise and timely one, and there has been general approval of his Majesty's decision... The prejudice attaching to anything German is intense, and we hope that when the war is over, neither the German or his goods will be seen in this country.[11]

King George V made a final break from his German ancestry on 17 July when he decided to change the name of his Royal House from Saxe-Coburg-Gotha to Windsor. The decision was announced following a Privy Council meeting held at Buckingham Palace and was well-received throughout the country. To commemorate the adoption of the name Windsor, the King and Queen presented their State Portraits to the Royal Borough. In Berlin, the Kaiser joked that he would be attending a performance of Shakespeare's play The Merry Wives of Saxe-Coburg-Gotha.

When the Duchess of Connaught died in March, the King and Queen had attended her funeral in St George's Chapel. She was the first member of the British Royal Family to be cremated, and her ashes are buried at Frogmore.

The Queen paid a visit to River Street in early September 1917 to see the conditions in which the poor of the area lived,. Later in September, she visited the Windsor Communal Kitchen where it was reported that she spent nearly an hour

IN HOT WATER.

THE KAISER:—"Boo Hoo! It's too hot!"
MARSHAL FOCH:—"There's more coming. I'm not going to stop until you're properly cleaned up."

11. *Windsor Express 23 June 1917*

inspecting the premises, and helping to serve the dinners.

When in Windsor, the King often visited his uncle, HRH Prince Christian, at Cumberland Lodge. The Prince died aged 86, on 28 October 1917, and the King and Queen travelled to Windsor by train for the funeral. Prince Christian, as a general in the British Army, was accorded full military honours and his coffin was carried by gun carriage, and escorted by soldiers to Frogmore. In December, the King assumed the office of Ranger of Windsor Great Park, vacated by the death of Prince Christian. The other vacant office was High Steward of the Royal Borough of Windsor; this was accepted by HRH the Prince of Wales in March 1918.

The German Spring Offensive on the Western Front began on 21 March and severely dented the Allied front line. In late March 1918 the King travelled to France to discuss the current situation with Sir Douglas Haig, and visit wounded soldiers. As a result of this unplanned visit to France, the King was unable to be in Windsor in time for Easter. The King and Queen, with Princess Mary and Prince Henry, arrived at Windsor Castle from Buckingham Palace on 6 April and stayed until 14 May. Three days after their arrival, the Germans launched a second major attack in a different sector of the front line, and the King kept in close contact with the Government during this period. In mid-April the King noted in his diary that the news from France was 'not good'.[12]

On St George's Day 1918, the King gave the Mayor a cheque for £100 for local charities and the Queen, once more, drove through many of the streets of the town A week later, the Queen sent out a message from Windsor Castle addressed to the men of all three services telling them 'how much we, the women of the British Empire at home, watch and pray for you during the long hours of these days' stress and endurance'.[13]

The King and Queen, and also Princess Mary, used their time at Windsor to receive servicemen at the Castle and to visit wounded soldiers in hospital The *Windsor Express* reported:

12. *GV/PRIV/GVD/1914-1918*
13. *Windsor Express 4 May 1918*

Last Sunday evening, whilst the King and Queen, accompanied by Princess Mary, were returning from Divine Service in St George's Chapel, they noticed two wounded soldiers, one of whom had lost an arm and was being wheeled in a bath chair by a lady. Their Majesties were passing the Lord Chamberlain's office at the time; but much to the surprise and delight of the two men, immediately crossed the road and entered into conversation with them… Not only were both men delighted with their interview, but it appears to have done them good and aided in their recovery.[14]

Parties of overseas soldiers were entertained weekly at Windsor Castle and at the end of the month it was the turn of over 150 men from the American air squadrons quartered in Ascot. The visitors were shown over parts of the Castle before being entertained at tea in St George's Hall. A few days later, the Queen visited the Soldiers' and Sailors' Institution in Victoria Street, Windsor.

In early May, at her first function in Windsor since her twenty-first birthday on 25 April, Princess Mary, the King and Queen's only daughter, visited King Edward VII Hospital and opened the new orthopaedic department for discharged and wounded servicemen.

Nearly four years of war was beginning to take its toll, and people were feeling war-weary. The King also felt the strain, and in his diary on 6 May 1918, written at Windsor Castle, he noted the eighth anniversary of his accession, 'I don't think any Sovereign of these Realms has had a more difficult or more troublous 8 years than I have had.'[15]

The King and Queen returned to London on 14 May but were back in Windsor, accompanied by Princess Mary and Prince George on 16 August; they stayed until 21 September. The Prince of Wales, on leave from his regiment, joined his parents in Windsor shortly after their arrival and Prince Henry, who had left Eton, and was now studying at the Royal Military College, Sandhurst, also arrived.

On 18 September, the King, Queen, and Princess Mary visited

14. *Windsor Express 20 April 1918*
15. *GV/PRIV/GVD/1914-1918*

King Edward VII Hospital again, where the King presented four Military Medals and shook hands with each recipient. The Royal visitors spoke to every wounded soldier in the ward, enquiring as to their wounds and wishing them a rapid recovery.

Kaiser Wilhelm II abdicated on 9 November, two days before the armistice on the Western Front. In his diary for 9 November 1918 King George wrote:

> We got the news that the German Emperor had abdicated, also the Crown Prince. 'How are the mighty fallen.' He has been Emperor just over 30 years, he did great things for his country but his ambition was so great that he wished to dominate the world & erected his military machine for that object.[16]

Later that month, Princess Alice, Countess of Athlone, attended a thanksgiving service at the Parish Church in Windsor. Town and Castle gradually emerged from over four years of war; at the end of December the gates on Castle Hill and at the Hundred Steps were opened to the public for the first time since 1914, and the State Apartments of Windsor Castle were re-opened to the public from January 1919.

Unlike many European monarchies, the British Royal Family not only survived the war, but emerged strengthened and was more popular and respected for their compassion, dedication to duty and willingness to share the hardships and sacrifices demanded.

16. *GV/PRIV/GVD/1914-1918*

The Berkshire Regiments

The Royal Berkshire Regiment

The regiment has its origins in the 49th Foot, which was raised in 1743 as Trelawney's Regiment, and the 66th Foot, which was raised in 1756 as the 2/19th Foot. These two regiments were merged in 1881 to become the 1st and 2nd Battalions of Princess Charlotte's (Berkshire Regiment). The Royal title was added in 1885 and the regiment later became the Royal Berkshire Regiment (Princess Charlotte of Wales's).

Prior to the First World War, infantry regiments comprised four battalions; the first and second battalions alternated between home and foreign postings, the third was a reserve battalion and the fourth was a Territorial Battalion, for home defence. At the outbreak of war the 1st Battalion was serving at Aldershot and the 2nd Battalion, together with a large portion of the British Army, was in India. The battalions in the UK were mobilised, and reservists called up, and the 1st RBR was sent to France on 12 August 1914. In October 1914, 2nd RBR returned to England and was sent to France the following month.

The Territorials, including the Windsor 'D' Company of 4th Royal Berkshire Regiment (RBR), were also mobilised on 4 August. Every man of 'D' Company turned up at the local drill hall the next day and, accompanied by an enthusiastic crowd, marched to the Great Western Railway station to travel to the RHQ in Reading. There was an urgent need for more men to be sent to France and the Territorials volunteered en masse for active service abroad. The 4th RBR was renumbered 1/4th RBR and a new 4th Battalion, numbered 2/4th RBR, was raised.

The Berkshire Regiments were always foremost in the mind of the *Windsor Express* and their fortunes were followed closely. On 3 April 1915 the newspaper reported that the Royal Berkshire

Regiment's Territorial battalions had been completed up to establishment; even a third line unit for the 4th Battalion RBR was to be formed, but 'recruits were coming in slowly for this.' In the same edition it was reported that the 1/4th RBR, stationed at Chelmsford, 'has left for an unknown destination'; this battalion fought on the Western Front throughout the war. The Berkshire Yeomanry advertised in the *Windsor Express* of 3 April, for 200 recruits who were willing to serve abroad, as did the 3/4th Royal Berkshire Regiment (Territorials).

On 17 April 1915, the *Windsor Express* reported the losses suffered by the 2nd Battalion during the four-day battle at Neuve Chapelle. Six officers were killed and eight wounded, 45 other ranks were killed and 207 wounded. Sadly, similar losses would be reported throughout the war. Many Windsor men served in the Royal Berkshire Regiment, mostly on the Western Front.

The Berkshire Yeomanry

The Berkshire Yeomanry can trace its roots to the mounted units formed in 1794, during the French Revolutionary War, to resist an invasion by French troops. In 1828, the Yeomanry was disbanded but soon re-formed following outbreaks of civil disturbances in the county. After the Haldane Army reforms of 1907, the Berkshire Yeomanry became part of the Territorial Force. There were three squadrons at the time; 'A' (Windsor) Squadron being the local unit. When war was declared in August 1914, the Yeomanry was mobilised and on 5 August every member of the 'A' (Windsor) Squadron was present for a roll call at the drill hall. They left Windsor for Reading on 11 August and the *Windsor Express* reported that 'they were asked if they would volunteer for Foreign

Service if required and nearly all answered in the affirmative.'

On 3 April 1915 the *Windsor Express* reported that the Berkshire Yeomanry sailed to join the British Mediterranean Force. A local well-wisher sent the Squadron a telegram wishing them good luck. Letters from the Windsor boys were soon received by their friends and families after they arrived in Malta. One praised 'this beautiful-looking place' and told of singing and cheering with French sailors and a corporal described the arduous voyage in a ship designed to carry 320, into which 1,100 and their horses were cramped.

In May and June 1915 a number of letters were printed in the *Windsor Express* from the Berkshire Yeomanry in Egypt. Most complained about the heat, flies and bugs. A Windsor trooper reported that they were busily engaged in fighting a different foe:

> Our first exciting engagement was the wholesale slaughter of the pests usually associated with lodging-houses, the enemy lost heavily, but now we have night attacks.

Another Yeoman wrote: 'A liberal use of Keatings has saved me from bites, I think'. The same issue, dated 29 May 1915, carried the advertisement: 'Keating's Powder Kills with ease, Bugs and Beetles, Moth and Fleas.'

The regiment remained in Egypt, on garrison duties, until sent to Gallipoli in August. Within days of landing at Suvla Bay on 18 August they were in action, as dismounted troops, against the Turkish army. The Yeomanry sustained severe casualties at Hill 70 on 21 August while attacking a heavily defended enemy position.

Trooper Alfred Blane of New Road, died of wounds received in this terrible charge and is buried in Egypt. Three other local men were killed in the same action: Cpl Reginald Davenport, L/ Cpl Harold Jefferies and Trooper Herbert Hiley. They have no known graves and are remembered on the Helles Memorial in Gallipoli. The Windsor Town Council congratulated the Berkshire Yeomanry on their heroic charge in Gallipoli on 21 August, and expressed their sympathy with relatives of 'those brave lads who lost their lives.' A memorial photograph of the Windsor 'A' Squadron, taken before the Squadron left for active service was presented to the

Mayor in April 1916. The group photograph was surrounded with enlarged portraits of their Commanding Officer Major Gooch, and the four Windsor men killed at Hill 70.

In October 1915 the headquarters of the 1/3rd Berkshire Yeomanry were moved from Aldermaston to Windsor, using the new Drill Hall in High Street.

Many Windsor men fought with the Berkshire Yeomanry in Egypt, Gallipoli, Salonika, Palestine and, towards the end of the war, on the Western Front. An obelisk memorial on the corner of Barry Avenue, records the names of the members of 'A' Squadron of the Berkshire Yeomanry killed on active service during the Great War.

Windsor Barracks

With the construction of two barracks during the wars with France at the end of the eighteenth century Windsor became a major garrison town. The Infantry Barracks in Sheet Street were built between 1798 and 1799 on a site of one acre, and were designed to house 750 infantry soldiers. In 1803, an additional building which was to provide a canteen with kitchens, bake-house, parlour, bar, tap-room, sergeants' rooms and bedrooms for 100 men, at a cost of £925[1], became in fact an extra barrack block for a further 250 men. Infantry soldiers had to wait for such comforts as separate kitchens or recreation rooms for several more decades. Housing 1,000 soldiers, often accompanied by several hundred women and children, in such a small space, was made possible by the use of wooden bunks arranged in two, sometimes three tiers, with two men per bunk. Of course, such overcrowding had a damaging effect on the health of the soldiers and their families, who were regularly crammed into these buildings, especially during times of war.

In 1865 the size of the barracks was quadrupled with a large extension over Spring Gardens, and married quarters were first made available to soldiers in the Georgian part of the barracks. Another extension, over Love Lane, was approved at the end of the nineteenth century.

Love Lane had 39 houses and the borough surveyor's store yard. Thirty seven houses were still occupied in 1902, but by 1907 the street was empty and demolition had begun. A new barrack extension was started in 1908 and completed by January 1911 at a cost of between £50,000 and £60,000.

The new extension of the Infantry Barracks, now called Victoria

1. *National Archives WO 40/18, Plan for Sutling House at Infantry Barracks Windsor, 1803*

Barracks was described as the finest and most luxurious buildings for soldiers in the world: 'the new building marks a revolutionary change in the conception of barrack construction'. Each man had a cubicle to himself, and there were shaving rooms, shower baths, ordinary baths, footbaths, recreation rooms, a theatre, dining halls, study room, billiard rooms and grocery stores. It was lit by electricity throughout.[2] No longer did up to 25 soldiers have to sleep, clean their kit, dry their clothes, dine and socialise in one room.

In 1912 a medical centre was built on the site of the former police station, which had moved to St Leonard's Road in 1909. It included two small emergency wards; previously the hospital for infantry soldiers was sited at the Cavalry Barracks. The Coldstream Guards who stayed in Windsor throughout the Great War moved into barracks which were the best of their time.

Victoria Barracks were completely rebuilt during the 1980s.

The Cavalry Barracks were built between 1800 and 1804 on a site of 14 acres in Clewer, half a mile from the Castle, to house a cavalry regiment and its horses. The stables were underneath the soldiers' quarters, and men had to wash in stable buckets in the stables, but overcrowding was not as severe as in the Infantry Barracks. The Household Cavalry made Windsor barracks their headquarters in 1820. They were extended and improved in 1896, and included married quarters and better sanitary arrangements. In 1900 they were renamed Combermere Barracks after Viscount Combermere, Wellington's comrade-at-arms at Waterloo and Gold Stick in Waiting of the Household Cavalry. During the 1960s the barracks were pulled down and re-built, and have been improved again during recent years. Each soldier now has a single room.

The 2nd Life Guards were stationed in Combermere Barracks in 1914, and marched from there to the station to be entrained for the front. They suffered great losses at Mons, where 18 officers and men lost their lives.

Once again as war broke out, like one hundred years earlier, the town was flooded with soldiers. But the overcrowding of

2. *Windsor Express 21 Jan 1911*

108

the barracks and unhealthy conditions of former times were not to be repeated. Soldiers were instead housed in temporary accommodations in private houses and in the summer months, in tents in the Great Park.

The Coldstream Guards

The Coldstream Guards were raised as Monck's Regiment of Foot in 1650, becoming the 2nd Foot or Coldstream Guards in 1670. They are the second in seniority of the five Foot Guards regiments. Although not a Berkshire regiment, the Coldstream Guards have a long association with Windsor because of their presence at Victoria Barracks and on ceremonial duties. Their recruitment area is all parts of England and local men enlisted whenever the regiment was stationed in Windsor.

All reservists were called up the day war was declared. Victoria Barracks were occupied at that time by the 2nd Coldstream Guards and the battalion was despatched to France on 12 August 1914. More detachments of reservists, and men who had been wounded and were returning to the front, left Windsor over the following months. Of the approximately 1,000 officers and men who left the barracks with the battalion at the start of the war, very few returned in February 1919. Victoria Barracks continued to be occupied by battalions from the Coldstream Guards, including the

1st Coldstream Guards, Windsor.

4th (Pioneer) and 4th (Reserve) Battalions. In July 1915, the latter battalion became the 5th (Reserve) Battalion and was stationed at Windsor until the end of the war.

The Household Cavalry

The Household Cavalry, in 1914, comprised three regiments, the 1st and 2nd Life Guards, raised in 1660 and 1661, and The Royal Horse Guards, raised in 1661. Like the Coldstream Guards, they are not Berkshire regiments but have a long association with Windsor because of their presence at Combermere Barracks and on ceremonial duties. Their permanent location in Windsor ensured that many local men joined the cavalry.

At the outbreak of war, Combermere Barracks were occupied by the Royal Horse Guards. After mobilisation, the regiment went for training on Salisbury Plains, and landed at Zeebrugge in October 1914. The 1st Life Guards were stationed at Hyde Park, London and the 2nd Life Guards were at Regent's Park. The 2nd Life Guards marched through Windsor on their way to war in August 1914.

The 2nd Life Guards Reserve Regiment was formed in August 1914, and was stationed in Windsor throughout the war. The Household Cavalry Composite Regiment was formed on mobilisation, with one squadron from each of the three Household Cavalry Regiments, but this new regiment was broken up in late 1914 with the personnel returning to their original regiments. All Household Cavalry regiments fought in France and Flanders.

Letters From The Front 1914

In August 1914, the British Expeditionary Force (BEF) landed in France and advanced into Belgium to meet the invading German Army. The first contact between the two was at Mons, 23-24 August. Although heavily outnumbered, the BEF repulsed the initial German assault and inflicted severe casualties, but subsequent attacks forced the British to withdraw from Mons and, with their French allies, fight a rear-guard action across Belgium and into northeast France. On 26 August, the BEF made a heroic stand at Le Cateau, 30 miles from Mons, halting the German advance. Heavy losses, however, forced the BEF to fall back towards Paris, and by the end of the month the Germans had advanced to around 20 miles from the French capital.

After the initial setbacks in August, the BEF and French Army made a determined stand on the Marne where they succeeded in forcing the Germans to retreat to the River Aisne. The German Army dug in, taking advantage of the Aisne heights to face their pursuers, and both sides pushed northwards in a bid to outflank the other, in what became known as 'the race to the sea'. The BEF handed their positions to the French and marched to Flanders to assist the Belgian Army in holding the town of Ypres, where heavy fighting took place between October and November. By the end of the year, both sides had created elaborate trench systems to protect themselves from attack and shell fire; both Allied and German trenches stretched from the Belgian coast to the Swiss border.

Windsor men serving at the front wrote about their experiences and some of these letters were published in the *Windsor Express* under the heading 'Letters from the Front'. All letters included here are from the *Windsor Express*, unless otherwise stated. One of the first letters published, on 5 September, was from Tom Husted, 'son

111

of the Old Windsor Phoenix goal-keeper'. He was serving on HMS *Fearless*, which was in the thick of the naval fight at Heligoland, where on 28 August British cruisers engaged the German High Seas Fleet and sank four German ships. He wrote to his uncle, Mr Fred Husted, at Eton:

Just a line or two to let you know that I am quite well and happy. I am pleased to say that we were in action yesterday, and we came out on top. I cannot tell you anything more about it, but you will be able to read all about it soon.

On 19 September, a letter from a wounded soldier serving with Captain C H Browning, Royal Field Artillery, who was the prospective Liberal Candidate for Windsor, gave more details of his death. The *Windsor Express* reported:

Bombardier Bennett, of Captain Browning's (124th) Battery, who was among the wounded in Plymouth Hospital, wrote that the gallant officer was first wounded in the head, but he at once got up, and while cheering on his men, the fatal shot came.

In the same edition, there was a letter from L/ Cpl J O Beavers, Army Service Corps, who was attached to the 5th Cavalry Brigade Supply Column. He wrote to his parents at Clewer Village:

We have had not a few narrow escapes. One of our captains was riddled with bullets. One night I lost the column with my lorry, and was left to the mercy of the world in a jungle. I have had to fix my bayonet on my rifle twice since I have been here, as I have got so near the enemy… Our men almost weep here when they see the poor women and children fleeing from their houses. I should like to see an English paper to get the news. I only know that day after day we are cutting up the Germans in thousands.

Pte F Golding, 1st Battalion Royal Berks Regiment, from 23 River Street, had been sent home wounded, but was making a good recovery. He told of his experiences in the firing line near

Mons on 26 September:

> … The Germans came on in dense masses, and it was like the sea – there seemed to be no end to them. Our Maxim and rifles started, and we piled up the dead so high that we could not see the troops beyond. In one place the Maxim I was working got through 16,000 rounds… At last the German soldiers had to climb over their own dead. The German officers held a revolver in each hand, and drove forward the five or six firing lines at the point of the revolver. The Germans fired thousands of bullets, but as they discharged their rifles from the hip, the bullets went harmlessly over our heads. It fairly rained bullets. For five hours this went on. There was plenty of water for our Maxim guns, and plenty of ammunition, and the Germans must have lost thousands. Near to us were the Middlesex Regiment, East Surreys and Gordons, and at the end of five hours we were told to retire. We did not want to, but as we were told that it was part of the scheme, we marched and fought until we got to Le Cateau… I got hit with shrapnel in the knees, and my chums at once put me on the gun limber. I wanted to stick with my section, who were mostly Windsor lads, but they would not let me. The officer said I should lose my legs if I did not go into hospital, and so I had to go…

Trumpeter Albert McCarthy wrote to his parents at the Doubles Gates Lodge in the Long Walk:

> We were present at the battle of Mons, and have been in every engagement during the war. We are capturing prisoners by the hundred every day.

Pte A Gould, Army Service Corps, writing to his wife at 36 Oxford Road on 19 September, from 'Somewhere in France', said:

> Just a few lines to let you know that I am all right and enjoying good health…We have bully beef and biscuits for dinner, biscuits and jam for breakfast and tea, but as we go through towns we can buy bread, etc. The worst of it is, however, the Germans have looted all the tobacco shops and we cannot

get any for love or money, and I have not seen a match for a week.

Bombardier C Bilbo, 37th Brigade, Royal Field Artillery, wrote to his wife at 2 Acacia Cottages, Old Windsor. In his letter, published on 17 October, he said:

It is just two months today since I donned a uniform. How much longer I wonder? If all reports are true, we are giving the Germans beans, and I am still of the opinion that the war will be over by Christmas. However, as I am prepared for anything, I shall not be disappointed if it lasts longer. All the German prisoners seem very glad to be captured – 'fed up' I suppose. It is stated on very unreliable authority that some of our infantrymen in the trenches have been chaffing the Germans to come out and fight, but that not succeeding they shouted out in a peremptory manner 'Waiter!' Immediately, some heads popped up at the well-known command...

He survived the war.

Pte C Bird, Somerset Light Infantry, was taken prisoner and treated in a German hospital, he wrote to his mother, at 20 Arthur Road:

I am in a German Hospital, wounded in both arms and head. We are getting treated very nicely indeed, so you need not worry about me. I am quite all right where I am.

Writing from an Allied Hospital, Pte Barnett, Royal Berks Regiment, wrote a letter to his mother at 4 Charles Street, from the Segregation Camp, St Nazaire, France. It was published on 31 October:

I suppose you would like to know how I got wounded. It was on the 17th of September. We were in the heart of the big battle of Marne, and we could not get the Germans out of the trenches, so our officers said, 'We must move them, boys.' A bayonet charge was proposed, and just as we got up ready for it I was shot through the hand, and my rifle was broken.

But we went into them, 'neck or nothing', and cleared them out after a tussle. I got a bayonet through my left side. The Germans cleared with very few left to tell the story. Instead of occupying the trench we drove them from we retired back to the old position, and as we were running back a shell burst close to us, killing three and wounding seven. I got hit in the leg, which finished me off for a time, so my fighting is done for the present. Will you please send me some smokes?

A letter to the Household Cavalry Regiment in Windsor published on 7 November told of the death of Cpl Charles H White, Royal Horse Guards. He came from Frome, but had served in Windsor, and had been active with the Windsor and Eton Football club as left full-back.

On 12 December a letter from Pte A McFarlane, 12th Royal Lancers, to a friend at Windsor was published:

As you have no doubt seen by the papers, the cavalry have been taking turns with the infantry in the trenches. We have had a spell of rest lately, and are now in support just in rear of the firing line. Things are comparatively quiet in this vicinity just now, and, in fact, our worst enemy at the present moment is the weather. We were honoured by a visit from the King last week, and the old 12th gave him three English cheers... We all appreciate the confidence that Britain has in us, and I can assure you the Windsor lads will do their share to justify it... I look forward to spending many happy civilian days in the Royal Borough when we have finished off the Kaiser and his hordes.

Pte McFarlane had a subsequent letter published in March 1915, and he appears to have survived the war as his name is not on any casualty list.

Under the heading 'Windsor Boy's Narrow Escape', a letter from Pte A Hawtree, 2nd Battalion Royal Berkshire Regiment to his uncle at Windsor was published on 19 December:

... I had a very narrow escape from one of their shrapnel

shells. Two of us [from the Signal Company] were sent out from headquarters to repair the wire, which we found was cut in two by the (German) shells. Just as we had finished they started shelling the town again, and naturally enough we made a dash to get out of it, but they followed us along, and we had nearly got out of the town when a shrapnel burst immediately above our heads, about 30 feet high. I said to my mate, 'Now for it' as we expected it to strike us both, but as luck would have it, not a little bit touched us. We could hardly believe it after bursting so close as that…

One of the saddest letters from the front was published on 19 December, five days after the death of the writer. Pte George Groves, 2nd Battalion Royal Scots Regiment, to his parents at Hundred Steps Lodge, Windsor Castle, said:

You will see by my address that I have joined my old battalion, but I don't know how many are left, as we have had 32 officers and 700 men killed, wounded or missing. We are at a place in Belgium, and have just come out of the trenches, after being in them three days and three nights with water up to our knees and so cold. The German trenches are only 200 yards from us. We are getting plenty of clothes. I shall not be sorry when this war is over.

Killed on 14 December 1914, aged 27, at Ypres, Pte Grove's body was never found and he is commemorated on the Menin Gate Memorial. The *Windsor Express* included his name in the casualty list on 16 January 1915. His brother Frederick, also serving with the

Royal Scots, was wounded in both legs on 28 March 1917, and killed on 7 June 1917.

Letters From The Front 1915

At the start of 1915 trenches stretched along the entire Western Front, from the North Sea to the Swiss border. The BEF repeatedly tried to break through the German defences with attacks at Neuve Chapelle in March, Ypres in April (when the Germans used poison gas against British troops for the first time), and Aubers Ridge and Festubert in May. A combined British and French offensive was made at the end of September, and while the French Army concentrated on the Artois and Champagne areas, the BEF attacked at Loos, where in turn the British Army used poison gas for the first time. After sustaining severe casualties, the Loos offensive ended in stalemate.

When Turkey joined the war on the side of the Central Powers, British and Indian troops were sent to Mesopotamia (now Iraq, then part of the Turkish Empire) where a plan was devised to knock Turkey out of the war and re-open the supply line to Russia by taking control of the Dardanelles. The failure of the original naval bombardment brought about a badly-planned and mismanaged invasion of the Gallipoli Peninsula, and among the Allied units sent to Gallipoli was the Berkshire Yeomanry, which arrived via Egypt, in August. Windsor men fought in campaigns all over the world, including South West Africa and at sea.

Letters from the Front continued to be quite detailed, and although there was some censorship, harrowing accounts often found their way into the newspapers. One of the first to be published was on 9 January, from Pte E Price, a Reservist of the 1st Battalion Grenadier Guards, who had been employed at the *Windsor Express*. On 26 December 1914, he wrote to friends:

We have had very rough weather all the time in the trenches, with the frost and snow. We happened to be lucky and got relieved out of the trenches on Christmas Day and Boxing Day. We are billeted on a farm, and I expect we shall have to return on Sunday night and fire a few more pills at the Germans. We have held the one position ever since we have been out here, and in some parts of the trench we are not more than one hundred yards from the German trenches, in fact, we can nearly speak to one another, as it is just the width of the field that parts us – rather too close to be pleasant… There are several Guardsmen here from Windsor, and we are all hoping to get back together.

W J Wood, who had left his post as porter at the Old Windsor Workhouse to enlist in the 6th Dragoon Guards, still thought that the war would be over soon. He wrote to the Master of the Workhouse to thank him for a gift of tobacco and cigarettes, and said:

…You have seen by the papers that the cavalry are doing trench work… At one time when we were in the trenches the weather was so severe that every man and officer had frost-bitten feet. We were in the trenches 72 hours on that occasion. It has left my feet very tender, but otherwise I am all right with the exception of rheumatism. The position that we hold now is quiet safe. The enemy has made several rushes everyday but to no purpose. The general idea out here is that the war will be over by the end of February. Anyway we are strengthening our positions every day, and there is no possible chance for the enemy who have been beaten ever since we retired from Mons…

Bombardier C A Bilbo, Royal Field Artillery, of Old Windsor, did not share the belief that the war would soon be over. Writing from 'Somewhere in the mud on the Frontier of Belgium and France' he said:

…The war in my opinion will last a long time yet, and when the advance comes, as it seems to me it must do in the early spring, well, someone will get hurt… I have not seen any of the German atrocities, except in one case; no doubt a lot have occurred, but I think also that this matter is exaggerated. The case I refer to is of a young volunteer motor cyclist, who was bayoneted and burnt with his bike on a haystack; whether he was dead when put there I do not know… If I was allowed, you would have a letter containing more interesting matter from me, but it would not pass the censor.

A letter from Bombardier H Alderman, 46th Royal Field Artillery, of Eton, was published on 16 January. He wrote that they 'had a very hot' time in November with severe losses, but proudly claimed that 'our infantry are, without a doubt, the finest in the world; the manner in which they have held their ground against overwhelming odds, time after time, can never be forgotten.' He concluded:

On the 23rd of December we were recalled to the firing line to relieve the Indian troops, who were a little fatigued after the hard fighting they have had… We had a very happy Christmas; we sent the enemy our greetings (a few rounds of gun fire) but they did not return the compliment, so we had a very quiet day. Christmas cards from the King and Queen were issued, also pudding, and Princess Mary's gifts, so we did very well indeed.

Ambulance Driver Streamer wrote a harrowing account to his brother in Albert Street, about the day he had to go out to an Artillery Battery, which had received a direct hit:

…a dreadful sight met my eyes – a sight I never want to see again… the poor men were blown to pieces; we identified them by their identity disc, so we gathered up the pieces and put them into a grave we had previously dug in the moonlight.

By the end of January, reports of the 1914 Christmas Day truce had reached home and the *Windsor Express* published several letters from local men who had spent Christmas in the trenches. On 23 January a letter from a soldier in the 2nd Battalion Royal Berkshire Regiment described how the Germans had initiated the temporary ceasefire:

At about 6 pm, the firing on both sides was very desultory and the Huns put some lights and lighted up Christmas trees up on the parapet of the trench, which was about 200 yards from the trench of the corps on our left. After a few minutes they shouted 'English, Merry Christmas' to which our chaps replied, 'Same to you. Want some duff?' Then a German said, 'Yes; come half way' to which our people replied 'Right oh!' Firing seemed to cease all along the line, and then a couple advanced from each side, met in the centre, shook hands and exchanged gifts. All that they could give was rotten black bread and cigars for our bully and Christmas duff. My position was roughly 400 yards from where this took place. Soon afterwards there was shouting to the right and left of me. It was freezing hard at the time and so you can tell that sound carried well. Some of our chaps sang the National Anthem, and the Germans cheered and clapped and then sang theirs and were suitably applauded. Nearly all night both sides were singing carols. I don't think any of this took place in my battalion.

The next morning... I saw all the Germans on top of their trenches. Naturally enough we did the same and shouted greetings to one another. Several Germans came over to our lines and stopped about 20 yards from our wire entanglements, and several officers of 'ours' met them. The Germans stood to attention and saluted, and then shook hands. Anyone away from the firing line could not imagine such a thing. All day long they were walking backwards and forwards. Heaps of our chaps shook hands with them, but I did not get a chance myself. From one source and the other, we learnt that they were tired of the war and they said that they would not shoot if we didn't... The state of friendliness existed for several days, but now we are at the old sniping business, or I should say that they snipe while we take no notice of them...

A similar story was told by a soldier of the 2nd Battalion Scots Guards, writing to a friend at the Ship Hotel, Windsor.

I am going to relate to you what happened to us on Christmas morning. Of course, it hardly seems real, but at about 8.30 on Christmas morning we were in the trenches, when I heard someone saying something about a football match between us and the Germans. I thought they had gone mad when I heard it, but it was right. I happened to look over our trenches and saw about forty of my Company talking to the Germans in between their trenches and ours, which are about 80 yards apart, so I thought I would go over too. When I got over, a German held his hand out to me, wishing me a merry Christmas in broken English, and handed me his cigar box to take one, which I did. Then one of our officers came over, and the Germans sang one of their hymns in their language. Then our lot started singing 'It's a Long Way to Tipperary', all of us smoking cigars and cigarettes. They also gave us sweets, etc; one of them gave me one of their coins for an English penny. We had a jolly time with them for over an hour; then we both went back to our trenches again, and went over to them in the afternoon. When you read this you will think I am mad, but it is quite true; if  I had not been there I would not believe it. They say they are 'fed up' with it. They are wishing for peace. We are back in the trenches firing on one another again.

A private in the 2nd Battalion Coldstream Guards, however, had quite a different story to tell and described how his battalion had fought off an enemy attack on Christmas Eve. In a letter to a friend, published on 23 January, he wrote:

…We had a very rough Christmas. I have read letters in the papers about Christmas in the trenches… All I can say is that if what they say is true it was very different to our part of the line. Talk about shaking hands with the Germans. I can tell you that the boys in No 4 Company of the 2nd Coldstream Guards are not so fond of them… About December 22nd we received orders to advance as the Germans had broken through the French lines. At dawn we let them have it, and drove them back and took their advance trenches. They were reinforced, and a terrible fight commenced and lasted till Christmas night. We were told that it was important that we should hold their advance trenches, and hold them we did, although God knows how. They had something up their sleeve. As it was getting dark on the 23rd and they found they could not drive us out with bombs, etc, they broke a great dyke and tried to drown us out. But they found that it took more than cold-streams to beat the Coldstreams. The water was about four feet deep in our trenches, and they started an all-night attack, thinking that we should never stick the night in four feet of water and freezing very hard. But our boys didn't half let them have it. Their cries were terrible. They tried for about four hours, and then retired beaten…

On 20 February a letter from Cpl E Bayliss, South Staffordshire Regiment, who lived in Victor Road, said he had been in the thick of the fighting at Mons, was hit in the head with shrapnel and shot through the neck. After time in hospital, he joined the line at Ypres, where he lost his left arm in a desperate hand-to-hand fight in a Redoubt:

The German artillery found us with shrapnel, and they simply peppered us. Still we held on, but our men went down one by one. At the finish there were four Germans against Pte Grundy and myself. Two Germans got in the redoubt and I had a fine

122

bayonet encounter with a huge fellow. He stabbed me in my right arm, but I finished him off with my left. Meanwhile the other German had shot poor old Grundy, but I avenged his death… It must have been an explosive shot that hit my arm and shattered my elbow so badly that I had it amputated at Rouen.

In the same issue was a letter from Pte William Blackford, 2nd Battalion Norfolk Regiment, which had been stationed in India, written to his mother in Leworth Place, from an entirely different field of war:

We are now somewhere up the Persian Gulf in Mesopotamia, just seeing the Turks off, and I never saw a more chicken-headed lot of people in my life. When we boarded our big liner we thought we were bound for Europe… The Indians with us are the very essence of splendid fighters, and we get on well with them, although not being able to understand each other.

He recounted a skirmish involving British and Indian soldiers against Turks and Arabs. Pte Blackford spent his war in Mesopotamia, where he was killed in action on 30 July 1917 and buried at Kut-el-Amara War Cemetery.

After the battle of Neuve Chapelle in March, Cpl Downey, 2nd Battalion Scots Guards wrote a letter to a friend at the Ship Hotel, which was published on 20 March. He said:

…We lost heavily. I was the Company's Orderly during the fight, running messages under tremendous shell-fire; but we beat them – yes, still another victory. Ah, but what a price the victory cost the Division… The Germans (cowards as they are) when the last trench was taken, surrendered; they would not fight us, but held their hands up waving white flags, and came running towards us… Our Commanding Officer was wounded and my Captain was killed, and a few more officers wounded, in all about 300 or 350 killed and wounded.

Pte W Pither, 2nd Battalion Royal Berks Regiment was also at

Neuve Chapelle, and a letter published on 3 April told his uncle in Oxford Road about the battle:

> … It commenced with a half-hour bombardment by our artillery… After the bombardment we made a glorious charge, many of our lads running to death, but all so bravely. On reaching the German trenches a terrible sight met us, for we saw the awful result of our artillery fire. Many of the Germans were still alive but soon surrendered, and seemed only too pleased to get out of it. On we went with the Germans flying before us, and then we were reinforced by another regiment who came through the middle of us and continued the attack… I think the days of trench fighting are over, for the weather is changing and the ground getting fit to move upon. Many of the Windsor boys were wounded and I don't see too many of them knocking about.

Pte A McFarlane, 12th Royal Lancers, wrote to a Windsor friend on 7 March, that they had to leave their horses behind, before going into the trenches:

> … We are doing turns of duty in the trenches at intervals again now, and expect to go in again very shortly, but as the weather is gradually improving, it is not so trying as before. The last time we went up to the trenches we left our horses behind and were conveyed in motor buses to within a short distance of the firing line. We were then held in support for five days, being billeted in the remnants of a once prosperous and beautiful city… At the end of the five days we went up to the trenches for another five… The trenches which we occupied were very close to those of the enemy, and at some points only fifty yards separated the two… I have not met many Windsor men myself, but I know there are plenty of them doing their little bit in various places, and I see that the list of names in the Express continues to lengthen.

Many of the letters home exaggerated the bravery or bravado of their side and the lack of it in the enemy line. This was not only to re-assure the folks at home, but as a means of self-preservation. Pte A Boyce, 2nd Battalion Royal Berks Regiment, who had been working at the newsagent's in Peascod Street, wrote to his old employer about Neuve Chapelle:

> The order came down for us to advance, and with no hesitation we went for all we were worth, under heavy shell and rifle fire, but we did not care – it had to be done. When we got to the German lines, the Germans were like a lot of frightened kids. They didn't run away, but gave themselves up. We lost a few men, but their casualties were ten times greater than ours.

Pte A Betteridge, 1/4th Royal Berks Regiment, expressed similar sentiments in a letter published on 8 May:

> As I write, our artillery are pounding away over our heads into the Germans. We are pretty safe here, as the Saxons haven't much heart. Sometimes we don't fire a shot all day, as they keep their heads below the barricades. The trenches are lovely – like being at home- only the shells remind you that business is at hand… I am glad to say all the Windsor boys are safe, though we have had some narrow escapes. We get the Express every week, which lets us know how the old town is getting on.

Other letters showed a great deal more realism; Gunner G E Kadwill, 7th Battery Canadian Contingent, writing to his parents at 5 Victor Road, said:

> We are doing fairly well, but are getting quite a few killed and wounded. I have been lucky so far, and hope to keep it up. It is something awful to see the wounded keep coming along in one great big stream. We were nearly captured the other night, but managed to get out of it. We keep smiling, and each day when we wake up, that is if we get any sleep, we always say 'Good morning' to the sun, and thank God for letting us live another day.

Gunner A E C Meade, Royal Field Artillery, wrote a rather grim letter from Belgium to his mother at 32 Bolton Road, published on 15 May:

I am in a big school writing this letter, and it is in ruins. The Huns are shelling us from morning to night and with 17in shells, too. They are coming over now. The sights one sees out here are too terrible – it's nothing but murder! I shall never forget the poor fellows who were killed and wounded by my side, when I was blown out of a trench. One of them had his legs blown off, and his groans were awful. Three of them were killed by the fumes in the same dug-out as I was blown into, but I did not lose control of myself and managed to crawl along the trench into the communication trench, and was taken from there. At the same spot, a poor chap had both his legs broken, and lay there until late at night in dreadful pain. We often can't get our wounded away until dark. My Battery has suffered a lot lately, and the night before last one of our chaps went mad as the enemy started to shell us. It's enough to make anyone go mad at times, especially when all your comrades are falling round you...

During May and June more letters reached Windsor showing just how global the conflict had become. The Berkshire Yeomanry arrived safely in Egypt at the end of April and Windsor Yeomen wrote letters from Malta and Egypt. A corporal of the Berkshire Yeomanry, in a letter published on 22 May, said:

...We are getting used to the climate, but I can tell you it wants some getting used to. We just exercise the horses and little things like that, so far. Work has to be done in the early morning or in the evening. In the middle of the day one just lies down and sweats! We are somewhere near the sea, and able to bathe fairly often, so that makes up for a lot... We are in a town (I must not say where). It is a fine place in parts, but the native quarter is the limit! In fact, some of Windsor's back streets are 'kings' to it.

A trooper in the Berkshire Yeomanry wrote:

We are now doing garrison work [in Egypt], so what with the extra duties and our forces to care for, you can guess what kind of time we are having. Please don't imagine we are in anything like the two Barracks at Windsor! We have to find guards for all the public buildings, Foreign Embassy, Hospitals, war prisoners and the High Commissioner's house. All the hospitals here are full of wounded – mostly Colonials. In talking to them they say it was awful work landing at the Dardanelles.

Another trooper of 'A' Squadron wrote:

Only eight men per troop are allowed out of barracks every evening, and they all have to get a pass. There are plenty of military police about to see that you do not transgress... I have been on horse guard today, and a hot job it is too. It makes you sweat if you are only sitting down chasing the flies off your face...

In June, a Windsor trooper of the Berkshire Yeomanry wrote:

...It was good news to hear that a landing had been effected on the Gallipoli Peninsula, and the fact was emphasised by the incessant stream of motor ambulances passing through ---- --- from the docks to the hospitals, but the sight of the poor fellows merely served to fire our enthusiasm...

On 5 June a number of letters were published from Petty Officer F L Harding, Royal Naval Air Service, to his parents at 2 Balmoral Villas, New Road. He wrote about his voyage to German South-West Africa (now Namibia) and skirmishes with the enemy:

Six were killed and about twenty injured on our side and about three times the number on the enemy's. One German officer was working a machine gun and wanted our men to take him prisoner, but our men saw the trick and simply peppered him to bits with their maxim... Our chief pest here is flies and our chief want is good water. The flies nearly drive one mad. The temperature goes up to about 110 degrees in the shade every day and drops a good bit at night. It never rains, so one is always safe here to sleep out on the bare ground. The chief complaint here is dysentery, brought on through drinking too much water…

Pte Richard Jamieson, 6th Battalion Seaforth Highlanders wrote to his mother at 3 Albert Street, on 16 June, from No 9 General Hospital in Rouen:

We had a terrible time yesterday, as you will no doubt see by the papers, but I am not badly hurt. I am suffering chiefly from shell shock, and have a slight wound in the left hand caused by shrapnel. It was just before 7 o'clock yesterday morning when it happened. The Germans started shelling us like anything, and I was resting in my dugout, whilst Arthur was making tea for the five of us in his, next door. A high explosive shell came and hit the parapet just above me, and of course I was buried underneath the lot, and got slightly squashed. After a time I was dug out very little the worse, but poor Arthur had some terrible wounds caused by splinters of the shell. At this time there was quite a stream of casualties, and no stretcher-bearers were available, so three more chaps and myself volunteered to take Arthur across to the dressing station. We were being shelled all the time going across the open, and a sniper also had a pot at us. We were just in time to get Arthur into a motor ambulance, but of course I could go no further myself, and dropped out. Afterwards I was sent on, and learned that poor Arthur died just as he was being taken into hospital…

Five days later he wrote again:

I am now almost convalescent… I have lost almost everything and shall have to be equipped again. My rife was blown to atoms, but I suppose it is just one's luck, and I am considering myself lucky to be alive… Even now I think I could tell you enough about the war to fill a book, but perhaps it is best not. I am down on the board suffering from 'Multiple contusions, concussion and gunshot wound in left hand'. Sounds terrible, doesn't it, but really that is all.

Gunner A Springford, Royal Field Artillery, wrote to his brother at Eton Wick, about 'the slaughter at Ypres':

When we were coming through the town of Ypres, the first thing we saw was a lance-corporal sitting in a crouched position with his full pack and his rifle up against his chest, stone dead. The next we came across were horses, mules, carts and waggons all blown to pieces. I shall never forget it, or anyone else that was there. It was absolute slaughter, nothing else. The dead were laying three or four deep… I can tell you people in England do not understand what we and our brave infantry have to go through…

Bombardier F Thomas Smith, Royal Field Artillery, continued the theme of 'the inhuman Germans', in a letter to his sister at 10 Goswell Cottages, published the same month:

…they are shelling us day and night with dirty big 'coal boxes'. All the civilians were there, until one day they started sending them over and a great many women and children were killed. It was a pitiful sight to see them; some of the young men and girls were carrying their aged parents on their backs to safety; some wouldn't go without we took them away. I can tell you it brought tears to many of our lads' eyes, and a great many thoughts were on dear old England… I once saw at a place called St Ellis a poor old woman who had been bayonetted, and a girl lying by the side of her naked, so you see what inhuman swines we are dealing with. Our chaps are only too glad to have a good scrap with them, so that they can have revenge, but it's the German officers who are to blame, not the men.

An appeal for more men to join up came in a letter from Bombardier A D L Meade, Royal Field Artillery, to his sister at 32 Bolton Road, published on 17 July:

… They (the Germans) are nowhere near beat yet either with men or munitions, and if the young chaps who are fit for service could only realise the state of things out here they wouldn't slack.

There were more letters urging men of military age who had not enlisted yet to join up and help defeat the Germans. L/Sgt Walter William Payne, 11th Battalion Royal Scots Regiment, writing to his parents at 2 Prospect Place, Eton Wick, said:

... if some of our young fellows were to see some of the sights out here I feel sure they would quickly stand up and fight for England's pride and glory. The Belgian people, who have now settled down in houses wherever they can get, always pay us chaps a hearty welcome, but most of them have lost their homes, and in most cases have not their husbands or sons.

Payne, who lived in Clewer, died aged 22, on 12 March 1916 and is buried in Hainaut, Belgium.

In October, a letter appealing for men to enlist was published from a private serving with the Windsor Territorials:

Having been given to understand that there are still some men in our district who have not yet responded to their country's call, I now appeal to them amidst the hail of 'Huns' Bullets'. I appeal to their manliness. Are they content to stand by and read of men much younger and much older than themselves fighting to uphold the honour of our dear old country? We out here have come to the conclusion that they will not respond until they see their own homes in ruins, like those we see daily out here. We can hardly credit what we read in the papers of the slump that has recently occurred in recruiting. If some of the chaps who are responsible for this would just for a moment try to imagine what we daily see and go through, I am sure they would go to the nearest recruiting office straight away...

Several letters in June and July from men serving in the Royal Berks Regiment told of life in the trenches in France and Flanders. Pte W Ranscombe, 1st Battalion, writing to his parents at Dedworth Green, said:

I suppose you have read in the papers about the gallant Berkshires, who have driven the Germans from their winter home. We had a night attack and took two German trenches.

130

The bullets were flying all ways. The Germans cried for mercy, but we gave them what they asked for with the bayonet, as it was a bayonet charge. There were a tidy lot of our fellows killed and wounded. My mate is killed, for which I am very sorry. Thank God I am safe, but I had a narrow escape. A bullet went into my pack and into that tin of tobacco you sent me out. I daresay if it had not been for that tin I should not be writing this. We are out of the trenches now for four days' rest. I shall be thankful when this war is over, to see you all again.

Pte A Betteridge, Windsor Territorials (1/4th Royal Berkshires), wrote:

Just a few lines to your paper, which we all appreciate out here, to let you know that all the boys in the Windsor Terriers are quite well and safe, although we have been shelled out of our 'dug-outs' two or three times. But I am glad to say all have come out alive. At present we are at a place near Hill 60, where no one can move a limb safely by day and not often by night. It is not very pleasant, as we can only get one drop of tea for the day by a fatigue party of six men, fetching it at one o'clock in the morning; then we have to make do till one o'clock next morning. Our meal consists of a tin of bully biscuits and jam sometimes. I am sure the people of Windsor cannot understand the hardships and endless duties we have to do…

Pte W Hall, 1st Battalion Royal Berkshire Regiment, told of life in the trenches in a letter published on 10 July:

…The German trenches are facing ours about 300 yards between, but we haven't seen much of them yet, but they are firing often and we have to keep low. At times the artillery fire is deafening and last night I counted 100 shots fired at an aeroplane… We live very well indeed in the trenches, getting hot tea for breakfast, and good stew made from bully beef for dinner. We are not allowed to light fires in the trenches, so we get two candles lighted and stand them under our canteens, which boil them all right…

On 18 September Trooper H E Kirk, Berkshire Yeomanry, who had been wounded in Gallipoli, wrote from a hospital ship about the regiment's operations on 20-21 August:

…The din and noise were so great that it was quite impossible to hear any orders. Men were falling fast. We, however, advanced steadily until reaching a gully a hundred yards or so from the crest of the hill, which afforded fairly good cover, and as we laid there we were simply smothered with dirt from the bullets hitting the bank in front of us... Whilst we lay there one man was killed and two wounded, and without a leader we were in a dilemma as to what to do or how to act. However, when the sun had set we moved, under heavy fire, with the objective of getting in touch with our regiment or other troops. We went to the right and then forward again, along another gully, until we were quite near the enemy's trenches. Here we found a row of dead Turks, and some of the bodies being in a state of decomposition the stench was awful… No reinforcements arrived, so we decided to retire down the hill, and we did so until we came in touch with a party of Borderers, who were digging themselves in well up the hill…

An NCO of the Windsor 'A' Squadron Berkshire Yeomanry wrote from Gallipoli to a friend at Windsor about 'an awful night':

I suppose by now you have heard all about our first time of going into action and the disastrous results. All I can say is that it was a most awful afternoon and night, and I trust I don't have to go through anything like it again. When you see the list of casualties you will understand what it was like. We had to advance over about two miles of open country swept by shrapnel fire, and then we got under cover of a hill, and had five minutes 'breather'. Then we had the order to fix bayonets and charge, and take the Turks' trenches in our front. We went on under a regular rain of bullets from rifles and machine guns. How I got through I don't know! Well, what was left of us went on and took two trenches, and got into the third, but we were driven out. We held the others for a time, but had to leave them as we were not strong enough to hold them, there being nobody to back us up from behind. We dropped back in the early hours of the morning, or, I might say, crept back. What were left of us were beaten to the world – all had the 'nerves' very bad. We have been out here nearly six weeks now, and have been under fire the whole of the time…

In October Pte L Buckell wrote to his mother at 9 Bolton Road:

Am pleased to say I am quite well, and, thanks to God, safe. We got a long way through their lines, but they got reinforcements up. They opened up a most murderous fire on us, both with artillery and rifles… The shells were bursting all around us, the ground shaking continually with the terrific explosions. It was terrible to see one's pals falling around us crying for help. Some of the wounded that were being dressed in our lines were blown to atoms by a shell. The roar of our guns, massed behind our lines, the shells bursting, and a huge mine of ours seemed to throw the ground from under our feet. Great masses were flung high in the air, and blew that part of their line to smithereens. They used their gas against us, but with the latest smoke helmets few casualties occurred from it. Though we lost heavily, they lost very many more, their dead lying about everywhere in masses…

Pte A Ives, Grenadier Guards, wrote to his parents at 17 Church Terrace, Dedworth from 'somewhere in France' on 2 October:

I'm the luckiest man living. We have just been through one of the most fearful fights that have been fought since the war began. We went into action on Monday, and we drove the Germans out of their trenches, and then we drove them over the open country for about a mile and a half. The bullets and shells were falling around us in thousands, and we lost a lot of men, but I was one of the lucky ones. While I was lying on the ground a bullet went just over my head and pierced the pack that was on my back. It must have been my luck, as had I moved I should have been killed, but, thank God, I got through without a scratch…

His luck held as he is not on any casualty list, but two other members of the Ives family were killed. All three appeared on the Roll of Honour on 28 August. William Henry Ives was killed in November 1915 in Iraq, and George Robert Ives was killed in June 1915 in Gallipoli.

Another soldier whose luck held was T Hobbs, Berks Yeomanry, writing from Cairo to a friend in Windsor on 8 October:

> I am just writing to tell you of a very narrow escape I had. Owing to a little pocket book I had from you in 1913 – a Charles Letts' Diary – a bullet went through the right sleeve of my tunic into my right breast pocket. It then passed through the pocket book and into a pocket the other side. The bullet next went through another book and out, without my getting a scratch. I showed the doctor, and he said if it hadn't been for the books I should have been a 'goner'. I am sending you one of your son's cards, which was in the book at the time (the bullet passed through one end of the card). After being in the Peninsula seven weeks and having some very narrow escapes, I am back in Hospital in Cairo with rheumatism. Most of the trenches out there had a foot of water in them. I expect you have had all the news about our charge by now. That was an awful night, and I lost a lot of my best pals.

Bombardier B Powell, Cavalry Brigade (Ammunition Column), wrote from the Persian Gulf to a friend at Windsor about the unbearable heat which affected even the men who had served five years in India, although they were used to the burning sun. 'The flies are the great pest of existence. Food is black with them the minute it is put on the table'. Even worse was disease:

WINDSOR MEN IN INDIA.

Sickness, I am sorry to say, has accounted for a good percentage of our force being sent back to India. Heat stroke is the commonest complaint, while enteric and malarial fevers, dysentery and colic have claimed a good number of men.

Pte W Blake, Coldstream Guards, wrote in October to Mr A H Clelland of Queen's Road, giving a graphic description of a recent engagement in which he took part in France. His letter was published on 30 October:

… About ten days ago the Germans bombarded our front line and support for five hours and then commenced to attack. They flattened our front line, and we had to retire for a short time, but not for long. We had three companies in the firing line and one in support. I was lucky to be in support. The attack commenced at about 4 o'clock by the Germans. They sent the 57th Regiment in front of the wonderful Prussian Guards, and they knew it. Some of them got into an advanced trench of ours and never got back again. The Prussians then came and there was 'hell to pay'. They never knew who was in front of them, for some others went back as fast as they could. Our men caught some of them in a sap and then charged across the open and finished them off with bombs. Then they [British troops] brought up their reinforcements and one of the finest bits of artillery work was done. They caught them napping. They put up a screen of shrapnel behind them and mowed them down like corn. The eighteen-pounders played direct on them, and the observers estimate the German losses at about 2,500. They were piled up all around. The German reports say we attacked and were repulsed, but that's nothing of the sort, and they knew it to their cost. That finished them for that day or a few days to come…

In November a letter was published from Pte H Rowland, 8th Royal Berks Regiment, to his mother at Surley Hall Road, Clewer and dated 3 October:

It is rather doubtful whether there is any 8th Royal Berks

now, we were so cut up... We advanced 6.30 Thursday night, September 23rd, from the reserve trenches into the second line of trenches, which were a foot and a half deep in mud. We were all wet through, but we Tommies did not mind that, we were all cheerful. After remaining in the second line until the following evening, we went into the firing line… It was 3.30 the next morning the order came long to stand to arms… It was 6 o'clock the order came along to fix bayonets, which was done in great silence, and was broken by a terrible bombardment of the enemy's trenches, which were 250 yards away from ours. Then the enemy replied; the din was fearful, shells dropping everywhere, shrapnel flying, gas shells bursting; it really was indescribable. We were all worked up into a pitch to kill all the Germans in the world. A few of our men were dropping here and there in the trenches… Over we went, hundreds and thousands of us, yelling like madmen; then came my first sight of death in battle; a shell burst a few yards from me, killing my officer and nine men. … My blood roused, I went like mad towards the first line of the trenches we had to capture, but the Germans had all fled, leaving their dead and dying behind…

On we went, like a wave, sweeping everything before us; then we came to the Germans' second line, and we were under a heavy fire from their Maxim guns. Though our men were falling fast, on we went…We cleared the second trench of the cowards and still advanced until we captured all the trenches. On we went, until we got to Hill 70, where we checked ourselves, being very few of the front line left, and Hill 70 is a strong fortified post. A gas shell burst and I remembered no more until I came to in the hospital. Thank God I am going on well now… How I missed being hit I cannot say; bullets were like hail, but it was a glorious charge the Kitchener's boys made – victory from beginning to end…

Many correspondents used their sense of humour to cope with the horrors of war. A private in the Grenadier Guards, writing to a friend in St Leonard's Road, in a letter published 6 November, said:

…There are always a few 'ups and downs' in a game of this sort, and more downs than ups, but you can get used to it if they will only give you time, but the Huns do not seem to think that when they are sending those 'express trains' through the air that when they burst it might fill your mess-tin full of dirt and spoil your breakfast – no sense in it. It is no good telling him to knock off for meals, he won't, and it does make you wild just as you have taken the trouble to build a fire, boil some water and make the tea, and then a 'Jim Jackson' or one of 'Stevenson's Comets' comes over and fills it full of muck, and then the air is blue for a bit; you could cut it with a knife, it is that thick… It is not good for your health out here. When this place is under rain it is under water, and I have managed up to now as I have a swimming certificate, but you can get tired of bathing if you have too much of it…

The last letter of the year, published on 25 December, was from Pte G Foster who wrote to his father at the Castle Pumping Station in Old Windsor:

I have lost the use of both feet, only for a time though, I hope. I reckon mine is a charmed life. A shell hit the ground between my feet. It blew me about twenty feet into the air, and didn't do more than bruise me, but the shock has put my feet out of action. I am now enjoying the luxury of a bed – the first for four months. I don't know whether I shall be out this side of Christmas or not…

Letters From The Front 1916

In January 1916, the last troops were successfully withdrawn from Gallipoli, bringing this ill-fated campaign to an end, although British soldiers, including Windsor men, remained in Egypt and Mesopotamia and fought at sea.

Windsor men also took part in one of the lesser-known campaigns of the war, on the Salonika Front, and wrote home about their experiences. British and French troops, later joined by Italians and Russians, landed at the Greek port of Salonika in late 1915 to assist Serbia in its fight against the Austro-Hungarian Army. They arrived too late but faced a new threat when Bulgaria entered the war on the side of the Central Powers.

The main thrust of the war against Germany was still on the Western Front. It was planned that the Battle of the Somme (July–November) would break through the trench warfare system, as well as taking the pressure off the French, who were fighting a war of attrition at Verdun. Instead it is remembered as one of the costliest battles of the war in terms of lives lost. On 1 July, the opening day of the battle, over 19,000 troops were killed, making it the greatest loss in a single day in the history of the British Army. By the time the battle ended in mid-November, with little territorial gain for the Allies, it had become another war of attrition. Fortunately for Sir Douglas Haig, compulsory military service was introduced in early 1916 to fill the gaps in the British front line.

The first letter of the year, published on 15 January, came from Pte Ernest Habgood, Machine Gun Section, 2nd Battalion Royal Berks Regiment, thanking the *Windsor Express* for publishing the account of their football match.[1]

Descriptions of the mounted charge by the Berks Yeomanry in Egypt in December 1915, show that the regiment was in 'a hot encounter', which ended with the Arabs being driven off with heavy losses. According to the official account the enemy numbered 300, of whom 35 were killed and seven captured, while the British casualties were 16 killed and 18 wounded. Mrs Martin, of 41 King's Road, received a letter from Major E B Foster, Berks Yeomanry, with reference to her son, Trooper W Martin, who was killed in the action on 11 December. Major Foster's letter published on 22 January, said:

He met a soldier's death in very gallant fashion while helping to hold a position against great odds. A cavalry charge had taken place, as a result of which subsequent dismounted fighting took place. The Arabs admitted to a loss of 83 men killed. About 50 men of the Berks Squadron and an armoured car were the only troops seriously engaged. I feel his loss personally very much as he belonged to my old Squadron – the Windsor one. He was such a plucky little fellow: for such a small man he was full of grit. The officers and men of the regiment are subscribing for a memorial to be erected on your son's and his comrades' graves, which are situated in the little town of Mersa Matruh, which is now held by our forces…

On 19 February there was an appeal by Rifleman T Pocock of Bridgewater Terrace for hair-cutting implements to be sent to the desert: 'The weather is getting very warm out here and we are about 150 or 200 miles west across the desert, so we can't get our hair cut in town.'

Sgt A T Hughes wrote from the Prisoners' Camp at Erfurt, Germany, to the Mayor of Windsor, in a letter published on 4 March:

1. See chapter on Habgood family

139

At last I feel it is my duty to let you know of our welfare and health, also in acknowledgement of your right welcome parcels which we all receive quite safe and in good condition each week, the last dated 20th January. Everything sent is of remarkable value to us; there is no doubt the whole parcel is really too good for words… Up to the present we have had very mild weather, very little snow to what we had last year. Our camp and quarters are kept very clean and respectable. Everything is granted us, if it should be for our benefit. We have hot water pipes in our barracks, and a drying room to hang our clothes after washing them. We are allowed one hot water bath each week, and if we so desire we may have a second, or even a third. We have a daily roll call parade. After the roll has been called we break up into two parties, as we call it, 'the old and the young'. The old, as it were simply marches around; this is to keep all as fit as possible. The young do physical exercises...

There were a number of letters from the Berks Yeomanry in Salonika. Pte H Hunt wrote to his mother at 11 Bexley Street, in a letter published on 4 March:

After riding over the mountains all day, we came to a small village in which were about a hundred Greek soldiers. They made a great fuss of us there; some of them helped us to unsaddle our horses, while others took away the horses to water and feed, and also put them in a good stable. The officers, of course, went to a house where there were Greek officers, and we got a small room about a hundred yards away.

…We did about thirty miles that day, and stopped at a village in sight of the Bulgarian frontier. After two days there we started back for camp. The country here is one mass of mountains and we had to ride over these. It was dangerous work, as the mountains were all covered with snow and ice, and anybody who was not a good horseman would have been killed by falling over a deep ravine. At one part of the journey back one of the officers' horses slipped up on a frozen goat track, and fell about three hundred feet. We did not expect to see him alive again, but when we got down to him we found him smoking a cigarette and looking at his horse. The officer was none the worse for his fall but we had to leave the horse there. He rode a spare horse coming back. That was the only fall we had, but we were very lucky as we had to ride round the side of the mountains on a path sometimes only a foot wide, with a mass of rocks beneath us. We got back to camp quite safe, and the boys gave us a cheer when we came in.

A second letter sent to the editor asking for haircutting and shaving sets was published on 8 April. It came from two soldiers serving in the Royal Berkshire Regiment, Privates H Austin and John Tame:

We are having a quiet time at present in the trenches, but there is plenty of mud and water. Still we keep smiling. We were out for a rest from the trenches a month ago and had a very enjoyable time. We played the Buffs at football and beat them comfortably by 5-1. We have a fine football team, including some of the Windsor boys from the Clewer St Stephen School. We also have a good rugby team, and we haven't been defeated yet. We are urgently in need of a haircutting and shaving set, and if any of your readers would kindly forward the same to us we would be very pleased.

Sadly, Pte Austin, of Oakley Green, died on 27 January 1917, and is buried at Grandcourt Road Cemetery, France. Pte Tame died on 19 August 1917 and is remembered on the Tyne Cot Memorial, Belgium.

A letter from Pte Edward West Wackrill, Royal Berkshire Regiment, sent to Mr H Agent of 49 Sheet Street and published on 15 April, gives a long account of life in the trenches:

We left the base, last Thursday week, for the trenches and have been having the time of our lives. We stopped in the reserve trench for nearly two days, which although nearly 1½ miles from the frontlines is shelled by the enemy's big guns at all times of the day and night... On Saturday we moved up to the front, we relieved a Battalion who did not hide their satisfaction of being released, and gave us some rather disquieting remarks about Fritz. Our job was to watch the periscope by turns by day, and look out over the top by night in pairs. This is rather dangerous, as the devils keep sending up starlight shells, which light up the place like day, and they then blaze away like hell with rifle and machine guns. When it came to my turn with the periscope I noticed a lot of curious forms lying between the two lines of trenches, and soon found out they were bodies of the poor devils who attacked on September 25th last, and would have been buried long ago in any other war but this one. Well, they shell us, and our guns far away behind shell them and Tommy sits tight and swears… These trenches are so exposed that there has been no time to dig dug-outs, and we had to take our rest in the pouring rain day and night for 72 hours straight off. I managed to get seven and a half hours sleep all told and we were then sent back about half a mile for a breather…

Pte Wackrill was killed shortly afterwards, on 3 July 1916; he is remembered on the Thiepval Memorial.

Trooper Walter Eldridge, 'A' Windsor Squadron Berks Yeomanry, wrote to his parents from Egypt. His letter was published on 29 April:

I have been for the last four weeks miles from where mails ever get or go from. We have been trekking during that time continually, resting only for sleep and food, which, of course, is mostly 'bully' and biscuits. The greatest pain we suffer is from the lack of water. Of course we always stop at a well, but although it always does for the horses, it's more than I can drink – it has that sandy, salty, rank taste… I don't know if the censor will allow me to tell you, but we have been as far as the very north-west frontier of Egypt, to a place called Sollum (pronounced Salome), and here I've been in action. With the aid of four armoured cars and 'A' Squadron as a rear guard, we absolutely routed the Senussi tribe and drove them back into their own haunts, chasing them for over 20 miles over Italian territory (Tripoli). We captured from them 93 shipwrecked sailors from off the Tara, which was torpedoed last November. The poor devils looked just like the natives themselves, black and dirty, and half starved. They went fairly mad, and they shifted grub at an alarming rate. The following day they were taken by Red Cross motors and cars to Sollum and put straight on to a hospital ship, and by this time, I guess, are back with their people in dear old England. After we had captured a Turkish officer and three of the chiefs they surrendered. The armoured cars did much damage to the Senussis; in fact, I believe it put the lid on it…

Trooper Eldridge was killed in action on 19 April 1917 and, like Pte Wackrill, became a casualty without a known grave; he is remembered on the Jerusalem Memorial.

A letter from 'a gunner' about life in Mesopotamia was published on 6 May:

…The Arab boatmen sell tobacco, dates and Huntley and Palmer's biscuits at fabulous prices. Apart from that there is nothing to buy… The mules, heart-breaking animals though they are, work well, though I am thankful to say I still have a horse. I doubt if the appetite of the ostrich is as varied as a mule. They eat their saddles, their blankets, their ropes and even their neighbours' tails. One poor fellow died, apparently of debility, but it was found that he had eaten not only the saddlery but the buckles as well. Tobacco is easily got, but I should be very grateful for a stick of shaving soap and a towel. I cannot yet steel myself to leave my chin unscraped. It was a great disappointment when I could not get home for a few days. Our days end at sunset. Candles are as scarce as apple trees.

Bombardier Frank Welch, Royal Field Artillery, of 8 Eton Square, Eton, wrote from Salonika on 3 April:

I thought you would like to know of a little exciting time I had a few days ago during a German air raid. At the time I was in charge of a guard over a supply of meat. About a quarter to five the first bomb dropped, and I woke up at once; at first I thought I had been dreaming, but before I had time to get off my bed, which happened to be a side of beef and a few sacks, two more bombs dropped a short distance away. I then went out on to the road just as day was breaking, but it was not light enough to see the German machines. All along the road one could see Greeks doing the half-mile in record time. By this time it was getting nice and light and our guns were beginning to make things hot for the Germans. Suddenly a bomb dropped on a spot which seemed to send a ball of fire several hundred feet up into the air. It then spread out into a large cloud of smoke and started to blow over towards the hills, and the German airmen, seeing the good cover it gave them, at once flew into it. By this time they had finished dropping bombs and were making for home. While this was going on, four Frenchmen had gone up and were making battle with the Germans, who were now making for home as fast as they could, and that finished our part of the programme…

Frank Welch died on 18 May 1917 and is buried at Struma Military Cemetery in Greece.

Fred Weight, who was Captain's Steward on HMS *Tipperary*, witnessed the Battle of Jutland on 31 May. He wrote to his father, Mr J H Weight at 35 Oxford Road:

… We had a signal to take up a position behind the Grand Fleet, and then the big ships began to speak. We could see the flashes of Beatty's guns, but owing to a slight haze, we could not see the ships. By 6 o'clock practically all the Grand Fleet were firing. The sight was extraordinary and most impressive, for miles and miles there was nothing but big ships firing salvo after salvo; about 7 o'clock we saw the Invincible blow up. One huge blood red flame shot up into the sky, followed by a huge cloud of smoke and all sorts of wreckage, and when the smoke cleared there was nothing to be seen. One of our destroyers was within a quarter of a mile from her, and they said that ten seconds after the explosion there was nothing to be seen. A huge battle raged up to about 10 at night, when firing subsided a great deal, but there was intermittent firing all night. Soon after 10 o'clock we were proceeding on a night attack, and about 11 o'clock or 11.30, we were at our action stations.

I was at the after gun ammunition supply, three of us together, when suddenly a terrible fusillade at very close range caught our forecastle bridge and engine rooms; a few shells burst close to us, one killed the ward-room cook, injured another fellow badly, caught me a clout above the ear with shrapnel and knocked us all over. I fell down the wardroom hatchway, but came round in a quarter of an hour, and was carried up on deck. We found the firing had lasted nine minutes. They had knocked the foremast down and killed and wounded about 200, besides setting the bridge on fire and smashed up all our boats, leaving us with two rafts and a motor boat, which sank when we lowered it into the water; the three funnels were like colanders, holes all over them...

In June 1916 an Army Order was issued prohibiting letters home, which gave away too much information on the conditions at the front. Officers and men were 'forbidden, without special authority, to publish any article, whether purporting to be fiction or fact, which in any way deals with the war or with military subjects'. This was designed to stop the explicit letters published in newspapers (particularly on the eve of the Battle of the Somme); there certainly were none published for several weeks during June but it did not put an end to all letters home. One published on 15 July came from former Windsor Police Constable F Walker, then a L/Cpl in the Military Police. He did not say where he was, but from the description of a large town with a fine cathedral in ruins, it could have been Ypres:

… I am pleased to be able to say that I am 'in the pink' so far. I have been up this part of the line now for four months, and have only seen two local men all the time. One of them used to live next door to me at Spital, he is in King Edward's Horse; the other young fellow comes from Dedworth, he is in the Royal Engineers. I expect some people have the idea that the Military Police do not get anywhere near the firing line, but if not actually in the trenches we who are up here are very close behind, and well within rifle range and under shell fire every day. But Sunday seems to be the great strafing day of the week for the Boches; that is very often how we have to tell what day it is. I should think this place was a very busy town in peace time, but it is a sight to look on now – a sight that some of the conscientious objectors ought to be made to see. The Cathedral was a fine building, but now it is one mass of ruins with the exception of the chancel, although the roof is all blown in and there are great holes in the wall…

A letter published on 5 August, from Trooper G Bennett, Dragoon Guards, to his mother at 16 Red Lion Row, River Street, described a cavalry charge he was involved in:

…Three days they were shelling us, and we could do nothing. However, on the fourth day came the order and away we went. The infantry drove the Germans from their last trench into a valley, and weren't they surprised when we charged down among them. The Artillery tried to put us 'out', but the pace we were going made it impossible. It was fine, but rough going – nothing but shell holes, about ten feet deep and three yards wide – but we got there, right in the thick of it…The horses, frightened by the shells, went like devils, and more than once I rose rather high from the saddle when the horse leapt, but my knee was there like glue. I am glad to say – as does everybody else – that this is the luckiest regiment out here. We had very few casualties. Although we got away rather light – which surprised even the General – a tidy few horses went under. We took about fifty prisoners. I always said this war would last a long time, but in this part we had them on the run and they

146

had no trenches to drop into, only shell holes, a lot too deep for us...

On 12 August two letters received by Mrs Smith at Surley Hall Road, Clewer were published. The first concerned her son, L/Cpl Joseph Smith:

I am sorry that your son Joseph Henry has been wounded today doing a very brave action indeed. Fortunately his wounds are not severe... The act he was doing was to attempt to throw himself on a bomb that was about to go off for the purpose of saving the lives of his comrades, and to prevent the explosion of a large store of bombs. Fortunately the bomb exploded before he got to it, and the pieces wounded him in the legs and arms. If he had been in time to throw himself on the bomb he would probably have been killed. As it was he was able to save his comrades being wounded. This is not the first occasion on which your son has proved his gallantry, and the Regiment is proud of him... Rev J H Kempson, Chaplain.

The second letter was from her son, a well-known local footballer, married with one daughter, and he gave an account of the action described by the Rev Kempson:

I was in charge of a big bomb store for a time, and we were examining some of them when one of them fused, and I went out into the passage with it, and covered the other chaps and the bombs. Then it exploded and caught me about a hundred wounds all over my legs but none of them very bad, only small wounds. But the other chaps got off scot-free, so that was good.

L/Cpl Smith was recommended for a gallantry medal.

On 19 August, under the heading 'A Message From Russia', was part of a letter sent by Petty Officer W C Church to his parents at Beaumont Farm, Old Windsor telling about the welcome the British had received in Russia. There were placards everywhere which read: 'A Hearty welcome dear Allies', and 'England is with us and her sons are here'.

Pte A V Pullinger wrote to his parents at 37 Albany Road, about his experiences in the Somme Offensive. The letter published on 26 August described the scene after his battalion had captured a German trench:

…Looking around one was astounded to think that we had driven the Hun from it; once deep, well-dug trenches, dugouts splendidly excavated and timbered with three or more entrances, some twenty to thirty feet below ground level, and what were once immense redoubts of concrete and stone.

What was it all like now? One piece of churned ground, shell holes nearly touching one another (after our terrific bombardment at the commencement of the offensive) and not a brick of the village once standing in the vicinity above three feet from the ground. In all my time out here I have never seen such chaos. Lying partly buried in the trenches were corpses numerous, some 'Allemand', some ours. Also it was no joke to walk along at night suddenly to feel the earth give way beneath; quickly one stepped forward without hesitation. The most enjoyable sight I saw was about two hundred Germans driven along on either side by our bombers, suddenly leap from their trenches and come running towards us with their hands up. The enemy gunners the other side did not like to see their own men surrender, so they fired into them, consequently we made very few of that batch prisoners for the majority were killed.

Driver B Ryan, Royal Field Artillery, was transferred from Mesopotamia to Bombay after he had been injured, and in August wrote to his mother at 6 Acre Passage:

…All day long I have to stick in bed, and I can tell you it gets monotonous. This is the first time I have walked for three weeks, and I feel like a small kid just learning to stand on its feet. Since I have been here (the Victoria War Hospital, Bombay), I have picked up wonderfully. The temperature here is only 80 degrees in the shade. What a difference to the 120 [in Mesopotamia]. It seems as though I am in England I came here on the 29th July, now today is August 3rd, only five days you see, and I get plenty of food now... The only thing we can't get here is fruit. The authorities won't allow any to be brought into the Hospital on account of the disease it introduces, chiefly cholera... I have lost all my kit. I was lucky to get away from Mesopotamia with my life, with all I have been through, as so many thousands of our poor fellows pegged out there. They call it the white man's grave...

This shed is not as hot as the tent I was in (Amara, Mesopotamia). It wasn't safe to leave the tent at mid-day. You would not be out long before you would have to be brought back with a tap of the sun. It completely knocks you down and your head feels as though an iron band has been tightly drawn across your forehead.

Harry James Hyde joined the Royal Flying Corps aged 19 and had seen service in Egypt and Mesopotamia. He wrote to his father at 13 Alma Terrace, in a letter published on 30 September, after a forced visit to India suffering from malaria:

No doubt you were surprised to receive a letter of mine from here. The fact is I hadn't been able to write you recently from up river Tigris, not feeling at all up to it, as I had been for five weeks somewhat queer and in an improvised hospital before I got sent down here with malaria. But I picked up a bit on the sea voyage. It was some trip, for I don't think the majority of us ever expected to reach Bombay, as on the journey we experienced one exceptionally rough night... The majority of us sick were sleeping, or trying to, on deck, using our great coats as pillows, there being no issue of blankets or bedding, and the rats playing leap frog over our faces and scampering about all night long. However, our 'bonny boat' eventually landed us outside Bombay, arriving there on the 1st of August. We were not taken off until the following day, in a pouring rain, which naturally added to our comfort. But when ashore we were got straight on to the train, which, after 30 hours, brought us here... We get as much food as we can hide away and first-rate too, it is. I'm glad to say I'm feeling a lot better in myself, and I'm mighty glad to get sent down from Basra, for the climate conditions made it a perfect hell there for three months. Still, the hot weather will have passed by the time I have to return, as the nurse informs me. I shall in a few weeks be able to go to a convalescent camp, and then, of course, there's no knowing what the programme will be.

Pte Jack Angell, who was formerly trainer of the Windsor and Eton Football Club, wrote to the *Windsor Express* in October:

Since writing my last letter to you, our Battalion have been moved to another front, but wherever I go I always run into Windsor boys. This time I have been fortunate to meet George Mason, of Albert Street, who is RQMS of the Royal Fusiliers, and before we could exchange greetings he said 'Come on, our meeting is not going to be a dry one this time, as I read about the last meeting you had, in the *Windsor Express*'... By the way, I am very pleased to inform you that our Windsor Company has gone down for a well-earned rest, but for how long I do not know, I had to sprint to catch them up and see our dashing left-half E Udell. I am pleased to say he is looking in good health, in fact the whole Battalion looked very smart and well after the excellent work they have performed...I am glad the Mayor has been presented with a new 'horse', and I hope he is well as he looks in the Daily Sketch.

Ex-Police Constable Weeks (Windsor Borough Police), was a sergeant in a Canadian Regiment and had been awarded the Military Cross and a Russian decoration; he was subsequently shot by a sniper and evacuated to Tooting Military Hospital. In his letter published on 14 October, he said:

... In April 1915 we experienced our first real fighting at Ypres, where, in addition to the Germans being about ten to one against us, they gave us a good dosing with gas. I was then a machine gun sergeant. I was wounded on April 24th 1915, and came home to hospital. I was awarded the Cross of the Order of St George, by the Czar of Russia for having kept my crew supplied with ammunition, although wounded. I returned to France two months later, and have been there up to the time of my receiving the present wound. In July last, and whilst the Battalion was holding trenches, the Germans blew up a big mine on us. After picking myself up and finding that I was OK, I rushed into the crater with a few men, and managed to hold it until reinforced. We got there before Fritz. For this I was lucky enough to get the Military Medal... A dirty sniper got me, and I am now in hospital with a hole through my right thigh...

Pte John Ottrey, of the London Regiment, whose parents lived at Acre House, wrote to a friend in October:

I have been engaged in pushing the Huns and am pleased to say that I came through all right, but had the misfortune to cut my thumb rather badly on a Maconochie[2] tin about an hour after we came out. I lost several of my pals and had a pretty rough time, and a full share of excitement, finishing up covered with mud, hungry, and tired out. I stayed behind two days after the battle with bad feet and was put on baggage guard, and so missed the cinematograph, which took the rest and will be published (so the padre says) in the 3rd edition of the battle films... There were plenty of souvenirs knocking about in the shape of caps, helmets, rifles, etc, the other day, but I did not trouble about them except for a pocket knife and some German tobacco. One of us found a German pipe – you know the style: long stem and cover to the bowl. It was a fearful time though and so were some of the sights there. Some things I should like to be able to tell you but they would not bear writing down.

John Ottrey was killed on 12 January 1917 and, like so many without a known grave, is commemorated at the Menin Gate Memorial in Ypres.[3]

Cpl E J Tilbury, who formerly worked for the *Windsor Express*, joined the RAMC at the age of 40. He had two sons serving in the Foot Guards and wrote to a friend on 11 November:

2. Maconochie was a meat and vegetable stew made by the Maconochie Company of Aberdeen

3. See also chapter on Windsor Boys' School

We have only been away from the firing line for a fortnight in the six months we have been out here. The Ypres line was bad enough but the Somme is much worse. My ambulance lost heavily last week and we gained three Military Medals, although I was not one of the lucky ones… The different ambulances are doing great and glorious work… striving to save the lives of their comrades, up to their knees in mud, marching into the danger zone.

A letter sent by Pte T Soen of Clewer, Royal Berks Regiment, to his sister in Houghton, Datchet was published on 11 November. He wrote of the terrible mud in the trenches:

"The Morning Toilet."
Some Windsor Lads "Somewhere in France."

After we had been in the trenches for four days and nights, in the front line too, with old Fritz shelling us all the time and rain coming down in bucketsful, we were told that we were going to be relieved, and I can tell you we were jolly glad to hear it, as I think it was the worst time I'd had in the trenches – all up to our necks in mud and water. When the relief party came we started off (or tried to) out of the trench, but a lot of us got stuck in the mud. I had at least three men getting me out, finally they managed it. After going a bit further I got stuck worse than ever, and they could not get me out, so they told me I could get myself out best and left me to it. After struggling for half an hour I managed to get out of it, and we stayed for the night in a dug-out. Next morning we started to find our Battalion. We got a ride up, and were given half a loaf and cigarettes. We then got on a bit and had a good warm beside one of the camp fires and some tea…

Letters From The Front 1917

In 1917 British troops were still fighting in Mesopotamia, Egypt, Palestine and Salonika, although the Western Front continued to be the main theatre of war. By April, the German Army had withdrawn to a new line of defence called the Hindenburg Line, where British and Commonwealth attempts to break through the German defences met with limited success. The Arras campaign in April achieved its objective at great cost of life, but was not followed through, while the Messines Ridge was successfully captured in June.

One of the most bitterly fought campaigns of the war was the Third Battle of Ypres, commonly known as Passchendaele. It began on 31 July, and ended after the capture of the Belgian village of Passchendaele in November, and was not one battle, but a series of military engagements which were planned to remove the Germans from their dominant positions overlooking the Ypres Salient, and ultimately capture the Belgian ports used as U-boat bases. The attack soon ran into difficulties, due to the determined German defence and the appalling weather. The Allied bombardment destroyed the drainage system and left the landscape covered in shell holes; the unseasonal heavy rain then transformed the area into a sea of mud, in which countless men died.

Although intended as a strategic breakthrough, the Passchendaele campaign turned into a war of attrition, with small territorial gains at a considerable cost in human life. It is estimated that between 60,000 and 80,000 British and Commonwealth soldiers were killed or missing, with total casualties in excess of 300,000. At the end of November, tanks were used en masse in battle for the first time at Cambrai, but failed to break through the Hindenburg Line.

There was just one letter from the front published during the whole of January, from Pte J Deacon, Royal East Surrey Regiment, to his sister in Windsor, describing his Christmas, from 'somewhere' in Salonika:

We had rather a good time this Christmas, as we were out of the trenches and in billets. We had managed to get some stuff up, such as nuts, oranges, and three turkeys, which each platoon raffled for as there was not enough for the company. Our platoon was lucky enough to win the turkeys, so we had fowl for dinner. The *Daily News* sent us some pudding, so we did not go without pudding for dinner…'

Writing a postscript on 29 December, he added:

I went to a pantomime last night, which I am sending a programme of. It was quite a treat. You would be surprised to have seen it. The theatre was a huge barn-like place, and the stage was as good as any in England. The scenery was very good too, all made out here by the men of the RAMC. The songs were fine, dealing with the troubles of life in the RAMC, and the high prices charged by the Greek canteen, which are gold mines to their owners… The pantomime was entitled 'Aladdin, a Field Ambulance'… There were a about a score of performers in the cast, as well as soldiers, tortoises and muleteers, while the orchestra was supplied by members of the band of a Welsh regiment.

A letter published on 24 March came not from the front, but a prison camp in Germany. Pte W Simmonds, Royal Berks Regiment, from Dedworth, wrote on 10 January to Mrs A T C Cowie at Clewer Rectory:

So pleased to receive your letter, dated 27th November, also to let you know that I am in splendid health. I have received the parcel with the card in it, and it is a very nice one… I have at the time of writing received one parcel from the Central Prisoners of War Committee, London, sent December 1st 1916, but it did not have the name of the donor on it. It was a splendid parcel. Of course I should like you to continue packing the parcel for me, but in war time orders are orders, and so we must obey them for the present – not much longer, I hope. You say in your letter that we must have patience, but I am afraid mine won't last out, as I have been here over two years, and it has tried my patience to the utmost. Still, with the help of those five parcels you packed for me, I have managed to pull through with flying colours…

E Lovegrove, Australian Imperial Force, in a letter to his father at 4 Albert Place, Clewer Green, published on 28 April, said:

I think you can feel sure that we were in some of the news you are reading about, as we have been very much to the front of late. In fact, since we made a start this way last July we have been regular visitors to the front line. This business beats the best of men in time. The weather here is what we should have had last month – cold winds and rain and sleet, and yesterday a fall of snow. Snow is no good for men in the 'line' as the sniper can see you plainer. Just now, though, it will be equally as bad for him as for us.

I remember very well, after a heavy fall, during that very cold spell, we had to relieve the men in the front line, and there were no trenches to go through. As luck had it, there was a lovely full moon. Of course, going across the open we were very easily seen by 'Fritz' and he gave us a lively time. Some crawled, others walked stooping, and others ran for it. I had no choice, as I had a machine gun to carry. I had to walk, and it was very uncomfortable going along. By rights we should have all been hit, but the only man who was hit was the man behind me. He was wounded, and is doing well. That particular bit of the line had cost us and the Huns many hundreds of lives. It is ours since the evacuation, and now we can see how much it cost the Hun to hold the place. None of the line is good, but that place was particularly bad… This year in France has taught me a lot. It's a very rough schooling and one that one will remember for life.

A letter published on 12 May was simply called 'A Windsor man writing to a friend':

To write of all I have seen and been through would keep me occupied for some considerable time, so I shall leave that for a later date. The first town of any size I saw when near the line was Albert, and I should say it will take about 'umpteen' years to put things straight and rebuild the place. Then the Germans shelled it while we were there, but now the civil population are returning and Fritz is miles away… It is the same with other places on the Somme, where the heavy fighting of the winter months have left their mark. If you could see a barrage by our artillery previous to an attack you would wonder how anyone could live under it all, but Fritz knows how to build a dug-out. One I went into contained passages and rooms for sleeping and officers' quarters at the far end. I can tell you he wanted some shifting. It was a cheering sight after so much trench warfare to see the cavalry moving up to the front. We began to think cavalry were a thing of the past, but they sprung to life when Fritz did a right about turn… Last evening a number of prisoners came through a certain village we happened to be occupying (not on the Somme), and they were the worst set of Fritzs I had ever seen, covered from head to foot in mud and chalk and utterly worn out. They looked properly 'fed up'…

On 26 May the *Windsor Express* published a letter received from a prisoner of war in Germany to a friend in Windsor. He had very disturbing news about British POWs being in the firing line:

…We are now on the frontier of the Russian-German firing line in Russia. We left Libau [now in Latvia], where we had been for nine months, about three weeks ago, and are not to be removed until the German prisoners are removed from the firing line in France. We have been very fortunate until now, as we have been under shell fire on several occasions and not one of us has been hit yet. The cold here is cruel and I have been almost freezing since I left Libau. The snow is very deep except in the roads, and we are living in a tent, so you can imagine what we have to put up with. The officials here tell us it is a reprisal for what our Government is doing to their prisoners, and I hope and trust we will not be left in this condition very long. It is agony, and no one who has not gone through it can imagine what it is like. There are 500 of us here, hoping day after day to be sent back out of it. We hope it will be very, very soon now, as everyone is in such low spirits and fairly well exhausted with the cold. Make this letter as public as possible so as to let all at home know what we are going through. Do not be downhearted; we shall all pull through, I hope, and our trust is in God.

This letter must, presumably, have been written with the approval of the Germans – perhaps to force the British to remove to safety German soldiers allegedly held at the front. The fate of the unnamed writer is not known.

A three verse poem by J Burke of Windsor, serving in the BEF in France, was published in early June under the heading 'In the Trench':

> Oh, I'm 'aving th' time o' me life,
> With a bit of a hell of a time,
> 'Cos me khaki's in rags,
> An' I've run short o' fags,
> But me 'ealth an' me spirits is prime.
> We're a mixed lot of sports at the front,
> 'Cos there's British an' Belgins an' French,
> All as gay as tadpoles,
> In our little mud-holes in th' trench.
>
> Tho' yer can't put yer 'tuppennies' out,
> W'en Jack Johnsons[1] is flying about,
> But they don't do no harm,
> If yer keeps yerself calm,
> An' yer digs yerself in yer dug-out.

1. *Jack Johnsons were large artillery shells. The large amount of dark smoke given   off by the powerful explosions were reminiscent of the black heavyweight boxing champion Jack Johnson.*

They're feeding us quite ally cart
(I'm a dabster at pickin' up French).
Th' cribs were we nestles,
We calls 'Hotel Cecils',
Our snug little holes in th' trench.

But yer feels it's nigh breakin' yer 'eart,
W'en yer best chum's put under th' sod.
'Till I gets this 'ere note,
Wot my dear ole gal wrote:
I wos arstin strite – Is there a God?
She writes as our two tiny kids
(I won't swear any more – 'cept in French)
W'en they toddles to bed,
Sez a prayer for dear Dad,
In 'is little mud-hole in th' trench.

IN THE TRENCH !

Oh, I'm 'aving th' time o' me life,
With a bit of a hell of a time,
'Cos me khaki's in rags,
An' I've run short o' fags,
But me 'ealth an' me spirits is prime.
We're a mixed lot of sports at the front,
'Cos there's British an' Belgins an' French,
All as gay as tadpoles,
In our little mud-holes in th' trench.

Tho' yer can't put yer " tuppennies " out
W'en Jack Johnsons is flying about,
But they don't do no harm,
If yer keeps yerself calm,
An' yer digs yerself in yer dug-out.
They're feeding us quite ally cart
(I'm a dabster at pickin' up **French**).
Th' cribs were we nestles,
We calls " Hotel Cecils,"
Our snug little holes in th' trench.

But yer feels it's nigh breakin' yer 'eart,
W'en yer best chum's put under th' sod.
'Till I gets this 'ere note,
Wot my dear ole gal wrote :
I wos arstin strite—Is there a God ?
She writes as our two tiny kids
(I won't swear any more—'cept in **French**)
W'en they toddles to bed,
Sez a prayer for dear Dad
In 'is little mud-hole in th' trench,
    J. BURKE, Windsor.
B.E.F., France.
26/5/17.

An article in the same edition analysed 'Humour at the Front'. It was said that conditions 'are often so nearly intolerable that if troubles were taken seriously, one would very quickly "go under"'. The article came to the conclusion that 'humour is a synonym for a sense of proportion and that the men who go farthest are those whose sense of irony carries them undismayed through the direst misadventures.' The author of 'In the Trench' obviously had a good sense of irony.

Cpl C C Martin, Berks

159

Yeomanry at Gaza, wrote to his sister at Windsor. His letter was published on 2 June:

> …On Monday night, April 16th, we moved out from our base, from which we have been working the various outposts, marched the best part of the night, and then taking up a position to await events… At dusk we took up outpost again, digging trenches, from which we could see the Turks on the opposite ridge, about two miles away… During the day we hid in one of the many deep gulleys (practically dry river beds), for directly you showed yourselves in any numbers you got shelled, and pretty accurately…
>
> In the afternoon we were called on to reinforce, and galloped into action about 2 o'clock. My word! What a ride! Talk about excitement, with shrapnel bursting all around. In about ten minutes we had mounted, ridden about two or three miles, dismounted, and were in the firing line. What a din! Every available rifle and machine gun was going all out to cover our advance. We arrived just in time for the Turks were attacking, and would probably have driven the brigade from their position. After a short time, during which we gave 'Johnnie' a good peppering as he retired to cover of gully, etc, we advanced across open ground to a hill on the left. They gave us a good dose of shrapnel as we ran, but fortunately the shooting was bad, but they got a few of the boys down. From our new position we could fire on them as they dodged out of the gulleys to the top of the ridge. Here several more fellows were hit… Things now began to get warmer, so we shifted again, taking up a position more to the left and on top of a ridge. This we expected to hold all night, so commenced to dig in with our bayonets…They kept trying to shift us by shelling, but we stuck it, and eventually saw them retiring up an opposite slope. There they had it as hot as we could put them in, and I think they felt one or two…

An anonymous Windsor soldier, serving on the Western Front, writing to a friend at home said:

… I am under the medical treatment for my feet and legs, which broke out into sores and gave me gip, I can tell you. There were numerous cases of the same kind, which just gives a rough idea what trench life does for one, no matter how he tries to keep himself clean… During the three weeks most of us had a spell in the famous Hindenburg Line. It is certainly a very strongly fortified line and must have taken months of toil to make. It is not at all like our system of trenches. In places it is wide enough for a small trap to pass along, and dug-outs are all along the track. It must have been easily visible to our aircraft and a splendid mark for our artillery. The dug-outs I mention are in reality one huge underground tunnel running for nearly nine miles underground. Stretcher cases are brought through parts of it from dressing stations in the fire zone to stations in rear. This makes the work of the stretcher-bearers less arduous and is a great boon. All the dug-outs are numbered and lead down to the tunnel. It is something to have seen and been in this fine piece of handiwork. I think it speaks wonders for the combination of infantry and artillery in getting Fritz away from this part of his line…

Well, I see by the paper, more lads are gone from the town, and in Percy Jones I have lost a chum who was with me at school and we were always the best of friends. I was sorry to hear he had gone. Others I knew well have also made the great sacrifice.

His 'chum' Rifleman Percy Jones, King's Royal Rifle Corps, died on 23 April. It was reported in the Roll of Honour on 12 May and as a news item a week later.

A letter from 'three Windsor boys' was published on 30 June:

Just a few lines from three of the Royal Borough's lads doing their bit in France, and also doing everyone they come across, especially Fritz. We have enclosed photo taken behind the lines, and hoping you will publish it to let the people at home see we are quite happy. By the time you get this we shall be in the thick of it again. You may guess it is a treat for us to meet as we have not seen one another for years. I think this is all

we can tell you this time as 'Lights Out' has just sounded, and woe-betide anyone with a light burning after 9.15. We get your good old paper every week and it is very welcome.
NOBBY, FUZZY AND LUCKY.

The *Windsor Express* did not publish the photograph mentioned in the above letter.

The following are extracts from a letter written by E C Bragg, Royal Flying Corps, to his parents at 15 Peascod Street, and published on 7 July:

… We are in a ruined village, which, to say the least of it, is not so bad, as we are a considerable distance behind the firing line; and the place has been severely strafed sometime or other. Just in front of us is a coal mine, and old Fritz is very fond of placing a few shells of varying sizes amongst the rubbish there. So far that is the nearest point to us that shells have fallen, which is about 400 yards away, so you see I am comparatively safe at present… The Station is a fairly comfortable Armstrong Hut, in the corner of the garden of a Chateau in which was once a pretty little village. Our work commences at dawn and finishes at dusk, which is at present, roughly speaking, from 4 am to 10pm. As there are two of us we divide the day up into shifts of about 4½ hours duration. So far since I have been here Fritz has left the village alone, but nevertheless we get a pretty regular strafe. As I said before, he is fond of shelling, and we often get a dose of splinters… The other day we were doing a 'shoot' and all the telephonists were out, so of course we had to do the work ourselves. We usually have a telephonist to send the orders to the Battery. I work the ground strips and my pal stays on the instruments. After acknowledging the aeroplane I had to go in and telephone to the Battery, so had rather a busy time…

Yesterday I went in the YMCA and who do you think I met? – The Rev L G Reed, who is senior Chaplain to our Division. As soon as I can get a pass and cycle I am going down to Division Headquarters to see him, as he was too busy to stop to talk more

THE NAVY KNOWS the sustaining value of **Mackintosh's Toffee de Luxe** —the food sweetmeat. It feeds and satisfies — and thus saves other foods.

than a minute or two. I was pleased to see him as he is the first Windsor man I have seen over here…

The Rev L G Reed was one of the Minor Canons of Windsor before the war. After enlisting, he was appointed Temporary Chaplain to the Forces and was awarded the Military Cross for bravery.

A V Middleton, an old National School boy, son of ex-Police-Sergeant Middleton, of Windsor, writing to Mr Lutwyche, Headmaster of his old school, in August said:

I hope you will excuse me taking the liberty of writing to you, but I am sure you will be interested to hear a little news from one of the old boys… On one Sunday evening at 5.45 pm something happened to our ship which caused it to sink very rapidly, which it did in seven minutes. I need hardly say that it was very sudden and we had to make the best of things. Most of us were knocked about pretty heavily, and some of those who I am very sorry to say we shall never see again, must have been served the same. I had several journeys beneath the waves, but at last, after a severe struggle, I managed to reach a raft and from that I got to a large life belt. I remained like that until 12 o'clock, when I was rescued, and I can assure you I was dead beat. It is a wonderful and yet terrible sight to experience, and drifting about on the sea on a pitch dark night is not very pleasant, but such was what I went through, and you may be sure I was thankful when rescued. I am pleased to say that I am now safely at my destination and doing my best to make up for lost time.

We are under canvas and close by the sea which is a great asset in this hot climate. It is very hot in the day time but cold at night, so we have to be very careful not to get chills. There is plenty of sand here and dust blowing about. We are supplied with eye masks to protect us against sand storms. The customs are very strange indeed, and I often smile at some of the sights I see. The dress is Eastern style, which of course is strange to us… We are paid in Egyptian coin so we have to know how to spend it… There are a number of places for soldiers here, like the YMCA, Union Jack Club, etc and we spend some good times in them…Should you care to drop me a postcard to say you received this safely, my address is: L/Cpl A V Middleton, No 181074, ASC (MT), Egyptian Expeditionary Force, c/o GPO, London…

L/Cpl Middleton is not listed as a casualty, so it would appear that he survived the war.

There were two Letters from the Front published on 25 August; both from men who had taken part in the Passchendaele offensive and both mentioned the appalling weather. One of them was from Cpl Dowsett, Machine Gun Section of a Canadian Regiment, and was an apprentice at the Windsor Electrical Company's Works, in pre-war days. He wrote to Mr T H Plowright, of Trinity Place, describing the last 'big push':

The night before the attack we slowly crept up, under the cover of darkness and the usual gunfire, to our positions not far from Fritz's wire, and as we halted there the gunfire slowly died away until there was only the occasional crack and screech of a long-distance shell sent over by our guns to some dump, or important point, behind the enemy's lines… The whole country was illuminated by a dull red glow, and almost at the same moment every gun behind us opened up; it seemed as though hell had been let loose – it was our barrage… The infantry moved forward over the smashed up lines, meeting with very little resistance, and by the time we had reached their third line he (Fritz) was able to see scores of tanks waddling towards him over ground which was practically impassable…

The mere sight of us slowly creeping towards their concrete positions made them come out and give themselves up… I can safely say that had the rain kept off for a week or two we should have been well on the way to clear the northern parts

164

of Belgium; but as it is, it looks as though we shall have to wait until next year. I only wish the weather would clear up, because there is no doubt that we have the upper hand now and it will only continue to get stronger as time goes on… The Somme shelling was bad enough, but this is awful over all the ground of the advance. I do not think there was a square inch, which had not been hit by a shell.

The second letter, written by Windsor man Pte S Lawrence to a friend, said:

…A tot of rum and some tea worked wonders, and when the order to go over was given the feeling passed off and we wished each other the best of luck and a safe return. The barrage which preceded the attack was the heaviest I had ever heard, and Fritz must have had an awful time. As it was his first line trenches and dug-outs were battered almost out of recognition, and parties of 'Jerry's' brought back prisoners and numbers lay dead and wounded amongst the wreckage of the dug-outs.

On we went accompanied by three or four tanks, when suddenly his artillery opened out on us, and we had a particularly warm time. Pieces of shrapnel and huge clods of earth flew about in all directions, and it was a puzzle to know how to dodge them. Numbers of lads fell, some wounded and others dead, and still the rest of us kept on. Then the order was given to dig-in, and an attempt was made to reorganise. All the rest of the day we were subjected to heavy fire from machine guns and artillery, and last, but by no means least two or three snipers. To add to our discomforts rain began to fall, and drenched to the skin we waited till dawn when the relief party arrived. The journey out was very hard going through the mud, and it was a relief to get on to the roads once more.

On 1 September a letter was published from Edwin Stanbrook, writing to his parents at 37 Devereux Road, from a hospital at Nottingham:

It appears to be a habit of mine… to get wounded directly our regiment goes to a warm place, and by strange coincidence it has been on the third day each time, first on the Somme, then at Arras, and now on that most delightful of battle fronts, the Ypres sector. It was on Thursday, shortly after midday a shell noticed me in the mud and was so amused at the picture that it split its sides with laughing at me, and a small chunk dived in between my third and fourth 'digets' and escaped through the back of my hand, making quite a nice, clean hole… Well, when I was hit, I made my way back, without wasting any time, I can assure you, and after calling at different stations included in the wonderful system for removing the wounded from the line, I reached the Casualty Clearing Station by motor 'bus in the evening, at each place food, drink and cigarettes are supplied in plenty, and of course the wounds are properly attended to. At the 'CCS' we waited in marquees (on stretchers with plenty of blankets) for the train, and we travelled down to Etaples, once again being well attended to en route. By 10am I was in a hot bath at No 7 Canadian General Hospital, then into 'blues' and sent to a ward, a big marquee with 80 beds. Next day I was marked for 'Blighty' so began to cheer up, especially when I was rigged out in khaki again for travelling… It was grand to pass through London again and see St Paul's, the river, and the rest of the sights of 'Lunnon Town', but you can guess I was a little disappointed to leave it behind and travel north, reaching here at 10pm, after a halt at Peterborough for refreshment.

On 17 November the newspaper reported receiving an interesting letter from Pte A Betteridge (formerly of Sun Passage), dated 15 October, from 'Somewhere in Palestine'. He had served in France with the Windsor Territorials (4th Battalion Royal Berks Regiment), and was anxious to get into touch with some of his old comrades. While in France he was injured in the shoulder and side, sent home for some months, re-examined and declared unfit, so was unable to re-join what he called his 'old crush'. He continued:

I did the next best thing and joined the ----- to serve in Egypt for garrison duty, which was at one time on the desert. It was marvellous to see old Windsor men, also Datchet men, tramping across the desert for days' marches in the broiling sun.

While on the journey out on New Year's Day the vessel he was on was torpedoed 60 miles from Malta, and 'after a few hours' soaking in the Mediterranean' he was picked up with others by a mine sweeper. He had once again been transferred to a fighting unit in a county regiment and said he would be much obliged to receive a few lines from any of his old comrades in the Royal Berks Regiment. He sent his address, which was: 260018 Pte Betteridge, EEF, Egypt.

Pte Alfred Betteridge served in the Royal Berkshire Regiment, then the Hampshire Regiment, when he wrote the letter, before re-joining the Royal Berkshire Regiment. He survived the war.

Another letter published in the *Windsor Express* was from Rosina Boxall and concerned her husband, serving in Mesopotamia. It was published on 22 December:

> I thought that it might be of some interest to the readers of the *Windsor and Eton Express* to know that two Windsor men have recently met one another while on active service in Baghdad, Mesopotamia, and are billeted within one hundred yards of one another in that town. They are my husband, Cpl Arthur Boxall, who, previous to enlisting, was for several years in the employ of Brown and Son, butchers of Peascod Street, and Pte Hall, who previous to joining was motor driver to Dr Skevington. They are both attached to General Headquarters, Cpl Boxall as a despatch rider and Pte Hall as a motor driver to Head Office. They have been friends for several years, but neither knew that each other were out in Mesopotamia, until they met

Sgt John C E Rogers, Berkshire Yeomanry, wrote to his mother at 19 Walton Terrace, describing part of the fighting in Palestine. He was taken out of active service on 16 November, on account of septic hands. It was the final letter of the year:

> …In about four days' time I shall be on my way to the base

to get a new rig out ready for the regiment again. This place I am at is an infantry rest camp, which has been turned into a hospital for walking cases. It is right on the shore so we are able to bathe. There are four in a bell tent and we each have a mattress, two blankets and a pillow a-piece. You must have seen in the papers how our brigade, I think it was, captured 1,100 Turks, etc after a glorious sword charge. Just my luck to be out of it – the one thing we all have been looking forward to perhaps it was for the best, who knows? I can tell you but very little of what we did. From the time the offensive started until I left I don't suppose I had more than two hours sleep a day on the average. We were on the go all the time chasing them from one place to another, then racing off to get water and supplies, then going off to help someone here and someone there. The poor old horses very often didn't have a drink of water for over 48 hours; the men as well often went 36 hours. One time we lost touch with our ration convey and so had to tighten our belts for a day and a half.

My word, the Turks did leave a tremendous lot of ammunition and supplies about. When the total is made I am sure everyone will be surprised. From what I could see of his defences he thought he was going to stop at Gaza. His casualties must have been terrible, because he was in many cases blown out of it. On the night of the 11th and 12th we had a very big thunderstorm and in the morning we found pools of water about, which we speedily put into our dixies and made tea with... That same morning the doctor sent me to hospital...

Windsor lads on duty
in Egypt

Letters From The Front 1918

The course of the war in 1918 was shaped by two events, which occurred in different parts of the world, during the previous year. In April 1917 the USA entered the war on the Allied side, although it would be another twelve months before American troops arrived in large numbers. The second was the Russian Revolution in November 1917, after which an armistice was agreed and Russia took no further part in the war. The German army moved its troops from the Eastern Front to the Western Front.

The first two months were one of the quietest periods of the war along the Western Front, but this changed on 21 March when the Germans launched their Spring Offensive, known as the Kaiserschlacht (Kaiser's Battle). Although such an attack had been expected, its ferocity overwhelmed the overstretched BEF and the Germans made substantial territorial gains. Further enemy offensives were made in April and May before the German advance ran out of momentum and could be halted. The British-led Amiens Offensive in early August was the turning point in destroying the enemy army. General Ludendorff, Deputy Chief of the German General Staff, admitted that 8 August was the 'Black Day of the German Army'.

With American troops joining the British, French and Belgian Armies, a combined offensive was launched and the Allies made great progress in defeating the badly demoralised German Army. The Hindenburg Line was breached in October 1918, forcing a German retreat, meanwhile in early October, the German Government made appeals to the USA for an immediate armistice, which were refused. At the end of the month the German High Seas Fleet mutinied, and strikes and demonstrations swept Germany. Collapse followed swiftly, with Germany's allies concluding separate ceasefires; Turkey on 30 October and Austria on 3 November. The Kaiser was forced to abdicate on 9 November and fled to Holland to avoid arrest. An armistice was negotiated between the government of the new German republic and the Allies, which came into force at 11.00 am on Monday, 11 November, thereby ending the war.

Pte William Simmonds, Royal Berkshire Regiment, wrote to the Mayor from a German prisoner of war camp, which was published on 26 January (a previous letter was published in March 1917).

I thank you all the members of the Committee which was formed by you to send parcels to me and comrades of my regiment – a kindness which will never be forgotten by us. I must now wish you and all in the dear old Royal Borough and district of Windsor a brighter New Year.

The first letter from the front published on 16 February, was from Kenneth Cartland, Berkshire Yeomanry in Palestine, sent to his father at 13 High Street:

…You must have heard all about Beersheba by now. Well, we were in reserve during that action, but have been in action practically ever since up to this date… our horses were taken from us and sent back as they were worse than useless in the hills… we were going forward to relieve one of the advanced posts which was on the top of the next hill in front of the village we were then at. Well, on the top of this hill there was a mosque or house which was our post; this particular hill was 2,400 feet high. We had to be very careful here as we were always under fire if we showed ourselves over the walls. Everything went well until the next day; then the Turks brought some artillery up and soon got us in line: at the same time their infantry began to advance on us. We were only fifty strong against hundreds; they began getting round us to try and cut off our retreat, so there was nothing for it but to send out a party to try and drive them back. I think there were about twenty odd of us went out. We managed to hold them for a while, but their numbers were too strong for us; in the end they rushed us, then it was a case of fix bayonets and into it. I saw several of our poor boys go down.

Then the order came to retire, but it was almost too late. It was a case of out of the frying pan into the fire; we got back into the house all right, but it was like walking into hell. The Turks began to blow the place about our ears with high explosives. We signalled back to HQ that we couldn't hold on much longer, but they said we must. We stuck it till about 12 noon: by that time the place had become impossible. They had blown in the roof, and battered down the wall in the front, leaving us no cover; there were only a few of us left by this time, and the Turks had already made a half- circle round us. It was a case of surrender or make a bolt for it, and we preferred the latter, but we found a machine gun waiting on either flank of us, so we had to run the gauntlet. Never have I been in such a hare-brained race: how it was I was not hit, or how I missed breaking my neck jumping down over the rocks, God alone knows, but all got away untouched and brought three or four of the wounded with us. We arrived back to the rest of the boys more dead than alive, not having had water for three days. I found one or two of our chaps with the pack horses sitting in a little cave; I had hardly crawled inside before a high explosive burst in front of us, killing two horses, but missing us in the cave. Now thank God, we are back, having a rest and getting fitted up again; we have lost several of our poor old boys, but our causalities were not really heavy…

There was a three-month gap before the next letter was published on 18 May, it was also from a Berkshire Yeoman serving in Palestine. The unnamed writer was 'a Windsor man who went to Egypt, and was in the Dardanelles episode, the re-capture of Sollum and the release of the *Tara*[1] prisoners. He afterwards volunteered for the Imperial Camel Corps, and has since had a good turn of travelling over the Holy fields of Palestine.' He wrote:

1. HMS *Tara, a former passenger steamer was torpedoed in Sollum Bay, in the Mediterranean, in November 1915 by a German U-boat. The surviving crew members were taken by the Germans to Libya and held in the desert by the Turks. They were rescued in March 1916 by British forces.*

I have seen Jerusalem, Jericho, the Dead Sea, Beersheba, and have washed in the River Jordan. But the heat and flies and all other bally insects are a fearful pest. Our last trip was on the eastern side of the renowned river when we experienced awful weather going out – rain for days and bitter cold with frosts. One time in the hills, the next in the valleys below the level of the sea, and then hills again. Over brooks which reminded one of the 'Water-meet' at Lynton, and having to negotiate these with our 'ships of the desert' was hard work, especially as the mud was worse than the water. Marching all night in the rain, dead beat, we were ready to lay down just as we were and sleep in the mud. One night I shall never forget, but we won through in the end. The sun appeared in time to save us from complete failure. Once away from the hills the going was better, for it was dangerous work trekking through the broken surfaces of the hills. I have no wish to visit the Alps now!

After a little rest we essayed to finish our job. I was ordered to carry through a special mission with a small detachment and everything went off A1. Elsewhere my company and section were having a warm time and I am sorry to say that I lost some good pals. Pte Bennett of Reading and L/Cpl Millar (a Devonian), a friend of Craig's, who lives at Wokingham, were both killed, while Walters, Hooker, Penfold, Johnson and Holloway (all Berks Yeomen) were wounded. My wound is going on fine, and I am still able to 'carry on.' The stunt was

hard work for, and with, our camels, but they have covered themselves with glory this trip. Some of the scenery was fine, and one village in particular seemed possessed with inhabitants to whom industry and cleanliness were not unknown. But their actions to our fellows after we had passed through spoilt the whole picture. I have an idea the place is not quite so beautiful now! Although I am time-expired and my month's leave is four months overdue, I am still looking forward for the war clouds to reveal the silver lining, which will allow me a trip to dear old England again.

The same edition of the newspaper contained a letter not from the front, but from Manchester, and offered assistance to wounded Windsor soldiers being treated in Manchester hospitals:

As there may possibly be many wounded soldiers from your district in one or other of our hospitals here, if any friends or relatives of such men care to write me (naming hospital), I shall be pleased to look them up, and do anything else I can for their personal comfort. CHARLES E SHARDLOW, MANCHESTER.

The treatment of British servicemen held in German Prisoner of War camps had been of great concern for some the time. First-hand evidence of ill-treatment was difficult to obtain as letters home were censored, and if any information of German cruelty was passed on, British prisoners were subjected to reprisals. A letter about conditions in a POW camp on the Eastern Front, published in May 1917, was an exception and may have been written with the blessing of the German Army. On 25 May, letters from two local POWs were published under the heading 'British Soldiers' treatment in Germany: What Windsor men say', confirming the allegations. Both men had been sent to internment camps in neutral Holland. The first letter was from an unnamed soldier to a Miss Bower, who used to pack a weekly food parcel for the man:

…This is a glorious place and very comfortable. We have good clean beds, which was a thing of the past in Germany: our linen is done weekly by a contractor, which is what I had to do myself in Germany with cold water and very often without soap. We have two baths in our billet, a spray and a full length, which we can use to our own convenience. In Germany we might get one once a month and then for a matter of two minutes spray. The food is very reasonable, clean, good and nourishing; bread at present is rather scarce. The food in Germany was disgusting and insufficient…

You will no doubt think this letter very different to those post-cards I sent you whilst in Germany. That was the only way one could write, that is, if he wanted correspondence to get through and not get 'strafed' which is very easy for them to do. They had some cruel ways of carrying it out. If anything should go wrong they would stop our parcels for 14 days, not allow us to cook the articles in our parcels, stand us on parade for several hours, and allow no light to our room for several nights. We only had one light in each room, 16 candle power, for 350 men. All men below the rank of corporal are compelled to work, unless they are actually disabled. I have seen men forced out to work, at the point of a bayonet, with one eye, running wounds, stiff legs and others crippled in general. One poor fellow was forced out with a running wound which turned gangrene and he died, a married man, 41 with four children. That is Prussian Kultur…

The Mayor of Windsor, who organised the weekly food parcels to local POWs, received a letter from Cpl Cecil Nicholls, of the Border Regiment:

Having been interned in Holland, from Germany, I thought it my bounden duty to write and thank you and all ladies who helped to relieve our dreadful sufferings by the sending of parcels from the Royal Borough. Indeed, they were highly appreciated by all who were favoured to receive them. They were up-to-date, were the very things we were in need of, and above all, they were of good quality. We used to receive them regularly and, in fact, I used to look forward to them.

The staffs at Windsor Town Hall must have worked very, very hard to get them to us, because they were so very neatly and securely packed, that I know of not one instance where there was anything deficient. This is a great thing to say, because, as you may know, there is a lot of thieving going on as regards the parcels, and as ours were securely sewn up in white cloth, we were able to receive them all intact, exactly as they had left the packers' hands at the Town Hall. I would kindly ask of you to tender to all who assisted in helping to comfort us in our 'Dark World', my heartiest thanks: and, indeed, their kindness I shall never be able to repay... Being as I am a native of Windsor (my father was a Castle policeman), I shall make it my business to give you a call on my arrival at the Royal Borough. Again thanking one and all for their great kindness, I will conclude.'

Pte H W Forder, 2nd Battalion Royal Marine Light Infantry, also wrote from a POW camp to the Mayor to thank him for the food parcels. His letter was published on 3 August:

It is the greatest pleasure to write and thank you for the food parcels. As a prisoner of war I am extremely grateful for the same; one would hardly realise the difference one feels in having good substantial food. No doubt you will be pleased to hear that I am feeling in the best of health...

More letters were published from British prisoners of war after the end of the war in November. Cpl H Carpenter, 3rd Battalion Rifle Brigade, writing from Holland to his mother at 16 Bridgewater Terrace, confirmed the statements being published of the Germans' cruelty to British POWs. Published on 23 November, he wrote:

...I am away from Germany. It has left its mark on me. At times I thought I was never coming out of the country. As you know, in 1914-15, Wittenberg was stricken with fever, and I caught it myself. I laid on a straw mattress swarming with lice and fleas, for we had no soap to wash ourselves with, and no clothes – not a shirt to change from one month to another. I was carried into hospital, or rather into a den, to die. There I lay 17 days unconscious with typhus fever and double pneumonia, with hardly anything to eat to help me through my illness. The food consisted of coffee or rather burnt barley and soup… Before I was taken ill I had to help pull latrine carts about, with no boots or socks on, in winter, through the snow, ice and mud. Clothing was scarce; I had an old blanket around my shoulders to keep myself warm. When the carts got stuck in the mud we had not strength to pull them out, so we were knocked about by sentries until we could not stand it. I turned round on one, but got knocked down unconscious and kicked, barely escaping with my life… When I got better I was sent to Halberstad, but I was not allowed to write to you. What a God-send these parcels were! I remember the first one I had. I nearly went mad with joy to be able to have something to eat and a cup of tea! I thought I was in heaven…

Letters from the Middle East began to appear more often than letters from the Western Front and letters from two Berkshire Yeomen were published on 29 June. The first letter was from a Windsor man who was attached to the Imperial Camel Corps in Palestine:

We left our resting camp at the foot of Palestine for a stunt, our objective being the eastern side of the Jordan…The morning break had not affected the weather, for it rained the whole day and it took us twelve hours to travel six miles. But this landed us on the plains again – we had crossed the mountains at last – but, oh, the mud, each step was an effort to lift the foot out of mire and advance it for another immersion in the mud. Riding being out of the question, as the camels had the same difficulty to extricate their long legs from their miry embarrassments, and even had one the heart to attempt to ride they would have found it impossible, even as it was, man had often to help camel to make progress. After a halt of three hours, off we went again, the rain having given over, but it recommenced after a few hours…

Clean socks eased the pain and one began to feel cheerful, when a Taube found us out and peppered us with shots from a machine gun, besides giving us way to his artillery at a distance, which soon made targets of us. Our going was now over boggy ground, and with loaded camels to get along, and shells falling in every direction; the situation was hardly heaven. We escaped further attention from the artillery by entering a valley, where all went well until we came to another morass, where we lost three camels and had to carry their loads as best we could. We were getting close to our objective and our pleasure was great when we beheld the steel rails. No time was lost in undermining a long stretch of the track and blowing it up into the skies. How I wished for more time and more gun cotton, for having tasted the sweets of success, it was difficult to stay desire. We had successfully completed our special mission and now made tracks to re-join the main body. My section of demolitioners had escaped casualties in spite of the dangers we had gone through, but other sections of the Imperial Camel Corps had not been so fortunate.

The second letter, dated 28 May, told of a very different experience:

… How glad we were to see the last (as we thought) of Egypt; but how glad 100 times more were we, nearly 24 hours after, to see the old lighthouse on the skyline, and then at last to get ashore! We had got about nine hours out. Nearly all of us were in bed and asleep. I was subconsciously aware of a sudden jar, but what I do remember was sitting on my berth and asking what had happened, and was told that if I didn't get out quickly I should pretty soon know what it was. I pulled on a pair of shoes, and tying on my lifebelt scuttled along the corridor, and slipped up at the foot of the stairs. I went straight to our emergency station, and found the other men arriving… The ship soon stopped. There was a very slight list. The boats were got off, and the rafts too and when all the men were off the ship, I said to about half-a-dozen others still there: "Well, now we'll go". The water was then awash in the after well deck. So clad in pyjamas, canvas shoes, and a wrist watch, I climbed down about six feet of ladder, held my breath, looked at the black water, and then dropped quietly in. I had a swim of about 30-50 yards. I had a lifebelt on – a splendid thing. When we got to the lifeboat (a canvas-sided collapsible boat), we rowed and rowed

round in circles till a motor launch came and took us in tow, and then we arrived at an auxiliary ship of war. A few minutes after the vessel went down with a rush. We made off back here, all out, with over 1,100 survivors on board. The night was wonderfully warm, and I never felt cold, even in wet pyjamas. However, some kind naval officer fitted me out in a naval tunic and a pair of trousers, and of course I was the butt of many jests… About ten hours afterwards we arrived here. On the quay we were given clothes, Army issue, and the Red Cross gave us tea and biscuits…

On 20 July the *Windsor Express* published a letter from Able Seaman W Banham, under the heading 'Ships that pass in the night: Windsor Boy's remarkable adventures in a derelict vessel'. In a letter to his parents at 12 Grove Road, Windsor, he wrote:

… Early on the following morning, the look-outs reported a ship on the horizon, and we were detailed off to examine her and make a report… On approaching the vessel (she looked just like an ordinary steamer of about 2,000 tons) not a living soul could we see with our glasses. Everything about her seemed mysterious and uncanny, and apparently she was drifting helplessly with the tide... In the teeth of a gale, the whaler was launched, taking with her the First Lieutenant, a signalman and an ERA [Engine Room Artificer] rating. The crew had a terrible time pulling across to her, but after what seemed an eternity, she finally got alongside the steamer, and somehow or other managed to catch a rope hanging over the side of her. It seemed every second that the little whaler would be dashed to pieces and throw her crew overboard, but luck was in...

Our officer made his way to her bridge and opened the charthouse and discovered, according to the ship's log that she had been abandoned about four o'clock that same morning, for her log was made up at that time. But nothing else was mentioned as to the cause of her being abandoned and not a living being could be seen on her; everything seemed still and eerie... it was decided to put a crew aboard and thoroughly search her. So our whaler pulled back to us – back through the terrible raging sea.

A call was made for volunteers to go aboard the steamer... Volunteers came forward, myself amongst them, and offered to go... As soon as the little whaler came near we jumped into her. Almost as soon as we started on our return journey, the storm increased and a thick hail-storm came on... As best as we could we climbed aboard, being greatly hampered by our oilskins, seaboats and lifebelts... The ERA and the four stokers made their way below to inspect the engines and stokehold, while we begin our search.

The gale seemed to increase every minute and the ship rolled and rocked dangerously. After a swift inspection below it was discovered that the throttle had been broken open, that the boilers were stone dry and that the feed pump had been rendered useless. Such was the state of things below. It was decided to take the ship in tow...

Signaller George Foster, serving with British Forces in Mesopotamia, wrote to his parents in Old Windsor on 7 June.

179

Foster was in France for over eighteen months, and was awarded the Distinguished Conduct Medal after the Battle of the Somme. Being wounded he was sent back to England, and six months later volunteered for service in Mesopotamia. In his letter, which was published on 17 August, he said:

I have only seen one lot of fighting out here and that was last month. I can hardly stop here enjoying myself while the boys are slogging away out there. I wish they would send my Division to France. Not that I exactly want to go, but I shall certainly be ashamed to tell people after the war that I was in Mesopotamia while the biggest struggle in the world's history was going on in France. I thought I enlisted to fight and not to have a gentleman's life. Still, I suppose someone has to garrison the Empire, and I have the consolation of knowing that I have been in France. I am safe enough out here, and illness is the only thing I have to avoid, which is simply a matter of looking after myself. The longer I am in this country the more interesting I find it... As I learn different things, I am writing them down, so I shall be able to tell you heaps when I come home.

The last two letters of the year were from local men serving in the Royal Navy. Able Seaman V Beswick, HMS *Agamemnon*, had been on the ill-fated HMS *King Edward VII*, which struck a mine and sank in 1916. Writing to his parents, his letter was published on 14 December:

Just a few lines to let you know that I have survived the war all right. No doubt you have read in the papers that the Allied fleets have entered the Dardanelles and got to Constantinople. It was a very nice journey up the 'Narrows' to the Sea of Marmora. The place where our troops landed was not a very nice place for going over the top; it is something like Dover, and at the back was Chanac Light – which no heavy guns could hit – and also the forts, which formed a formidable resistance, with batteries of twenty 6in guns. The scenery all the way along was very pretty. For the past year we have been lying off Mudros in the Isle of Lemnos, which is not a very pretty place – all hills and mud huts...The armistice proceedings with Turkey were held on board our ship, which is a great honour for 'India rubber ship', as the Turks call her. The day peace was signed we had a merry time aboard... Owing to the censor we have not been able to tell where we have been, but we never had much steaming to do. We had several 'spasms' owing to the *Goeben's*[2] movements, and proceeded once to meet her, but were recalled; that was when the Raglan was sunk by her.

William W Banham, serving on the destroyer HMS *Wrestler*, and who lived at 12 Grove Road, wrote to his friends about 'the Grimsby Trawlers', in a letter published on 28 December:

...A great many people are aware that some of our great fishing grounds lay near Iceland, and the Faroe Islands, and it was the usual thing for several fishing trawlers and smacks to get together and depart from our fishing ports to these places. The Hun submarines had been giving a great deal of trouble to these fishing vessels, and week after week the enemy made a heavy toll. So much so, that a few destroyers were added to the few submarine hunters that there were at that time endeavouring to destroy them... We had been at sea about eighteen hours, when the look-out reported a suspicious looking object off the starboard bow...

The same day, we picked up some more [survivors] in another small boat, one poor fellow with the calf of his leg gone and his other knee smashed... His last words were: 'Thank you, boys, you are all 'toffs' and don't forget the Grimsby fishermen.' It appears from survivors' tales that two of our fishing trawlers were returning home with a good catch, when a submarine gave chase and opened fire... A boat was lowered from the submarine and pulled across to the trawler. The officer and men then examined the catch of fish and picked out the best lemon soles and returned on board the submarine, taking the fish with them, telling the crew of the fishing vessel to take to their only boat as soon as possible. They were doing this when

2. *The Goeben was a German battle cruiser, which was transferred to the Turkish Fleet in 1914 when it was renamed the Yavuz Sultan Selim.*

the submarine commander got impatient, and commenced to open fire, with the results already stated...

I hope that any of you who had any love left for the Huns, to remember what I have written, to imagine the horrors of war, for these things have been happening day after day, the total loss of merchantmen being near 15,000...

Letters From The Front 1914-1918

By the end of the war, the letters full of patriotic fervour sent in 1914 had given way to messages of hate for the 'Hun', as demonstrated above in the last letter of 1918. In between these extremes, letters sent by Windsor men, from almost every theatre of the war, displayed a wide range of emotions on a variety of subjects.

There were few letters in 1914 as the war began in August and it took a while to establish lines of communication. Also in the opening months, many soldiers thought the war would be short-lived and they would be home soon, so did not write. 1915 saw the largest number of letters from the front during the entire war, and the editor of the *Windsor Express* had a wide range to choose from.

In 1916, the number of letters published fell significantly. The Army Order of June that year, forbidding the publication of 'any article, whether purporting to be fiction or fact, which in any way deals with the war or military subjects' no doubt slowed down the publication of soldiers' letters. The stringent censorship in the build up to the Battle of the Somme had a similar effect. Idealism died in the disastrous Somme offensive, and soldiers in the trenches began to lose faith in their military leaders and politicians. Their families at home seemed to be remote and unable to comprehend what they had been through, and furthermore, they did not want to share with their families the true extent of their suffering. Loyalty to their comrades in the battalion was all that mattered. As a result the number of letters published was reduced yet again in 1917. Another reason could be that the general public were becoming war weary after three years of bad news, and restrictions at home; and editors did not publish letters detailing the horrors of war. There were even fewer letters published in 1918.

The Battle of the Somme

The Battle of the Somme began in July 1916 when the British Fourth and Third Armies attacked German positions to the north of the River Somme in France. The British advance over a twenty mile wide front, with French troops to the south, marked the beginning of the 'Big Push' which, it was hoped, would end the war. In preparation for the new offensive, Allied artillery had bombarded the German trenches for a week before the attack started and it was confidently predicted that nothing could survive such fire-power.

At 7.30am on Saturday, 1 July 1916, on a fine summer morning, British troops left their trenches and walked into no-man's land. The advancing troops were instructed to walk, not run, with a one-minute interval between each battalion, and capture the shattered enemy positions.

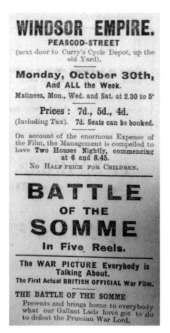

In many areas, however, the German defenders were ready for the attack. They had taken shelter in their deep underground bunkers at the start of the artillery bombardment and emerged unscathed at the end of it to set up their machine-gun positions. Wave after wave of British soldiers advanced, only to be mowed down by the machine-guns they had been told were destroyed. Many did not manage to cross their own wire before being killed. The new offensive, despite some small gains, was to prove a tragic miscalculation. There were 57,470 British casualties on the first day,

184

including 19,240 deaths. Despite these severe losses, Sir Douglas Haig, Commander-in-Chief of the British Expeditionary Force, was determined to continue the offensive. With both sides bringing up reinforcements, the battle soon turned into a war of attrition. The Somme offensive dragged on until mid-November 1916, by which time British and Dominion casualties were 420,000 for the gain of just over eight miles along the whole front. The French had 205,000 casualties and German losses are estimated to be about half a million.

The *Windsor Express* in its editorial of 8 July 1916, commented on the new Somme offensive:

> The general offensive against the Germans appears to have commenced in earnest, and all the world is looking on at the terrible struggle with breathless interest. Following the blows on the Russian and Austrian Fronts, the British and French troops leapt from their trenches on Saturday morning, after a week of terrific bombardment of the enemy lines, and they have now advanced some miles, over a twenty mile front, with gratifying results...

In truth, the results of the first few days were hardly 'gratifying'. The casualties for the first day alone were the worst ever suffered in any single day by the British Army, but reporting restrictions were in force at the time and reports from the front were censored.

The following week, on 15 July, the *Windsor Express* advised that 'the advance of our Army from the line so long held has given further evidence that the men of our New Armies are splendid fighters.' This was a reference to the newly raised 'Kitchener Battalions' which bore much of the fighting.

There were weekly Rolls of Honour published but rarely sufficient details of where the fighting took place. It is, however, possible to piece together information on Somme casualties. The Killed in Action list in the *Windsor Express* of 15 July, for example, contained two casualties on the opening day of the Somme offensive:

> Curtis, Thomas (of Old Windsor), Pte, Royal Berks Regiment, killed by a bullet from a German machine-gun 1 July.

Traill, Kenneth R (younger son of Dr and Mrs Traill, Cooralee, Sunningdale), Lieutenant of the Royal Berks Regiment; killed on 1 July, aged 22 years.

Commonwealth War Graves Commission records reveal that Pte Curtis served with the 2nd Battalion Royal Berkshire Regiment (RBR) and is buried at Ovillers Military Cemetery in the Somme region. Lt Traill served with the 6th Battalion RBR and is buried at Carnoy Military Cemetery, also in the Somme region. The Regimental History of the Royal Berkshire Regiment confirms that both 2nd and 6th Battalions took part in the opening attack on the Somme.

Lt Traill took part in the first wave of the attack from trenches at Carnoy. The Battalion War Diaries for 1 July includes an entry timed at 7.50 am (twenty minutes after the attack began) noting that he, and other officers, had been killed. A report in the *Windsor Express* noted that Pte Curtis was killed in action at 3.00 pm on I July and that 'he took up the duties of officer's servant to Lt Traill, who also gave his life for his country on the same date.' (It is not known why the two men are listed as belonging to different battalions.)

Another Windsor casualty of the first day was Pte Frederick Ash, 6th RBR, who lived in Clewer New Town. He was a married man with a wife and six children and re-joined the Army on the outbreak of war. He is remembered on the Thiepval Memorial, which contains the names of over 73,000 men who died on the Somme and who have no known graves.

Pte Frederick Cox, 6th Battalion RBR, also died on 1 July 1916. He was a sniper who had been wounded slightly as he was leaving a sniping post three days before the start of the Somme offensive. He returned to his battalion just in time to take part in the battle, and he is also remembered on the Thiepval Memorial.

On 15 July, it was reported that Pte George Habgood had died of wounds, aged 21, on 5 July. He was one of five serving sons of Mrs Habgood of 86 Bexley Street, Windsor. (*See chapter on the Habgood family*). He joined the 10th (Service) Battalion West York Regiment and took part in the capture of Fricourt on 2 July. Pte

Habgood was severely wounded in the attack and died three days later.

As the human cost of the new offensive became clearer, the weekly casualty lists became longer. The list published on 5 August contained 90 names, including 29 men either killed in action, died of wounds or missing believed killed; though not all with Windsor addresses. This compares with 11 names published three weeks earlier.

Amongst the dead was Pte Ayres, the third *Windsor Express* employee to be killed in action in the war. He served in the 1/4th (Territorial) Battalion, Royal Berkshire Regiment. After training in England, the battalion went to France and landed at Boulogne at the end of March 1915. It was attached to the 145th Brigade, part of the 48th South Midland Division (Territorial Force), which was in reserve at the commencement of the Somme offensive. On 14 July 1916 a fleet of buses carried the whole of 145th Brigade to the La-Boiselle sector of the Somme to be ready for an attack planned for 23 July.

Their objective was the German trenches just south-west of Pozières, but the attack was met with an intense bombardment. Despite this, several companies of 1/4th RBR charged the trenches and fierce hand-to-hand fighting followed. Reinforcements from other battalions helped to clear the captured enemy positions, while the Australians seized the town of Pozières. The German shelling continued in the afternoon of 23 July causing many British casualties.

The War Diaries of 1/4th RBR for 23 July 1916 noted that:

> Our attack began at 4.00 am. Their shell fire was incessant from dawn to dusk. The captured trenches, our right and all communication trenches being continually under fire… The Battalion did well in the attack and later when holding the captured trenches… Casualties 23 killed, 103 wounded, including shell shock 16.

That afternoon, during the heavy enemy shelling, Pte Fred Ayres was killed in action. He received a direct hit from an enemy shell while his battalion was holding a captured trench.

Fred Ayres' Army records, like 60 per cent of soldiers' records, were destroyed during the Blitz. His Medal Record gives his

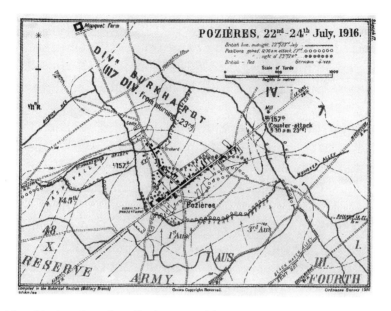

Map of Pozieres from the Official History of the War: Military Operations, France and Belgium 1916. (Compiled by Captain Wilfred Miles, HMSO 1938)

rank as L/Cpl, although his death notice in the *Windsor Express* in August 1916 quoted his rank as private. A member of Ayres' family said that when he was promoted he was put in charge of rations and discovered the way they were distributed was so unfair he refused to be part of it and returned his stripe.

On 9 September 1916, the weekly Roll of Honour recorded the death of Cpl Richard Wilson, 1/4th RBR, of 17 Victor Road. He was killed in action on 14 August during an unsuccessful attack on enemy trenches near Thiepval. (Captain C A L Lewis, the company commander, was wounded in the thigh in the same attack.) Cpl Wilson, an old National School boy and former member of the Church Lads' Brigade, had been due to come home on leave shortly to get married. He has no known grave and is remembered on the Thiepval Memorial.

On 26 August the *Windsor Express* published a letter from the front, under the heading 'Helping in the Great Advance. Windsor

Man's thrilling experience.' The letter was from Pte A V Pullinger to his parents at 37 Albany Road. In it he wrote:

… Once again we are out of the line on a rest more than earned, for we have been in the hottest part of the 'front' helping in the advance… It seems wonderful to me that we had so few casualties, for 5.9 shells seemed to rain on the captured line, bursting at every yard. It took men with nerve to stand it, which the higher commands fully recognised… Before advancing we had two or three days to look about the position we were holding. It was all enemy works, and in their hands not a fortnight previous. Looking around one was astounded to think that we had driven the Hun from it; once deep, well-dug trenches, dugouts splendidly excavated and timbered with three or more entrances, some twenty to thirty feet below ground level, and what were once immense redoubts of concrete and stone… I would certainly write you a lot about this new experience, but it has all to be censored so I must stop.

Although he was not permitted to disclose his location, he mentioned working with Australian troops and it is likely that this occurred in the Pozières area the previous month. Pullinger was fortunate enough to survive the war.

Sgt Oliver Brooks VC, 3rd Battalion Coldstream Guards, was seriously wounded at Ginchy on 15 September, during the new British offensive to break the deadlock on the Somme. Many local men were listed as wounded in action 'during the recent fighting in France.'

On 21 October, towards the end of the Somme offensive, the *Windsor Express* reported in its Roll of Honour the death of L/Cpl Luke Bowley, 3rd Battalion Coldstream Guards, aged 22 years. He lived at 18 Church Terrace, Dedworth and was killed in action near Ginchy on 15 September 1916. His name is recorded on the Thiepval Memorial.

Windsor's Victoria Cross Recipients

The Victoria Cross (VC) was founded by Royal Warrant on 29 January 1856 to be awarded to officers and other ranks of the Navy and Army, who, serving in the presence of an enemy, should have 'performed some signal act of valour or devotion to their country.' Queen Victoria was moved to introduce a decoration which was exclusively for acts of valour and to be differentiated from existing honours and awards. It was democratic in the sense that, unlike previous awards, it could be awarded to all ranks and that 'neither rank, nor long service, nor wounds, nor any other circumstance or condition whatsoever save the merit of conspicuous bravery' would  be sufficient to deserve this new decoration. The Victoria Cross remains the nation's highest award for bravery. Between 1914 and 1919 a total of 632 VCs were awarded, including two bars; over 30 per cent of the Great War awards were posthumous.

The VC was awarded to one soldier who was born in Windsor (Harry Greenwood) and another soldier, (Oliver Brooks), who was born elsewhere but later lived in Windsor after the Great War. A second Windsor-born man who won his VC in Sudan (Alexander Hore-Ruthven) served throughout the war.

Harry Greenwood VC

Harry Greenwood was born at Windsor Infantry Barracks, on 25 November 1881, the eldest of nine children. His mother, Margaret Abernethy, was a lady's maid from Co. Tipperary, Ireland and his father, Charles Greenwood, was a sergeant in the 2nd Battalion

Grenadier Guards. The Greenwood family would have lived in the old Georgian barracks, which had been turned into married quarters in the 1860s. The family moved from Windsor when the Grenadier Guards left the town in February 1882.

Because of the nomadic nature of army life Harry was seldom in one location long enough to attend school regularly and he was educated privately. Charles Greenwood left the Army in 1896, having completed his 21 years with the Grenadier Guards, and the family settled in Tottenham, north London. Harry joined the 1st Cadet Battalion, King's Royal Rifle Corps (KRRC) based in east London, while working as an apprentice compositor with *The Times.*

When the Boer War began in October 1899 he tried to enlist in a regiment going to South Africa. In December that year a new regiment was raised by drawing marksmen from all the Volunteer Battalions of the capital, including the KRRC Cadets. Greenwood, then aged 18, falsified his age on his enlistment papers and joined the new regiment, known as the City of London Imperial Volunteers (CIV). He served in South Africa, with the CIV and other units, for two years. Returning to England he worked as private secretary to a wealthy industrialist with business interests in Africa. He rejoined the KRRC and remained with them until his marriage to Helena Anderson on 9 January 1909. They later had three daughters.

At the outbreak of war in August 1914, Harry, then aged 32, volunteered for active service and joined the Regular Army via the Reserve of Officers. He was appointed to a Temporary Commission as Captain in the 9th (Service) Battalion of The King's Own Yorkshire Light Infantry (KOYLI) and, after training, his battalion left for France in September 1915. Prior to leaving for the front, 9th KOYLI had been in temporary billets in Maidenhead and was inspected by HM the King when the battalion passed through Windsor.

The battalion soon saw action and took part in the fighting at Loos at the end of September. For his part in this action, Greenwood was awarded the Military Cross and promoted to

Temporary Major. He was evacuated back to England suffering from a viral infection on 24 April 1916 and missed the opening attack of the Battle of the Somme on 1 July. Greenwood returned from sick leave on 5 July but not to his battalion – he was posted to the Training Reserve in England, where he helped to train new intakes. He returned to 9th KOYLI on 17 April 1917, almost twelve months after leaving France.

Major Greenwood was awarded the DSO, for a spectacular advance through early morning mist on 23 March 1918, to silence an enemy machine gun that was hampering the improvisation of a defensive line during a withdrawal; he also captured and brought back several prisoners. In July of that year, he was appointed to command the 9th Battalion KOYLI with the rank of Acting Lt Colonel.

The Battalion was back in action again in August 1918 on the Somme. Greenwood received a Bar to his DSO for leading an attack on 23/24 August 1918, on a German position and repelling two enemy counter attacks until relieved. He was wounded by 'friendly fire' in this action and four days later reluctantly reported sick; he did not return to command his battalion until 15 October.

By mid-October 1918, the Allied Armies had broken through the Hindenburg Line and were advancing towards the River Selle, where they met stiff resistance. They finally crossed on 20 October and the battle continued on 23 October, advancing over a wide area between the River Scheldt and the Sambre-Oise canal.

Lt Col Greenwood took an active part in the final advance, and was awarded the Victoria Cross for his conspicuous bravery near the village of Ovillers over a two day period on 23/24 October 1918. The VC award was announced in *The London Gazette* of 26 December 1918 and the citation read:

> For most conspicuous bravery, devotion to duty and fine leadership on the 23rd/24th October, 1918. When the advance of his battalion on the 23rd October was checked, and many casualties caused by an enemy machine-gun post, Lt Col Greenwood single-handed rushed the post and killed the crew. At the entrance to the village of Ovillers, accompanied by two

battalion runners, he again rushed a machine-gun post and killed the occupants.

On reaching the objective west of Duke's Wood his command was almost surrounded by hostile machine-gun posts, and the enemy at once attacked his isolated force. The attack was repulsed, and, led by Lt Col Greenwood, his troops swept forward and captured the last objective, with 150 prisoners, eight machine-guns and one field gun. During the attack on the Green Line, south of Poix Du Nord, on 24th October, he again displayed the greatest gallantry in rushing a machine-gun post, and he showed conspicuously good leadership in the handling of his command in the face of heavy fire. He inspired his men in the highest degree, with the result that the objective was captured, and, in spite of heavy casualties, the line was held.

During the further advance on Grand Gay Farm Road, on the afternoon of 24th October, the skilful and bold handling of his battalion was productive of most important results, not only in securing the flank of his brigade, but also in safeguarding the flank of the Division.

His valour and leading during two days of fighting were beyond all praise.

Harry Greenwood, like many VC recipients, was a modest and sincere man and was genuinely surprised to receive this award. He

HARRY GREENWOOD VC

· ·

Harry Greenwood in Pioneer Corps uniform, World War II

believed it should have gone to a fellow officer who had been awarded the DSO during the same action. He was presented with his VC, together with the Bar to his DSO, by King George V at an investiture at Buckingham Palace on 8 May 1919. By this time Greenwood had left the Army, having been discharged on 12 March 1919.

193

Between the wars, he worked for Sir Robert Williams and Co, a company he had been connected with since 1901, and spent many years working in Africa. During the Second World War, Greenwood was appointed a Colonel in the Pioneer Corps and was based in the UK. For his work in the re-organisation of the Corps he was rewarded with an OBE in 1944. Harry Greenwood VC DSO and Bar OBE MC died at his home in Wimbledon on 5 May 1948, after a long illness, and was buried in Putney Vale Cemetery. On 8 April 1997 a blue plaque was unveiled at Victoria Barracks, where he was born.

Oliver Brooks VC

One of the best known Windsor VC heroes is Oliver Brooks, who was not born in Windsor but settled in the town after the end of the Great War. In addition to his outstanding courage at the Battle of Loos in 1915, Brooks is remembered as the only man to receive his VC at the Sovereign's bedside.

This unique form of investiture was the result of a serious fall from a horse by King George V, who was due to review the First Army while he was in France in October 1915. It was normal practice for the King to walk down the aisles of troops, but he was persuaded by General Sir Douglas Haig that if he were on horseback the waiting men could see him better. Haig even lent the King his horse, a chestnut mare, for the occasion.

The horse had been crowd-trained, but was frightened by the sudden loud cheering when the King rode past a Wing of the Royal Flying Corps. The horse reared up, dismounted the King and landed on him. The King suffered severe injuries, including a fractured pelvis. He was taken by car to Château de la Jumelle in Aire before boarding a hospital train for the journey back to England. The King had heard how Oliver Brooks had led a bombing party, which re-captured an enemy-held trench and decided to decorate Brooks in person. The award had been gazetted on 28 October 1915, the same day as the King's accident.

Sgt Brooks was summoned to the King's hospital train. Accompanied by his Commanding Officer, he met it at Aire station on 1 November 1915 and the King held a private investiture ceremony at his bedside. If it had not been for the riding accident the investiture would have taken place publicly. Brooks knelt beside the hospital bed, bending over the King, who was lying on his back propped up with pillows, while Sir Charles Cust, the King's equerry, read the VC citation. Although the King was still in considerable pain he was determined to personally award the VC to Brooks, but he had overrated his strength, and could not manage to get the VC pin through the thick khaki of Brooks' tunic. Assistance had to be given before the unique investiture could be completed.

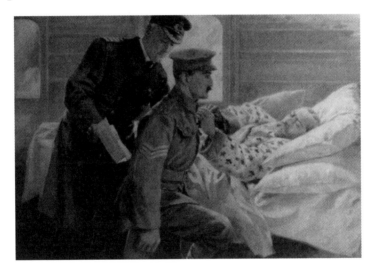

Oliver Brooks was born in Paulton, near Midsomer Norton in Somerset, on 31 May 1889. His parents were Joseph Henry Brooks, a local butcher, and his wife Mercy Brooks (née Snelling). Oliver was the youngest of their six sons. After leaving school he was employed at Norton Hill Colliery as a carting boy, hauling coal trucks by a chain harnessed to his waist. The work did not appeal to him, however, and at the earliest opportunity he left the coal mine and joined the Army. He enlisted into the Coldstream Guards at Bath in April 1906 and in August 1906 was stationed at Victoria Barracks, Windsor.

He completed his seven years with the Colours at various UK depots, and in April 1913 was discharged and transferred to the Reserve List. Brooks returned to the family home in Midsomer

Norton. He briefly went back to the coal mine, and later worked as a theatre manager.

Following Great Britain's declaration of war against Germany on 4 August 1914, all Army reservists were recalled. Brooks was mobilised in London on 7 August and posted to the 3rd Battalion Coldstream Guards. The battalion arrived at Le Havre on 13 August 1914, making Brooks one of the BEF's original 'Old Contemptibles'. Guardsman Brooks was promoted to Lance-Corporal on 25 November 1914 and to corporal on 12 July 1915. He was promoted to Lance/Sergeant the same day. On 9 October 1915, the day after the action for which he was awarded the VC, Brooks was promoted to Sergeant.

Despite earlier setbacks on the Western Front, the Allied Commanders were determined to launch a major campaign in the autumn of 1915. The attack began at dawn on 25 September 1915. By nightfall British troops had advanced as far as the village of Loos, but the Germans soon counter-attacked. Some of the heaviest fighting took place around the Hohenzollern Redoubt, a heavily fortified maze of German trenches to the north of Loos. On 8 October 1915 the Germans launched an attack on the British-occupied Redoubt, aimed at a section of trench named 'Big Willie', held by the Guards Division.

The 3rd Battalion Grenadier Guards were almost surrounded by the attacking Germans and bombed out of their forward position and forced to withdraw to a rear trench. The Germans were then in a position to take 'Big Willie' but were prevented from doing so by the 3rd Battalion Coldstream Guards, who were immediately to the right.

L/Sgt Oliver Brooks led a party of bombers armed with hand grenades, and a number of riflemen against the Germans and fierce fighting ensued. By this time the enemy had captured 200 yards of British trench, but by quickly leading his bombing party down the trench Brooks was able to force the Germans to retreat.

Oliver Brooks was recommended for the Victoria Cross for his part in the action and the award was announced in *The London Gazette* of 28 October 1915. The citation read:

His Majesty the King has been pleased to award the Victoria Cross to... No. 6738 L/Sgt Oliver Brooks, 3rd Battalion Coldstream Guards. For most conspicuous bravery near Loos, on the 8th October 1915. A strong party of the enemy having captured 200 yards of our trenches, L/Sgt Brooks, on his own initiative, led a party of bombers in the most determined manner, and succeeded in regaining possession of the lost ground. The signal bravery displayed by this non-commissioned officer, in the midst of a hail of bombs from the Germans, was of the very first order, and the complete success attained in a very dangerous undertaking was entirely due to his absolute fearlessness, presence of mind and promptitude.

Brooks received his VC from the King's bedside on 1 November 1915. He returned to the front and was, for a while, a bombing instructor at the Guards Divisional Headquarters in France. A new British offensive, planned to break the deadlock on the Somme, began on 15 September 1916. Sgt Brooks was seriously wounded that day; he received gunshot wounds to his head and left shoulder and was sent to England for treatment. After spending three months in hospital in London he was discharged and rejoined his regiment, but because of his injuries he spent the rest of the war in England.

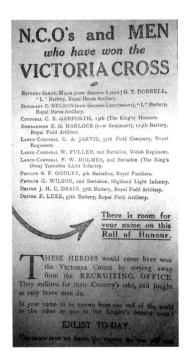

Brooks was demobilised at Victoria Barracks, Windsor on 27 February 1919. He married Marion Loveday on 17 August 1918 and they had four children – two sons and two daughters. When he left the Army he lived in Alexandra Road, and moved to Clewer Avenue in 1925. He became commissionaire at the White Hart Hotel, opposite Windsor Castle, where he was a popular sight in his greatcoat and medals.

Oliver died aged 51, after a long illness, at his home in Windsor on 25 October 1940. The funeral took place on 30 October. The Windsor branch of the Coldstream Guards Association, of which Brooks was an inaugural member, paid for a black marble headstone on his grave, and also dedicated a plaque to his memory in Holy Trinity Garrison Church on 24 April 1988. On 27 May 1998 a blue plaque was unveiled at Oliver Brooks' former home at 47 Clewer Avenue, Windsor.

Alexander Hore-Ruthven VC

Alexander Hore-Ruthven was born in 1872 at the Hermitage, but the family later moved to The Hatch, which was near The Willows on the Maidenhead Road. He grew up in Windsor, was educated at Eton College, and joined the 3rd (Militia) Battalion of the Highland Light Infantry in 1891. In 1898, Alexander, who spoke Arabic, travelled to Egypt, and was asked to join the Egyptian Slavery Department, which was established to break up the slave trade that was still widespread in the area. On 22 September he saved a wounded Egyptian officer from advancing Dervishes by picking him up, and carrying him to safety. For this he was awarded the VC. Queen Victoria presented him with his decoration at an investiture at Windsor Castle on 11 May 1899.

At the outbreak of the Great War he was at the Staff College in Quetta (now in Pakistan), but soon returned to England, and in February 1915 joined the newly created Welsh Guards as Major and second–in-command. He served throughout the Great War, in Gallipoli, where he was wounded, and on the Western Front. He was awarded the DSO and Bar, and was mentioned in despatches five times. In 1918 he was commanding the 126th Infantry Brigade, which crossed the Rhine on 4 December.

In January 1945, by then named Lord Gowrie, he was appointed Deputy Constable and Lt Governor of Windsor Castle, a position he retained until he retired in 1953. He died in 1955.

His only son was killed in action during the Second World War.

Belgian Refugees

The Germans advanced across Belgium and drove the Belgian army and government ever west, leaving towns and villages devastated. The advance came to a sudden halt east of the river Yser (Ijser) in October 1914, when Belgian patriots opened the sluice gates at Nieuwport flooding the low-lying area of Flanders as far as Ypres. This gallant and audacious act, carried out under the noses of the advancing German army, dramatically changed the course of the war, and stopped the Germans from gaining access to the main Channel ports.

Twenty per cent of the population, that is 1,500,000 Belgians, fled their homes and country. Many of these refugees left Belgium for the safety of England. King Albert I of the Belgians stayed with his soldiers to continue the fight against the enemy from the tiny stretch of country that remained of his kingdom, while his wife Elisabeth nursed wounded soldiers and their 14-year-old son joined the army as a private.

Belgian civilians fleeing the war zone were mentioned in a letter from the front by L/ Cpl J O Beavers in a letter to his parents in Clewer: 'Our men almost weep here when they see the poor women and children fleeing from their homes'. A feature in the *Windsor Express* on 17 October 1914 told readers: 'Germany has devastated the whole country and with the fall of Antwerp the poor Belgian's misfortune reached the limit'. Sadly it hadn't.

A number of articles told of atrocities, as the Belgians had bravely stood up against the German advance, and Windsor people were moved to give generously. The Mayor set up a fund for the Relief of Belgian Refugees, and a subscription list appeared in the *Windsor Express*. On 31 October the Slough Observer noted, that the Mayor of Windsor had invited the Slough Town Band to play in Windsor on Saturday 7 November during which a collection was made on behalf of the Belgian Relief Fund, and a 'Patriotic Concert' at the Royal Albert Institute added to the fund. By 12 December the total was £537 14s 10d, as well as promises of weekly subscriptions and gifts of furniture and provisions. The Vicar of Windsor was able to send a large amount of clothing to the refugees after an appeal in September, and two Windsor ladies offered to adopt three Belgian children who were orphaned. More was needed.

Slough received thirty refugees at Beauford House, and Eton College offered to accept a number of Belgian boys; in fact twenty-one boys received free education at Eton during the war. Windsor made St Swithin's house in Osborne Road available and it became known as 'The Belgian House'. Twenty-two Belgians lived there in 1915, which made it very crowded. The children of refugees attended the County School, the High School and St Bernard's Convent in Slough. Dr Hathaway gave medical services free of cost, and Messrs Russell and Co. of High Street provided free medicines.

On 29 June 1915, the Belgian refugees held an exhibition of their work at the Windsor Guildhall; Princess Alexander of Teck performed the opening ceremony. There was a fine collection of pictures, including local scenes, and items for sale ranged from 'the purely useful to the strictly ornamental.' The sum raised was £13 7s 6d, which was sent to the Belgian Red Cross Society, and the Belgian children collected £4 6d by selling flags and flowers. This all went to a fund to help disabled Belgian soldiers.

In August 1915 the Mayor's Fund for Belgian Refugees stood at £721 2s 8d, and by the end of the year it had reached some £1,550. In January 1916 the Belgian Relief Committee concluded its operations: 'The need which led to its formation having practically ceased'. Further money raised to December 1916 amounted to another £799 10 8d.

An article in the *Windsor Express* published on 15 January 1916, written by Emile Vandervelde, Belgian Minister of State, called for: 'Rebuilding a Nation once this war is over'. The author did not, however, want to rebuild Ypres: 'I am opposed to the idea of re-constructing the Cloth Hall, but leave the ruins and build a new city' It is a blessing that his advice was not followed.

In June 1918, the King of the Belgians conferred the Medalle de la Reine Elizabeth on the Hon Mrs Baillie, wife of the Dean of Windsor, for her work on behalf of the Belgian refugees.

The Military Service Bill
and The Military Tribunals

By the end of the first year of war, the Government realised that the ranks of the Army could not be filled by volunteers alone, but conscription was not seen as an option. Lord Derby, who was a supporter of National Service had become Director General of Recruitment in 1915, introduced the National Registration Act. It was known as the Derby Scheme, whereby men could give their voluntary assent to being called up if necessary, but the Government promised in turn to call up married men last. There were 46 groups in the Scheme: single men were put in the first 23 groups according to age, and married men put into the following 23 groups, also according to age (18-40). The National Register, which was set up under the Act was a means of stimulating recruiting and to discover what trades people were engaged in. On 15 August 1915, every male and female between the ages of 15 and 65 were required to fill in a registration form; the results of this Census were available to the Government the following month. This form of registration was the precursor to National Service. Lord Kitchener, Secretary of State for War, speaking at the London Guildhall on 9 July 1915, said:

When this registration is completed we shall anyhow be able to note the men between the ages of 19 and 40 not required for munitions or other necessary industrial work, and therefore available, if physically fit, for the fighting line. Steps will be taken to approach, with a view to enlistment, all possible candidates for the Army – unmarried men to be preferred before married men, as far as may be.

Lord Derby's canvas for recruits met with a good response, and recruiting authorities had to extend the attestation period by a day.

From the end of July 1915, the Windsor Recruiting Office could also enlist men (who had previously been rejected as unfit for services in the field) for garrison duty at home and abroad, and for home defence. On 5 January 1916 the Military Service Bill was passed. The Government finally decided to introduce compulsion which was one step away from conscription. All men of military age (18 to 40) had to register, although Ireland was excluded from the Bill. There were other exemptions which included some conscientious objectors, the medically unfit, and those engaged on work of national importance. Single men would start to be called up for service in March before married men, although this did not always happen. Compulsion began in May.

Notices were published in the newspapers in April 1916 which read:

> Men who come within the scope of the Military Service Act on 1st March who wish to escape the stigma attaching to those 'who waited to be fetched' can still be attested under Lord Derby's Scheme if they attest now and gain the inestimable privilege of being classed as volunteers. They lose nothing by so doing except the doubtful privilege of pleading for exemption on the ground of conscientious objection...

Conscription was finally introduced in May 1916, which included married men.

Military Tribunals

Many men clamoured to be exempted from military service, especially if they thought their trade or business to be indispensable, or they had pressing domestic reasons. As a result local tribunals had to be set up in May 1916 to give them a hearing and consider if a claim was a reasonable one. In Windsor the Tribunal met each Thursday at the Guildhall; it was led by the Mayor, but there always was a military representative present.

They were inundated with applications for exemptions or postponements, from tradesmen who wanted to keep the last remaining assistant, to parents who did not want to send their last son to war.

A number of early applications came from butchers in the town, both on their own behalf and for their slaughter men. One man who was 38 said he had now to do his own killing, all his men having gone. Another butcher, who applied on behalf of his slaughter men, said seven out of fourteen of his employees had joined up. In every case total exemptions were granted.

A garage owner aged 26 who said he was engaged on a Government subcontract for making caps for shells, but had lost all his mechanics to the war, was granted two months exemption. A fishmonger, who applied for exemption for the only assistant he had left, was granted three months. A young man whose brother had been killed at the Marne, and who was the sole provider for his parents, who would have to go into the workhouse if he joined up, was refused; so was postman Victor Squelch a married man with two children, employed by the Windsor Post Office, but a clerk employed by the Windsor Board of Guardians, and the only one with special technical knowledge of the Poor Law, was granted total exemption. Messrs Brown & Son applied for an exemption for their last remaining coach-maker, Caleb Sherwood aged 35, who was granted three months, Mr W Denney a baker of Peascod Street was given just one month's reprieve for his son, his only dough-maker. Two married *Windsor Express* employees came before the Tribunal for the second time in November 1916. George Pobjoy, a monotype operator aged 28, was given an exemption until the end of the month, and this was later extended until the end of the war. Harry Jeffries aged 31, a printer's machine minder, was granted a month's exemption before being called up. Jeffries died from enteritis, in Mesopotamia in 1918.

Frank Burlington, a widower aged 35 with two small children and a business in Alexandra Road as a firewood merchant and cab proprietor, who was now deprived of all male employees, asked for exemption in December 1916. He was granted just one month without further appeal. Windsor baker Mr H M Abbott, who had been given temporary exemption three months earlier to find someone else to run his business, was refused in April 1917. His shop had to be closed like so many others. Mr J M F Darville, 36 Managing Director of five grocery and provision shops in Windsor and Eton had been given a three months exemption in June 1917, to avoid closing all five shops, but he still had to find a representative to do his job. He was given another three months exemption in September.

In October 1917 all applicants for exemption were 'warned that they should get medically examined by the Area Medical Board before coming before the Tribunal'. This was to stop wasting time at the Tribunal if the man was unfit in the first place. Eligible men were reminded that very many more recruits were needed for immediate enlistment.

At a meeting of the Windsor Military Tribunal in November 1916, a resolution was proposed to ask the Recruiting Authorities why a large number of single men under 30 in Government employ had not been called up, while pressure was put upon married men with families to join the Colours. The King set an example by giving orders for every unmarried man of military age in the Royal Households at Windsor, Buckingham Palace, Sandringham, and Balmoral, no matter what the nature of his employment, to report himself to the military authorities for service with the Colours.

In April 1917, the new Military Service Bill for the review of exemptions passed through its final stage in the House of Commons. The measure was passed with much reluctance. The unpopular Bill had become necessary owing to the problems of providing substitutes for the men who were fit for the Services and ought to be set free to take their part in the war.

It became ever more difficult to gain exemption, as the military representative would appeal against the Tribunal's decision.

Local Tribunals were put under pressure to recruit half a million men by 31 July 1917, the day the Passchendaele campaign was to begin. The Director of Recruiting wrote:

> …Men who are fit to serve must come into the Army. It is no good talking and arguing that your fit men are indispensable… I would urge Tribunals to ask themselves: Are we providing our quota of this half million, and are we providing it quickly enough… Are we unconsciously allowing the pressure of local necessity and hardship to govern our decisions?

For this reason the military representative challenged almost every case of exemption, with the result that a number of Tribunals throughout the country, including the Windsor one 'came out on strike'. They felt this to be a reflection on the discharge of their duties, in short, that they were not regarded as competent. At a meeting in June, members of the Windsor Tribunal pointed out that they understood better than the military all the circumstances of each case that came before them; a number of men had their businesses destroyed, as there was no one else to run them, others who were the sole supporter of old or invalid relations had to leave their families destitute or to the care of the workhouse.

A select committee of the House of Commons decided in August 1917 to entrust control over Tribunals entirely to civilian powers and exclude military authorities. Now civilian authorities controlled recruiting, but Windsor had been sadly depleted of its business men and workers.

FATHER'S TURN.

"HOLD THE LINE, LADDIE! I'M COMING!"

In April 1918, the Man-Power Bill was introduced, raising the military age limit to 50, and in certain cases, for example doctors, to 55. Most exemptions were cancelled, which caused a great deal of upset to many businesses, and more shops were closed.

The Tribunal was busier than ever during 1918. Many men aged over 40 applied for conditional exemptions, Fireman John Hills, 47, was granted an exemption, but Working Man's Restaurant manager James Lowe, 46, was refused. However, he was asked to report for military duty in two months time, so that he could find a substitute.

A G Cullum, 45, caretaker at Barclays Bank, was granted four weeks adjournment to find a substitute, or he could find work of national importance. He obtained work at Hayes in the auto-screw department and his case was dropped.

One Eton tradesman, who could not get an exemption, displayed the following humorous notice in his shop window after he was called up to join the Army:

Notice. Owing to the British Government not being able to beat the Kaiser without my assistance, this business will be closed for the duration of the war.

Conscientious objectors also had to appeal to the Tribunal. William John Hetherington, 38 and married, would not fight on religious ground, but was told he had to serve, and would be called up in one month. The Tribunal recommended that he be employed on non-combatant services. As he was a skilled electrician this was a consideration.

Windsor Recruiting Sub-Area

As general conscription got under way, there were inevitably those who did not want to 'do their bit'. A list of local men and their last known addresses was published on the front page of the *Windsor Express*, each week during 1916 and 1917. In January 1917 there were 119 local names on this list, with 27 from Windsor. The list was called 'Recruiting Sub-Area'. The same names appeared week after week until it was last published in November 1917. Herbert W Acutt of 1 Alma Cottage, Alma Road, Michael Lawton of 23 Oxford Road, Patrick Reader, who had worked at the Canteen in Victoria Barracks or William Jones Woodward of 48 Thames Street were on the list for almost a year. It seemed that anyone who did not want to be found was able to avoid being called up. Where did they hide?

The public were asked to help trace these individuals, and were promised that 'the name of any person giving information will be kept secret'. Those men caught were fined £2 and handed to the military authorities, however the newspaper never published any successful prosecutions.

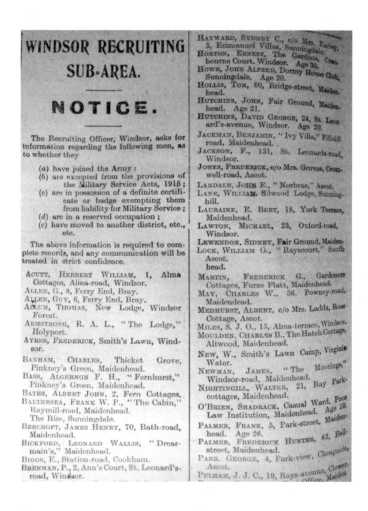

WINDSOR RECRUITING SUB-AREA.

NOTICE.

The Recruiting Officer, Windsor, asks for information regarding the following men, as to whether they

(a) have joined the Army ;
(b) are excepted from the provisions of the Military Service Acts, 1916 ;
(c) are in possession of a definite certificate or badge exempting them from liability for Military Service ;
(d) are in a reserved occupation ;
(e) have moved to another district, etc., etc.

The above information is required to complete records, and any communication will be treated in strict confidence.

ACUTT, HERBERT WILLIAM, 1, Alma Cottages, Alma-road, Windsor.
ALLEN, G., 8, Ferry End, Bray.
ALLEN, GUY, 6, Ferry End, Bray.
AILUM, THOMAS, New Lodge, Windsor Forest.
ARMSTRONG, R. A. L., "The Lodge," Holyport.
AYRES, FREDERICK, Smith's Lawn, Windsor.
BANHAM, CHARLES, Thicket Grove, Pinkney's Green, Maidenhead.
BASS, ALGERNON F. H., "Fernhurst," Pinkney's Green, Maidenhead.
BATES, ALBERT JOHN, 2, Fern Cottages, Maidenhead.
BALTERSEA, FRANK W. P., "The Cabin," Raymill-road, Maidenhead.
The Rise, Sunningdale.
BEECROFT, JAMES HENRY, 70, Bath-road, Maidenhead.
BICKFORD, LEONARD WALLIS, "Drearmain's," Maidenhead.
BIGGS, E., Station-road, Cookham.
BRENNAN, P., 2, Ann's Court, St. Leonard's-road, Windsor.

HAYWARD, SYDNEY C., c/o Mrs. Earley, 5, Emmanuel Villas, Sunningdale.
HORTON, ERNEST, The Gardens, Cranbourne Court, Windsor. Age 30.
HOWE, JOHN ALFRED, Dormy House Club, Sunningdale. Age 20.
HOLLIS, TOM, 60, Bridge-street, Maidenhead.
HUTCHINS, JOHN, Fair Ground, Maidenhead. Age 21.
HUTCHINS, DAVID GEORGE, 24, St. Leonard's-avenue, Windsor. Age 20.
JACKMAN, BENJAMIN, "Ivy Villa," Fifield-road, Maidenhead.
JACKSON, F., 131, St. Leonards-road, Windsor.
JONES, FREDERICK, c/o Mrs. Groves, Cromwell-road, Ascot.
LANDALE, JOHN E., "Norbrae," Ascot.
LANE, WILLIAM, Silwood Lodge, Sunninghill.
LAURAINE, E. BERT, 18, York Terrace, Maidenhead.
LAWTON, MICHAEL, 23, Oxford-road, Windsor.
LEWENDON, SIDNEY, Fair Ground, Maidenhead.
LOCK, WILLIAM G., "Rayscourt," South Ascot.
head.
MARTIN, FREDERICK G., Gardeners' Cottages, Furze Platt, Maidenhead.
MAY, CHARLES W., 56, Powney-road, Maidenhead.
MEDHURST, ALBERT, c/o Mrs. Ladds, Rose Cottage, Ascot.
MILES, S. J. O., 15, Alma-terrace, Windsor.
MOULDEN, CHARLES B., The Hatch Cottage, Altwood, Maidenhead.
NEW, W., Smith's Lawn Camp, Virginia Water.
NEWMAN, JAMES, "The Moorings," Windsor-road, Maidenhead.
NIGHTINGILL, WALTER, 21, Ray Park cottages, Maidenhead.
O'BRIEN, SHADRACK, Casual Ward, Poor Law Institution, Maidenhead. Age 39.
PALMER, FRANK, 5, Park-street, Maidenhead. Age 26.
PALMER, FREDERICK HUNTER, 42, Bell-street, Maidenhead.
PARK, GEORGE, 4, Park-view, Cheapside, Ascot.
PELHAM, J. J. C., 19, Rays-avenue, Clewer.
Office, Maiden

King Edward VII Hospital
and Other Local Hospitals

In June 1908, a commemoration stone was laid at the site of the new King Edward VII Hospital in St Leonard's Road, by King Edward VII, accompanied by Queen Alexandra and Prince and Princess Christian. Patients from the Windsor Dispensary and Infirmary[1] moved to the new hospital in March the following year and the two hospitals were then amalgamated. Men were treated in King Edward's Ward, women in Queen Alexandra's Ward and children in Helena Ward. Originally opened as a fifty-bed hospital, subsequent additions increased its capacity. A new building for pathology was built in 1910, and two years later a local benefactor, Mrs Elliman of Slough, donated £5,000 for a female surgical ward. In 1912, a statue of King Edward VII was unveiled at the hospital.

At the start of the Great War, many doctors and other medical staff left to serve in the Royal Army medical Corps (RAMC). One of the doctors was Angus MacNab, an Ophthalmic Surgeon who was commissioned into the RAMC and attached to the London Scottish Regiment. In November 1914, Doctor MacNab was attending wounded soldiers in a farmhouse when the British were forced to withdraw. He chose to remain behind with the wounded, who could not be moved. A British counter-attack resulted in the re-capture of the area, including the farmhouse, where Doctor MacNab and his wounded comrades were discovered dead. They had all been bayoneted by the Germans.[2]

Despite the hardships of war, the staff at the hospital ensured that patients staying over Christmas 1914 were as happy as possible. The *Windsor Express* recorded that:

1. *The Windsor Dispensary and Infirmary was established in 1818 at Church Street, Windsor. It moved to larger premises in Bachelors' Acre in 1834*

2. *Reported in the Windsor Express on 14 November 1914. Two other doctors who practiced at King Edward VII Hospital were also killed in action: Lt David Watson RAMC and Captain Archibald Cowe RAMC. Their names are recorded on a memorial plaque at the hospital*

Princess Victoria of Schleswig-Holstein paid a welcome visit to the Hospital and distributed gifts to everyone, from the House Surgeon (Dr A. Cowe), the Matron (Miss Wedgwood) and the staff downwards... As in former years, the gifts were provided through the agency of Princess Victoria's special fund for the purpose... Doctor Cowe carved the Christmas dinner for the women's ward, and he, together with Miss Wedgwood and the staff, accomplished all that lay in their power to ensure the success which undoubtedly attended their efforts...

Doctor Archibald Cowe later joined the RAMC and was killed in action in December 1917. Sister Agnes Brooks went to France at the end of 1914 to work in the X-Ray Department of the military hospital in Rouen. Following the retirement of Miss Wedgwood, she was appointed Matron.

Around the country, many hospitals were used for the treatment of wounded soldiers. Although King Edward VII Hospital had made a ward with twenty beds (out of a total of 68 beds) available to the military at the start of the war, it was not utilised as a War Hospital because the minimum requirement was then 100 beds. Local and Territorial wounded or disabled soldiers were received and treated as in-patients – sixty-five in the first eight months of the war – and sixty-seven were dealt with through the out-patients' department during the same period. Many soldiers who were billeted locally were admitted for hernia or varicose veins operations to ensure they were fit for active service. Belgian refugees were also admitted as in-patients.

At the hospital's annual meeting in May 1915, some of the problems of running a hospital in war time were revealed. Transportation was difficult because of the military occupation of the railways, but despite this, supplies at the hospital were well maintained, however, it was difficult to obtain certain items previously procured from Germany, such as special forms of glass for scientific use. The efficiency of the emergency arrangements was tested when the hospital received notice of a Zeppelin raid, and a telephone message from Uxbridge asked for 100 beds to be made ready to receive expected casualties. Directly afterwards the telephone system was disconnected and the electric and gas lighting was also cut off. The staff worked through the night and had everything ready before dawn for a possible inrush of patients – who happily did not arrive.

One of the main problems facing the hospital was funding. In July 1915 it had debts of approximately £3,000, but the liability was soon cleared, thanks largely to very generous offer made by Mr James Elliman to pay one half of the debt and the energetic response from the friends and well-wishers of the hospital who cleared the remainder.

War Hospital status was given in September 1916, when the minimum number of beds required was relaxed, and arrangements were made for sixty beds to be set aside for sick and wounded soldiers from the front. On 22 September, a party of twenty-seven wounded men arrived direct from the Somme battlefield. The *Windsor Express* noted:

> The cases are all gun-shot wounds and the men are from various units, comprising Guardsmen, City of London Regiment, Rifle Brigade, County Regiments, ASC, Trench Mortar Batteries, Ambulance, and last, but not least, three of our Canadian cousins, who have come over to stand shoulder to shoulder with the lads of the Mother Country.

The out-patients ward was altered in time for a further party of thirty-five wounded soldiers at the end of November. Some of the previous patients had been discharged, which left forty-nine wounded men and an additional five men from local depots to be cared for. In mid-December, when there were over fifty wounded soldiers in residence,

the hospital committee appealed to the owners of motor cars to take the soldiers for car rides. It was said that: 'Several owners have already generously placed their cars at the service of the hospital, but more are needed'. There were sixty-four wounded soldiers in the hospital over Christmas. By the end of 1916 the Board Room at the hospital had been converted to a recreation room, furnished with cards, games and a billiards table for the use of soldiers convalescing at the hospital.

On 29 September 1916, a week after the first wounded soldiers had arrived from the battlefield, King George V and Queen Mary made the first of three wartime visits to the hospital. They toured every ward and all the departments and spoke to newly-arrived wounded men.

Funding continued to be one of the biggest problems facing hospitals before the creation of the NHS. In April 1917 the hospital committee announced that it was again in debt; this time £1,925 needed to be raised by 31 May. The Elliman family came to the rescue again; Mrs Mary Elliman generously offered a donation of £1,000 on the condition that the remaining sum was raised through other donations. A local newspaper campaign helped raise the additional funds in just over three weeks. Among the donations received were £200 from King George V, £25 from the Mayor and £25 from Mr James Mason, the MP for Windsor.

Another thirty-four wounded men arrived in March 1917, bringing the number of men under treatment to forty-eight. In addition, sixteen other military cases were receiving attention, bringing the total to sixty-four. Over 400 soldiers had been admitted for treatment from the start of the war to the beginning of May but the percentage of deaths was small.

To cope with the large numbers, Alexandra Ward was set aside exclusively for the treatment of wounded soldiers from the battlefield. In June a veranda was erected outside the X-Ray Department to provide nine beds for soldiers to sleep there, the cost of this addition being raised by well-wishers. It was also necessary to convert the Out-patients Department to accommodate twenty-five additional wounded soldiers. Urgent out-patient cases, recommended by their doctor, were still seen but they had to attend at 9.30 am or make an appointment through the Matron. There was the lack of medical staff to run the department, as many of the hospital staff had enlisted or been called up for service in the RAMC. To help run the various wards the staff were assisted by Voluntary Aid Detachment nurses (VAD), recruited locally.

By the end of August there were eighty soldiers in the hospital, the largest number it had contained so far, and local residents responded to appeals for help, whether for cash or requests to entertain patients. In June, Mr Arthur Jacobs provided a river trip for wounded soldiers. Some 100 men and a number of nurses boarded the *Windsor Belle*, which took them to Bourne End and back, with tea and cigarettes provided, and they were entertained by the band of the  2nd Life Guards. On their return at 7pm Mr Jacobs told them that they could join in boat trips from Windsor free of charge from that day forward. In August the proprietors of the Empire Theatre, Peascod Street, invited all the wounded soldiers to a matinee, which they greatly enjoyed.

On 5 December Mrs Mary Elliman, who with her husband James Elliman was one of the hospital's principal supporters and benefactors, died. Sir Frederick Dyson, a Hospital Committee member and former Mayor of Windsor, represented King Edward VII Hospital at her funeral. The hospital lost another of its supporters in October 1917, with the death of Prince Christian.

There were eighty-eight wounded men in hospital over Christmas 1917, and the staff endeavoured to make their stay enjoyable. The *Windsor Express* recorded on 29 December:

The men were regaled with turkey, plum pudding and mince pies. In the evening a whist drive was held in the Alexandra Ward, which was attended by the other wounded men in the Hospital and a few friends, and a real good time was spent. The 'Soldiers' Ward', which was profusely decorated by the men themselves, looked very gay with its strings of paper chains, flags, and evergreens... Another interesting feature in the decorations was a series of well executed pen and ink sketches of the badges of the different regiments represented in the Hospital...

The U-boat blockade of Britain caused food shortages and people were urged to apply a form of voluntary rationing. As the situation worsened, compulsory rationing was introduced and hoarding food became a criminal offence. In February 1918 the Government announced that any householders who by inadvertence were liable to prosecution for hoarding would not be prosecuted if they voluntarily surrender their stocks. The hospital committee advised, through the local newspaper, that it would be glad to receive any excess stocks of food.

1918 brought new challenges, the German Spring Offensive caused many Allied casualties, and there was heavy pressure on the War Hospitals to provide as many more beds as possible. The military authorities had requested the hospital to increase accommodation for wounded soldiers, where space permitted. The *Windsor Express* summed up the problem on 6 April:

> The initial cost of each extra bed and its equipment of blankets and sheets is estimated at ten guineas. One or two of the residents in the neighbourhood have each kindly volunteered to give a bed and its equipment, and any further similar offers will be gladly received, so that the emergency may be met without increasing the indebtedness of the Institution.

In early May, fifty-two wounded soldiers arrived at the hospital from France. A total of 514 soldiers had received medical, surgical and nursing attention as in-patients during the twelve months to May 1918, in addition to a large number of out-patients. All this extra expenditure put severe strain on the hospital's finances and it found itself in debt again. James Elliman in the name of his late wife, sent a cheque for £736 to clear the deficit standing at the end of 1917, and the Mayor presented a cheque for £200 representing part of the proceeds received on St George's Day in Windsor. The hospital received further sums from the War Office for the care and treatment of wounded soldiers.

Arthur Jacobs, who had provided the river trip in June, made a similar offer a year later. In mid-June 1918, he gave 100 wounded soldiers and nurses a trip on his new boat, *Empress of India*, and provided tea on board. The problems of disabled soldiers were highlighted and an orthopaedic treatment room was constructed, which ultimately served as the Physiotherapy Department. In February 1918, the British Red Cross and the St John Ambulance Association made a grant of £1,000 for the building of the orthopaedic out-patient annexe for the treatment of discharged soldiers. A motor ambulance was bought that year to replace the horse-drawn one that had operated for the previous ten years.

Another Royal visit was made on 20 April, when the hospital had eighty-three wounded soldiers. The King and Queen spent an hour visiting the wards, and also spoke to the soldiers whose beds were situated on the veranda at the south side of the hospital. The King informed one soldier that he thought he had done his share when he discovered that the man was forty-eight years old and had been in France for two and a half years.

On 18 September, when the number of wounded soldiers was at a record figure of eighty-six, the King and Queen with Princess Mary visited the hospital again. They spoke to the wounded men, and visited the new orthopaedic department, which had been opened by Princess Mary on 3 May that year.

The war ended less than two months later, but as the soldiers left King Edward VII Hospital, their places were taken by the victims of Spanish Flu. This new and deadly form of influenza first reached Windsor in the summer of 1918, with the number of local deaths peaking in the late autumn.

From 1916 to the end of the war, the hospital treated a total of 1,044 wounded soldiers from the battlefield and a further 445 local troops. In addition, a considerable number of men were treated as out-patients, and of the wounded soldiers, most of whom required surgery, only nine died, (which is less than one per cent of the total admitted – a remarkable achievement).

Windsor War Hospital Supply Depot

Following a meeting at the Guildhall in November 1915, a Windsor War Hospital Supply Depot was established at 'Clydesdale', St Leonard's Road, Windsor. The Windsor Depot was opened in order to help supply the immediate needs of British and Allied Hospitals with surgical dressings, slippers, bandages, splints and clothing. The depot was run by local women who volunteered to work there on a part-time basis.

There was a fire at the depot in January 1917 when some tow (hemp fibres used for making pads) was placed in front of a fireplace to dry and a spark ignited it. The workers at the Depot successfully extinguished the blaze with buckets of water before serious damage was done.

In her diary entry for 4 May 1917, Queen Mary mentioned that she visited the Windsor Depot.

Queensmead (now Brigidine School)

The elegant Victorian mansion called Queensmead, which then belonged to the Spencer Churchill family was used as a VAD hospital from 1914 to 1918, and was staffed by the Berkshire Branch of the British Red Cross Society.

St Andrew's Hospital

This was staffed and run by the Clewer Sisters and had 81 beds. It provided medical rather than surgical care for the sick poor of Clewer and Windsor; only patients who could afford to do so were asked to pay for their treatment. There is no evidence that the hospital cared for wounded soldiers during the war.

Princess Christian's Hospital and District Nursing and Maternity Home, Windsor

The Princess Christian Hospital in Clarence Road was opened in 1894 by Princess Christian, (Princess Helena, third daughter of Queen Victoria). Five years later she opened the District and

Maternity Home in Trinity Place, for the wives of soldiers fighting in the Boer War. In 1909 numbers 3 and 4 Clarence Villas were purchased and added to the nursing homes. They continued to be used by soldiers' wives.

Princess Christian's British Red Cross Hospital, Englefield Green

In March 1916 it was reported in the *Windsor Express* that HRH Princess Alexander of Teck was devoting a day a week to work in the kitchen at Princess Christian's British Red Cross Hospital for wounded soldiers at Englefield Green. The Princess was said to have left the Castle at 8.30am and returned home in the early afternoon. While at the hospital she assisted with the cooking and also helped to wash up afterwards. The King mentioned in his diary entry for 20 September 1916 that he visited Aunt Helena's (Princess Christian's) Hospital in Englefield Green and saw 118 wounded men; they were accommodated in huts and said to be most comfortable.

Ascot Hospital

In her diary entry of 21 July 1915, Queen Mary mentioned visiting Ascot Racecourse to see the hospital. She wrote: 'We motored at 3.30 to Ascot to see the Hospital there arranged in the 5s Stands, most comfortable.' [3]

As more space was required, a number of wooden huts were constructed across the road. The 5s stands then became a reception centre for the wounded soldiers. After the war the huts across the road became Heatherwood Hospital, initially for the children of ex-servicemen who suffered from tuberculosis and orthopaedic diseases and it was supported by the United Services Fund.

Canadian Red Cross Military Hospital, Cliveden

In 1914, Lord Astor offered Cliveden to the War Office; they declined his offer. He then offered his house and estate to the Canadian Government, which declined the use of the house but had plans for other buildings. They requested the Covered Tennis Court as a hospital ward and Taplow Lodge for staff accommodation. Further buildings were erected to make a 600

3. QM/PRIV/QMD/1915,1917

bed military hospital, which was run by the 1st Canadian Army Medical Corps. The hospital was named the HRH Duchess of Connaught Hospital in honour of the wife of the Duke of Connaught, who was then the Governor General of Canada.

The King and Queen visited the hospital twice, on 20 July 1915 and 23 August 1917, and talked to all the men.

Actress and race-horse owner Ethel Clinton entertained wounded soldiers from the hospital at her house in Boulter's Lock, Maidenhead during the war.

Red Cross Hospital in Windsor Great Park

The Joint War Committee of the British Red Cross Society and the Order of St John decided to make a free gift to the American Red Cross of a fully-equipped hospital of 500 beds so that American wounded soldiers could be brought to England for treatment. The King was then approached for permission to erect the hospital in Windsor Great Park which he granted. In May 1918 preparations for the new hospital began, on high ground with a good view of Windsor Castle, however, the site was found to be impractical because of the clay soil and drainage difficulties. A replacement site was selected in Richmond Park.

Windsor Boys' School

Windsor Boys' School, then known as Windsor County Boys' School,[1] was founded in 1908. There were other schools in Windsor at the time, such as the Royal Free School, but the Education Act of 1902 compelled local councils to establish secondary schools. Mr George Wade, formerly headmaster of Wallingford Grammar School, was appointed headmaster of the new school when it opened and remained in this demanding post for the next eleven years. In its early days the school was in a house near Holy Trinity Church, Windsor and building work had not completed on opening day – something the Headmaster recalled at the annual prize-giving ceremony ten years later. There were only 46 boys registered when the school opened and it was not until 1917 that the number of pupils passed one hundred.

In 1914, many of the boys who were at the school when it opened were of military service age and enlisted in the Army. One hundred and twenty Old Boys served in HM Forces; fifteen of them died during the war and a sixteenth died a few years later from the effects of gas poisoning.

Raymond South, a former Deputy Headmaster, noted the difficulties of teaching during this time:

Despite the turmoil of war the school grew in numbers and importance. Nevertheless, so long as the war lasted, life was bound to be abnormal. Frequent and unsettling changes took place in the school staff. Men who fondly imagined that their days of teaching were over were brought back to fill the gaps – often to the delights of merciless schoolboys[2]...

In 1921 the four houses of the school were named after Old

1. *Windsor County Boys' School later became Windsor Grammar School, before becoming known as Windsor Boys' School in 1977*

2. *'Windsor Boys' School: The First Fifty Years' Windlesora No 13, published 1994*

Boys who had lost their lives during the war. The four chosen were Burnett, Lambdin, Ottrey and Woodland. (In the 1950s, when the size of the school had increased considerably, the number of

houses was doubled to eight; the new houses were named after former pupils who had died in the Second World War.)

A memorial to those who died in the Great War was unveiled at the School by Colonel, The Earl of Athlone GCB CVO on 28 June 1919. Still on display, it is a carved oak tablet inscribed with the names of the fallen. Fifteen were listed originally and William Huston was added in 1921 on his death from the effects of gas poisoning.

The 16 former pupils who died as a result of the First World War are:

Cyril Ashman

Cyril Arthur Ashman was born in April 1897 at Tidworth,

Hampshire. His father, Edwin Ashman, was a dairy farmer, and by 1901 the family had moved to Dairy Farm, Eton Wick. Cyril attended Windsor County Boys' School from 1910 to 1914 and after leaving school joined Barclays Bank in Southall as a clerk. He enlisted in the 2nd Battalion Honourable Artillery Company, at Windsor, on 9 December 1915, aged eighteen years and seven months. He was then placed  on the Army Reserve until April 1916, when he was nineteen, and posted to France with the BEF in November 1916. In late 1917, his battalion took part in the Third Battle of Ypres, commonly known as Passchendaele.

Wounded on 9 October 1917, but recovered, Cyril was killed in action on 28 October, aged 20. In a letter to his parents, his Company Officer wrote:

> It is with the greatest regret that I am writing to inform you of the death of your son, Pte Cyril Ashman, of this Company, who fell on the 26th October [sic] while performing his duty under heavy shell fire. His officers regret the loss of a good soldier and his comrades mourn one of their most popular comrades, and it is the wish of all that I should convey to you their deepest sympathy in the great loss which you have sustained.

He is buried at Tyne Cot Cemetery, in Belgium, and his name is on the Eton Wick War Memorial. His elder brother, Henry Douglas Ashman, was killed at Gallipoli in August 1915, whilst serving with the Berkshire Yeomanry. After the war his parents left the farm in Eton Wick to live in Slough.

Leslie Burnett

Leslie Cecil James Burnett was born in 1897 at Battersea, London, the only son of James Henry Burnett and Annie Louisa Burnett. The family later moved to Brighton and by the time of the 1911 Census they were living at 27 The Crescent, Slough. He attended the Eton College Choristers' School and later, in the autumn of 1911, went to Windsor County Boys' School, where he excelled in the classroom and on the sports field. An all-round sportsman, and captain of both the cricket and football teams, he was School Captain in 1915. Upon leaving school in 1915 he went to Banister Court School, Southampton, as a mathematics and science master.

Burnett enlisted in the Royal Field Artillery and was sent to France in early 1917. He was commissioned as a second lieutenant and was a promising young officer who had been twice mentioned in despatches. He was killed in action, aged 20, on 14 March 1918 by an enemy shell. Lt Burnett is buried at La Clytte Military Cemetery in Belgium. In his will he remembered Windsor County Boys' School by bequeathing them his book collection. His name is on the Slough War Memorial.

Harold Darville

Harold George Darville was born at Windsor in December 1897, the eldest son of Edwin George Mourd Darville, a grocer (Darville & Son Ltd), and his wife Mary Darville. He attended Windsor County Boys' School from September 1909 to December 1913. At the time, the family home was at 5 St Mark's Road. He enlisted with the Buckinghamshire Territorials, in January 1915, and served on the Western Front with the 1/1st Bucks Battalion of the Oxfordshire and Buckinghamshire Light Infantry. According to contemporary reports he was a much respected soldier and esteemed by all who knew him, and gained promotion to the rank of sergeant.

In August 1916, during the Battle of the Somme, 1/1st Bucks Battalion attacked German positions near Ovillers and suffered heavy losses. Of the 150 other ranks who went over the top in the unsuccessful attack on 23 August, 71 were wounded, 13 missing and 24, including Sgt Darville, were killed in action. He was aged 18. He has no known grave but is remembered on the Thiepval Memorial, France, and his name is also recorded on the Windsor War Memorial.

Francis Dawes

Francis George Dawes was born at Dewsbury, Yorkshire in 1898, second son of Henry Dawes and Alice Maria Dawes. The family moved from Yorkshire because of Henry Dawes' work as a teacher, and the 1911 Census records them living in the Industrial School at Portslade, Sussex. He attended Windsor County Boys' School 1912-1913. Francis Dawes enlisted at Brighton in the Royal Army Medical Corps, later transferring to the 2nd Battalion Dorset Regiment.

The 2nd Battalion fought in Mesopotamia, where the heat and disease contributed to many deaths. While there, Pte Dawes became ill and was evacuated to India, where he died in hospital on 17 March 1918, aged 20. He is remembered on the Kirkee 1914-1918 Memorial, Poona, India. His parents were living at Chichester, West Sussex at the time of his death, which may be the reason his death was not recorded in the Roll of Honour in the *Windsor Express*. Pte Dawes' name is not recorded on any local war memorial, other than the school's.

James Frame

James Frame was born at South Shields in July 1899, the second son of Alfred Frame and Maggie Frame. In 1901 the family were living at 2 Berwick Street, South shields. His father, a captain in the merchant navy, died in 1909 and his mother is believed to have also died. In the 1911 Census, James Frame, aged eleven, was an inmate at the St Augustine's Boys' Home in Clewer. St Augustine's was an Anglican charity home, with a strict regime, for orphans and under-privileged children. Frame attended Clewer Green C E School before going to Windsor County Boys' School on a scholarship placement, granted by Berkshire County Council in 1912-1913. He is said to have joined a Royal Navy training ship after leaving school and, after going absent without leave, enlisted in the Army under an assumed name. The memorial board at his school details James Frame as a guardsman in the Irish Guards. The Irish Guards, however, have no record of him ever serving in that regiment.

Frame is said to have died on 21 January 1918 although he is not listed in the weekly Rolls of Honour in the local newspaper. He is not listed on the website of the Commonwealth War Graves Commission either. His old school appeared sure that he had died and he was mentioned by name in the annual prize giving at the end of July 1918, when the headmaster of Windsor County Boys' School said: 'Lt Woodland... and J Frame both fell in action in the same month as Burnett'. (Woodland and Burnett both died in March 1918). Frame is recorded on the memorial board at Windsor Boys' School but has no other known memorials and it is not known where he is buried.

Christian Harnack

Christian Frederick Charles Harnack was born at Windsor in 1893, the only son of Johann Harnack and Marie Harnack. Johann Harnack was born in Germany and is listed in the 1901 Census as a 'German subject'. He was in Royal service at Windsor Castle as Groom of the Chamber and died in March 1917. Christian, who was a godson of Princess Christian, received his early education at the Royal Albert Institute before attending Windsor County Boys' School when it opened in 1908. After leaving school, later the same year, he worked for a while as a clerk at the Great Western Railway offices at Paddington before joining the London County and Westminster Bank in Lombard Street.

He had joined the Windsor 'A' Squadron of the Berkshire Yeomanry soon after leaving school and served in the Yeomanry when war broke out. Trooper Harnack proceeded to Egypt but suffered from an attack of enteric fever and did not go to Gallipoli with the rest of his regiment. After returning from leave at home, he served in Egypt and Palestine and was one of the Yeomen on board a ship which was torpedoed at night, and was in the water for three hours. He later transferred to the Machine Gun Corps on the Western Front and took part in the final Allied advance. Pte Harnack died in a casualty clearing station, of gunshot wounds, on 30 August 1918. He was aged 25 and is buried at Aubigny Communal Cemetery, France.

Herbert Hiley

Herbert Henry Hiley was born in 1894, the third son of John Malcolm Hiley, the Court Postmaster, and Sarah Hiley. The family home was in New Road. He was educated at Windsor County Boys' School 1909-1911 and was School Captain 1910-1911. He was captain of the school football team as well as playing for Windsor and Eton Football Club; he also belonged to Eton Excelsior Rowing Club. Hiley joined the Westminster Dragoons but on receiving an appointment in South America he obtained his discharge. He returned to England at the outbreak of war and joined the Windsor 'A' squadron of the Berkshire Yeomanry in the week ending 15 August 1914.

After several months training in Norfolk, the regiment sailed for Egypt in April 1915 and then proceeded to Gallipoli, as dismounted troops, arriving at Suvla on 18 August 1915. The Yeomanry took part in the action at Chocolate Hill on 21 August, when the regiment incurred serious losses; Trooper Hiley, together with three other Windsor Yeomen, was killed in action. He was 21 and had been in Gallipoli for only a few days. He is remembered on the Helles Memorial, Gallipoli. In Windsor his name is recorded on the Windsor War Memorial, the Clewer War Memorial and the Berkshire Yeomanry Memorial.

William Huston

William Edward Huston was born at Farlam, Cumberland in July 1895, the third son of Joseph Huston and Mary Huston. Joseph Huston, a civil engineer, was born in Ireland and the family lived there for some time; William's two older brothers were born in Ireland. Joseph's work took him all over the UK, William's younger sister Mary was born in Monmouthshire, and at the time of the 1901 Census the family lived in Queenborough, Kent. By 1911 Mary Huston and the children had moved to Wellesley Road, Slough. Joseph Huston is not listed on the Census document, although Mary is still shown as 'married'. William was educated at Windsor County Boys' School 1910-1912 and after leaving school he found employment as a bank clerk. (His elder brother Arthur was already working in a bank.)

During the war he served as a gunner in the Royal Field Artillery and was very badly wounded in an enemy gas attack. He survived the war but suffered from illness relating to gas poisoning and died as a result on 12 January 1921, in the Ministry of Pensions Hospital, Camberwell, London. Huston is remembered on the Slough War Memorial.

John Lambdin

John Reginald Lambdin was born in 1897 at Aborfield, Berkshire, the eldest son of John George Lambdin and Ellen Elizabeth Lambdin. His father (like several others of the boys' fathers) was in Royal service and in 1911 was House Steward at Cumberland Lodge, Windsor Great Park, before moving to Prince Consort's Gate. In 1908 John Reginald Lambdin entered Windsor County Boys' School, where he distinguished himself both in the class room and on the sports' field. He was successful in the Oxford Local Examinations in 1912-1913. He was good at both cricket and football and captain of his House football team. Lambdin was also a chorister at the Royal Chapel of All Saints, Great Park. Upon leaving school in 1913 he joined the National Provincial Bank of England, in London.

He enlisted soon after the start of the war and served in the 7th Battalion, West Yorkshire Regiment (Prince of Wales's Own). He was seen to have officer potential and after training was promoted to lieutenant. In one of the many actions in which he played a part he was awarded the Military Cross. Lt Lambdin was later attached to the 2nd Battalion Durham Light Infantry (DLI) and was serving with that unit when he was killed, aged 21, on 24 September 1918. During an attack by 2nd DLI on the Hindenburg Line, he received a serious gunshot wound and was admitted, unconscious, to a casualty clearing station. He never recovered and died a few hours after being admitted. Lambdin is buried at Brie British Cemetery, France. His name is on the Roll of Honour and commemorative window at Royal Chapel of All Saints, Great Park. After the war his parents moved back to the Reading area.

John Ottrey

John Anthony Ottrey was born at Windsor in 1895, the only son of Harry George Ottrey, a painter and decorator, and Kate Violet Elizabeth Ottrey. He was educated at Mr Wicks' Commercial School and in 1909 entered Windsor County Boys' School, where he was fond of cricket and cycling. In 1910 he was successful in passing the Oxford Local Examinations. After leaving school in 1911 he joined the Civil Service and was employed as an assistant clerk in the Claims Department of the Inland Revenue at Somerset House. At the time, the family home was at 30 St Leonard's Road. On the outbreak of war he made frequent requests to his office to be allowed to enlist and eventually received permission. He enlisted in the 1/15th Battalion London Regiment (Prince of Wales's Own Civil Service Rifles) in June 1915 and went to France the following May.

Pte Ottrey took part in the advance on the Somme in September 1916. Describing his experiences in a letter to a friend, which was published in the *Windsor Express* in October 1916, he said: 'I have been engaged in pushing the Huns and I am pleased to say that I came through all right… I lost several of my pals and had a pretty rough time, and a full share of excitement, finishing up covered with mud, hungry, and tired out… It was a fearful time though and so were some of the sights there.' He was killed in action near Ypres on 12 January 1917, aged 21. He has no known grave and is remembered on the Ypres (Menin Gate) Memorial in Belgium and on the Windsor War Memorial.

James Pearce

James Hale Pearce was born at Datchet in 1897, the only child of James Hale Pearce, an electrician, and Ellen Annie Pearce. The family home was at The Links, Buccleuch Road, Datchet. James was educated at Windsor Boys' School 1911-1913 and after leaving school is believed to have worked for the Post Office as a telegraphist.

He enlisted, at Windsor, in the 3rd Home Counties Divisional Signals Royal Engineers, a Territorial Force unit, in April 1915 and agreed to serve abroad. He initially failed his medical examination 'owing to defective vision', but it was noted that this was corrected by wearing glasses and a second doctor certified him as fit for service. He served in the UK as a telegraphist until 28 June 1918, when he was transferred to 62nd Divisional Signal Company on the Western Front. He was awarded the Military Medal, although the details are not recorded. On 22 October 1918, during the closing stages of the war, Sapper Pearce was wounded and gassed. He was taken to No 3 General Hospital, Le Treport, France, where he died of his wounds on 26 October 1918, aged 21. Pearce is buried at Mont Huon Military Cemetery, Le Treport. His name is recorded on the Datchet War Memorial.

Frederick Pusey

Frederick Walter Pusey was born at Buckland in Hampshire in 1899, the eldest son of Walter Pusey and Ellen Jane Pusey. He lived at various addresses in Bishops Waltham and Southsea, often without his father (who was in the Royal Navy), before his parents moved to Flying Barn, Windsor Great Park. After retiring from the Navy, his father was appointed His Majesty's Fisherman at Virginia Water; his duties included making arrangements for Royal fishing parties and teaching the children of the Royal family to fish. His service to the Royal family meant that his son, Frederick, was able to be a chorister at the Royal Chapel of All Saints, Great Park. Frederick was educated at Windsor County Boys' School 1912-1914.

He served in four regiments during the war. He enlisted originally in the Dorset Regiment and was sent to France with them in July 1915. He was then transferred to the Hampshire Regiment, then the Notts and Derby Regiment and, finally, the 1st Battalion Essex Regiment. By 1918 he had been promoted to L/Cpl. Pusey died at No 3 Canadian CCS, on 10 September, of wounds received on 9 August. He was aged 19 and is buried at Varennes Military

Cemetery, France. Frederick Pusey's Army records were destroyed during the Blitz, but it would appear from the known dates that he was under age when he enlisted. His name is on the Roll of Honour and commemorative window at Royal Chapel of All Saints. His father, Walter Pusey, was appointed gatekeeper at Queen Anne's Gate, King's Road in 1921.

Charles Sangster

Charles William Sangster was born at Willesden, Middlesex in 1898, the eldest son of Charles Sangster, a chemist and druggist, and Annie Bertha Sangster. By 1911 the family were living at 88 High Street, Slough. The young Charles was educated at Upton School and then Windsor County Boys' School 1910-1914. He was successful in the Oxford Local Examinations in 1914 and after leaving school he entered his father's business. When the war started he was eager to take part but was too young to enlist. He took an interest in the work of the YMCA among the troops then billeted in the area and worked with the Congregational Church in Slough. In November 1915, aged 17, he volunteered for service and enlisted in the 1/8th Battalion Middlesex Regiment (Duke of Cambridge's Own) at Willesden.

The battalion arrived in France in March 1915 and served on the Western Front for the rest of the war. Pte Sangster was killed in action, aged 20, during the Battle of Albert on 24 August 1918. He is buried at Bucquoy Road Cemetery, Ficheux, France, and he is remembered on the Slough War Memorial. An obituary in the *Windsor Express* noted that: 'young Sangster was a boy of singularly attractive personality: though not brilliant in an academic sense, he possessed excellent judgement for his years…'

Herbert Simmons

Herbert Arthur Simmons was born in Sussex in 1897. His parents, Arthur Herbert Simmons and Marian Simmons, resided at the Old Windsor Union Workhouse, where his father was the Master, at the time of the 1911 Census; their son did not live with them. Herbert was educated at Windsor County Boys' School 1911-1913 and was 17 when he enlisted soon after the outbreak of war. He joined the 12th Battalion Royal Sussex Regiment (one of the Kitchener battalions) at Hove.

The battalion went to France in March 1916 and on 30 June took part in a hastily planned attack near Richebourg designed to distract the enemy from the main Somme offensive which began the following day. The attack, which lacked effective artillery support, was unsuccessful and 12th Royal Sussex incurred heavy losses. Pte Simmons was killed in this action; he was 18.

A comrade, writing to his mother, said: 'Arthur and I were great chums ever since we joined the Signal Section; in fact he was liked by everyone, as he was an ideal soldier and a good and brave man. His last words were to a stretcher bearer immediately after he was wounded: "Do you think I shall get over it?" but he died almost immediately afterwards...' Simmons is buried at St Vaast Post Military Cemetery, Richebourg-L'Avoue, France.

Arthur Widcombe

Arthur James Widcombe was born at Datchet in 1898, the only son of Arthur Charles Widcombe, a coal merchant, and Agnes Mary Widcombe. The family home was at Selwood Cottage, Montagu Road, Datchet and he was educated at Windsor County Boys' School 1908-1915. During the war he enlisted at Slough in the 1st Battalion Duke of Edinburgh's (Wiltshire Regiment).

Pte Widcombe served on the Western Front and was killed in action on 12 April 1918, aged 19. His battalion held a position around Neuve Eglise, Belgium under heavy fire and after dusk supported troops fighting near Bailleul. There were heavy casualties from enemy shellfire, with 282 men missing in action. Arthur Widcombe was reported as missing before his death was confirmed and his name appeared in the weekly Roll of Honour on 11 May 1918 in the *Windsor Express* under the heading 'Reported Missing'. He is buried in Strand Military Cemetery, Belgium and he is remembered on the Datchet War Memorial.

Leslie Frank Woodland

Leslie Frank Woodland was born at Hooley Lodge, Chipstead, Surrey in March 1897, the second son of Edmund Arthur Charles Woodland and Annie Elizabeth Woodland. The family moved to Windsor around 1909 and lived in Grove Road – for many years Edmund was the proprietor of a livery and hunting stables in Francis Road before moving to Southampton. Leslie was educated at Windsor County Boys' School from 1909 to 1911 and after leaving school trained as a veterinary surgeon. He was a second year student at the London Veterinary College when war was declared in August 1914.

In January 1916 he enlisted in the Honourable Artillery Company, a territorial regiment, at Finsbury. He was subsequently posted to the Royal Horse Artillery for training as a driver, and was sent to France at the end of June 1916. In January 1917 Pte Woodland was evacuated to a hospital in England suffering from severe ulcers to his legs and back, brought about by the appalling living conditions in the trenches. He was discharged from hospital at the end of February and then applied for a commission. After successful completion of an eight-month gunnery course, he was commissioned as second lieutenant and posted to 180 Brigade Royal Field Artillery, arriving on 20 March 1918.

Second Lt Woodland was killed in action on 21 March 1918, aged 20. On that day the Germans launched their spring offensive making large territorial gains and inflicting serious casualties on the British Army. Leslie Woodland has no known grave and he is remembered on the Pozieres Memorial.

Eton College

Eton College's contribution to the war was considerably greater than any other school in the area; not only was it larger but it had been in existence much longer. In the 1920s, Eton College published a record of the school's part in the Great War, entitled List of Etonians Who Fought in The Great War MCMXIV-MCMXIX. It recorded the names of 1,031 Etonians 'whose deaths are attributable to enemy action, were killed or received a fatal wound'. The compiler, Mr E L Vaughan, acknowledged that the list may not be up to date – the figure has since been updated to 1,157. A total of 5,650 Etonians served in the war, in all services and theatres and almost one in five of them were killed – a much higher percentage than the national average for men who served in the Army. More than 1,000 Etonians were wounded during the war.

In common with other public schools, Eton provided military training for its pupils through the Officer Training Corps (OTC) and this together with its emphasis on patriotism and duty, resulted in a great number of former pupils enlisting as soon as war was declared. At the end of 1914 there were over 600 members of the OTC, and the *Windsor Express* reported on 19 September:

> A large number of Eton boys have asked for nominations for Sandhurst, where after three months training, they will be eligible for commissions. Some who recently left the school have joined the ranks. Many others are joining the Public Schools Brigades.

Most were eligible to become officers and after receiving commissions found themselves leading men into battle. Casualty figures for junior officers were higher than for other ranks, as they were expected to lead from the front, and the enemy always shot the officers first. In late 1914, in an article in the *School Guardian,* the Headmaster of Eton wrote:

> Outwardly, the school life seems to be going forward much as usual. But an observant eye would note a disturbance of the age balance. The place is alive with young boys, but where are the young men, the leaders of society, the seasoned captains of games, and the shapers of public opinion? Gone: about 110 of them over 17 years of age have vanished at the sound of their country's call, and are now either manning the trenches in Flanders, or finishing their training near some unknown French rail-head, or teaching the best of our recruits in a southern depot, or gathering brawn in the Sandhurst gymnasium… Of those who have already served at the front, several have been given temporary commissions, others are in the ranks, and others were in the Regular Army before the war began…

A preliminary list of Etonians on active service in France, Belgium and parts of Africa, and in the Naval Forces, was issued by the *Eton College Chronicle* in November 1914; it contained 736 names. The previous month it had been announced that the bell at Eton College Chapel would be tolled for a quarter of an hour every day for the fallen Etonians. By February 1915 there were 1,495 Etonians serving on all fronts, of these, 179 had been killed in action or died of wounds, 32 were missing, 227 wounded, 18 were prisoners and 32 were wounded and prisoners of war. Old Etonians continued to rush to enlist, and at the beginning of December that year the number serving had risen to 4,254, of which 3,250 were overseas. In the first sixteen months of the war, over 75 per cent of the total who served during the whole war had enlisted. The *Windsor Express* noted at the time that it was: 'A splendid war record'. Casualties also increased and by December 1915, 462 Etonians had been killed in action or died of wounds and the number of wounded had increased to 658.

Eton masters were also casualties. In March 1915, 2nd Lt Walter George Fletcher was killed in action. At the beginning of the war he had joined the Intelligence Corps, and later was attached to the Royal Welsh Fusiliers. A French flag, which he captured from the German trenches was hung in Eton College Chapel in December

1915. Lt Fletcher crawled all night between flare lights to climb a tree in the German lines where they had hung the captured French flag, and he succeeded to return to his own trench with his trophy. Shortly afterwards he was wounded in the head during an attack on his trench and never regained consciousness. He was the first Eton master to die in the war

In September 1915, the *Windsor Express* reported that Assistant Master, Captain Arthur Charles Sheepshanks, 8th Battalion Rifle Brigade, had received the Distinguished Service Order. By the end of the war, Etonians had been awarded 13 Victoria Crosses[1], in addition to over 400 DSOs, over 550 Military Crosses and other awards and Mentions in Despatches. The first Eton VC of the war was awarded to Captain Francis Grenfell, a nephew of Lord Desborough, for an early encounter with the Germans on 24 August 1914.

Lord Desborough

William Henry Grenfell, later Lord Desborough, was a great sportsman and local benefactor. When he became the President of the Olympic Games in London in 1908 he was responsible for bringing the Marathon to Windsor. On his death in 1945 the title became extinct as all his sons had predeceased him.

The death of Captain Julian H F Grenfell DSO of the 1st Royal Dragoons was announced in the *Windsor Express* on 29 May 1915. Lord and Lady Desborough had gone to Boulogne to be with their eldest son as soon as they heard that he was taken to a hospital there, seriously wounded, but he died on 26 May 1915.

1. *Etonians have been awarded a total of 37 VCs, which is more than any other school*

A second tragedy hit the family in July that year with the death of another son, Second Lt Gerald W Grenfell of the 8th Rifle Brigade, who was killed in action in Flanders on 30 July 1915.

The family had previously mourned the death of two nephews, twins Riversdale (Rivvy) N Grenfell who was killed on 14 September 1914, and Francis O Grenfell VC, killed on 24 May 1915, two days before his cousin Julian died of his wounds.

Many of the war's Generals, including Julian Byng, Herbert Plumer and Henry Rawlinson, were educated at Eton. The most famous Etonian soldier, was Field Marshal Earl Roberts of Kandahar VC (1832-1914). He had been awarded his VC during the Indian Mutiny in January 1858 and spent 41 years in India before serving in Afghanistan and South Africa. Although he had retired before the start of the First World War, he was a much-respected military hero and continued to work for the national interest. In a tribute in October 1914, following his 82nd birthday, the *Windsor Express* noted:

> Lord Roberts is one of Windsor's most distinguished freemen [he was living in Ascot at the time]... His knowledge and experience made him aware that our Army was not big enough to meet the exigencies of the situation, and a few years ago he proposed a system of national service, which would provide us with well-equipped and well-trained men to meet such an emergency as the present. He was not listened to by the nation, however, and we have now got to pay the price...

In November 1914 Lord Roberts went to the Western Front to welcome newly-arrived Indian troops. He caught a chill and died at Field Marshal French's HQ in France on 14 November. After receiving a state funeral, he was buried in St Paul's Cathedral Crypt.

Because of Eton's reputation, the school attracted pupils from all over the world, few of them lived locally. There were, however, several casualty reports of Etonians with local connections, the first of these being Captain Charles Hunter Browning, Royal Field Artillery, who was killed in action on 26 August 1914. Captain Browning, the prospective Liberal candidate for Windsor at the start of the war, had addressed only two political meetings in the town, but was a very popular candidate. A King's scholar at Eton from 1891 to 1897, he was gazetted to the Royal Artillery in 1898, and served in the South African War in 1900. At Le Cateau in August 1914, while the guns of his battery were in position with gun-pits on the right, a greatly superior body of German artillery shelled them from the left. They were obliged to swing their guns round in the open while under heavy fire and almost the whole of Browning's battery – 124th RFA – was killed.

Another Etonian with a Windsor connection was Major Charles Matthew Kemp DSO, 21st Battalion Manchester Regiment, who was killed in action on 9 October 1917, whilst in command of his battalion. The youngest son of Mr and Mrs W A Kemp, of Gloucester Place, he was married to Winifred May Kemp (nee Gunton), of 28 Alma Road. Major Kemp was educated at Eton College Choristers' School and was a chorister in the Chapel Choir. Writing to Mrs Kemp, the Commanding Officer of his battalion said:

> He was beloved by everyone who knew him and especially by the men of his Battalion, whose welfare and comfort were ever his first thought and consideration. As a second-in-command I never want anyone better; he was always our right-hand man, and his advice was always sound and welcome…

On 10 July 1915, the *Windsor Express* reported that a number of Eton boys who were too young to join the services, but who were anxious to do something for their country, were being employed in a munitions factory at Slough. Employed in various workshops, they took their place side by side with the other workers, most of them had been on a training course at the Eton School of Mechanics and had a good knowledge of the work. The *Windsor Express* editorial that week advised that:

> …thirty thousand more volunteers are wanted for munitions work. The Munitions Work Bureaux are aiming at raising the total number of workers enrolled to 100,000 … In the Windsor district a good deal is being done by voluntary workers, and

this week a number of Eton boys have joined in the work at a neighbouring factory…

Clara Butt, a popular recitalist and concert singer, organised and sang in many concerts for charity during the war. In 1915 she gave a concert in aid of the French soldiers, at Eton College with tickets from 5s to 12s 6d.

In May 1916 the King and Queen, accompanied by the Prince of Wales and Princess Mary, paid an informal visit to Eton, where their third son, Prince Henry, was being educated. They walked through the Playing Fields, and watched a scratch cricket match in progress. The war meant there were no professional cricket matches, all fixtures were dominated by public school matches and the occasional game between local regiments. Eton had a good team and won matches against Harrow in July 1917 and Charterhouse in June 1918, amongst others.

The headmaster of Eton, the Rev Dr Edward Lyttelton, resigned in 1916. He had been headmaster for eleven years and was an outspoken critic of Germany. His successor was his brother-in-law, the Rev Cyril Argentine Alington, then headmaster of Shrewsbury.

In December 1916, seventy-three Old Etonians of the II Army Corps, on the Western Front, celebrated Founder's Day by a dinner. General Sir Herbert Plumer presided, and in proposing the toast of 'Floreat Etona', said:

> We are proud of Eton and of our association with it; because we know we have every right to be proud… It is indisputably true to say that at every period of the history of our country, notably at every time of stress and trial, Eton and Eton's sons have taken a leading share in national service. In this war we have played, and will continue to play to the last, a part of which future generations of Etonians will be justly proud…

In June 1917, over two hundred Old Etonians held the Fourth of June[2] celebration at a special gathering in France. 'Absence'

2. The Fourth of June celebrates the birthday of King George III, who was a patron of the College, but it always takes place on the Wednesday before the first weekend in June

was called, and several school songs were sung accompanied by the Coldstream Guards' band. Major-General the Earl of Cavan presided, and among those present were Brigadier-General Prince Alexander of Teck, General Sir H Gough, and Brigadier-Generals J Ponsonby and the Hon J F Gathorne-Hardy.

Food restrictions facing the population of Windsor also applied to Eton College. From February 1917, boys were placed on war rations, with three meatless days per week and stewed fruit served instead of puddings. Furthermore, boys were not allowed to supplement their food supplies with items bought from the tuck shop; tarts, buns, scones, biscuits and all kinds of confectionary were declared 'out of bounds.' Before Christmas that year many of the boys voluntarily cut down their consumption of milk on the understanding that the supplies saved should be devoted to the use of the poor of Eton town. A large number of Eton boys, together with several of the assistant masters, were engaged the following month in digging up the playing field known as 'Mesopotamia', for the purpose of planting vegetables. The work was voluntary and done in their leisure time.

In addition, a number of the Eton boys contributed to the war effort by helping as agricultural labourers. One party of twenty-five, led by an assistant master, went to a farm at Wraysbury, and a similar contingent was drafted to a farm in Cippenham. The shortage of labour on the farms meant the offer of Eton boys was gladly accepted, particularly during the harvesting season, and they received ordinary workers' wages.

Despite the many problems created by the war, Eton continued to flourish. It was reported in October 1917 that there were 1,070 boys, including eight Belgian refugees, which at the time was a record attendance for the school.

As the number of Etonians dying in the war continued to rise, thoughts were given to some form of memorial. In February 1917, when over 5,200 Etonians had enlisted and nearly 800 had died, a provisional council was set up to provide a suitable Eton War Memorial. The Provost and Fellows undertook to contribute £10,000 by instalments from the College revenues, spread over a period not exceeding twenty years, subject to certain representation on the Council. It was hoped to raise a minimum of £100,000 in order to carry out the following objectives:

1. To provide for a permanent and visible record at Eton of those who had fallen.
2. To enable the sons of Etonians who had died in the service of their country during the war to be educated at Eton.
3. To create, with the surplus after a sufficient sum has been allocated to these objects, an Endowment Fund for the purpose of helping Old Etonians who could not otherwise afford it, to provide an Eton education for their sons.

By October that year, the Eton War Memorial had reached £135,000 – including about £40,000 promised for 1918 and future years. Of this sum £10,000 had been set aside for a 'permanent and visible' Memorial, and £20,000 for an endowment fund to help Old Etonians, who could not otherwise afford it, to provide an Eton education for their sons.

In July 1917 it was announced that between fifty and sixty members of the Eton College Choristers' School had joined up and seven had been killed. One of those who had died was L/Cpl H G Jefferies, Berkshire Yeomanry, who was champion swimmer of the school for three successive years. The death toll rose again in October when Major C Kemp DSO was killed in action.

Later that month, Lt. General Sir Francis J Davies made the annual inspection of the Eton College Officers' Training Corps, and among those on parade was HRH Prince Henry, the King's third son. Addressing the Corps at the close of the inspection, General Davies was quoted as saying the public schools had done magnificently well in the war in supplying the Army with the right class of officer and no school had played its part better than Eton.

He continued that this was perhaps something to do with what they learnt at Eton; they played the game to the last. When the Eton College OTC proceeded to Tidworth shortly afterwards, to train at the Public Schools Camp, Prince Henry was among 400 pupils taking part.

Application was made by Eton College, in August 1917, to the Food Controller regarding the resumption of hunting with beagles. The Food Controller replied that he had no objection provided the food regulations were strictly observed and the hounds were therefore brought back. It was later suggested that although hunting might be legal, it was not appropriate at a time when food economy was so important and in November the College authorities decided to disperse the beagles until the end of the war.

In common with the rest of the country, Eton had a good potato harvest in 1917 and the Eton crop was above average. The *Eton Chronicle* noted:

> From the one and a half acres, just on 15 tons of potatoes were produced, selling for £100, with a net profit, after paying of all expenses of £45 19s 8d. There was also a profit on the hoeing done, on neighbouring farms, of £9 6s 7d. A cheque for £55 6s 3d has been handed by the Headmaster to the Captain of the School, who will forward it to King Edward VII Hospital in Windsor, to be spent in aid of additional comforts for the convalescent wounded there. By the sale of the potatoes locally, carriage on at least three truck-loads was thus saved.

In February 1918 it was reported at an Eton Urban District Council meeting that King George V had sent venison to Eton College to relieve the meat shortage there. The King allowed a number of bucks from Windsor Great Park to be sent each week to the College. The money that the college houses paid for their supply of venison was sent to the Red Cross.

Towards the end of the war German prisoners were engaged in threshing operations on the Eton playing fields. There was an excellent harvest on the ground where the previous winter the Eton boys played their football matches.

Armistice Day, 11 November, was declared a half-day holiday at Eton; jubilant Eton College boys, decked with flags, marched round the 'burning bush' thumping foot baths. There was no regular work done the following day – a special service of thanksgiving was held in the College Chapel and in the evening songs were sung in the School Hall.

The first private memorial tablet to Etonians fallen in the war to be placed in the Cloisters at Eton College was erected in December 1918 on the East Cloister wall, in memory of nine 'sons of Eton and descendants of Thomas Smith, of Nottingham, 1631'. The names of all 1,157 Etonians who died during the First World War are now recorded on the Cloister walls.

The *Windsor Express*

The *Windsor Express* in 1914 had changed a great deal since it was first published just over 100 years earlier on 1 August 1812, when it carried mainly national and international news. It cost just one penny rather than 6 ½d, which had put it out of the reach of working people. By 1914 most people would have bought a national newspaper as well as a local one, thus the *Windsor Express* was now dedicated to local and regional news with Windsor and Slough dominating. There were sports reviews, situations vacant and wanted columns, cinema and entertainment notices, and reports from the sessions and assizes. When war came, the paper reported not from the battlefield but from the town, on recruiting, soldiers in the town, air raid precautions, food shortages and allotments, care of refugees, the Defence of the Realm Act, and much more. Many letters written by soldiers at the front to their families at home were published.

The *Windsor Express* printed frequent Rolls of Honour during the war, detailing local men who had enlisted, and those who had been wounded or killed. It often published long obituaries of local men killed in action in addition to the bare facts in the casualty lists. Many of the newspaper's employees enlisted and went off to war, and some of them never returned.

In February 1916, owing to government restrictions on the supply of paper, the size of the *Windsor Express* was reduced from eight to six pages, and separate Windsor and Slough editions were published. The six-page format proved inconvenient to readers, owing to the loose insert page, and the paper reverted to eight pages in January 1917. At the same time, the size of the page was made smaller. Two months later the first price increase of the war was made, to 1½d. The rising cost and serious shortage of paper caused by unrestricted German U-boat activity, made the increase necessary, and were responsible for a further price increase to 2d in February 1918. A reduction in the number of pages to six followed in March, with condensed reports and limited space for advertisers. Various editions in 1918 were smaller in page size but contained eight pages.

The printing staff of the *Windsor Express* enjoyed a holiday at Southend, on the Essex coast on a Saturday in July 1917. They got more than they bargained for; they watched a squadron of 22 German Gotha aircraft returning from a bombing raid on London in which 42 people had been killed and 197 injured. When the party returned to London, they found that the restaurant they had breakfasted at that morning had been a victim of the raid. In Windsor, Councillor Dyson raised the question of air raid warnings and he said that to be forewarned was to be forearmed.

Windsor Express men go to war

At the beginning of the war four men working at the *Windsor Express* office were called up for active service: L/Cpl Harold Jefferies, Berkshire Yeomanry, Ptes Frederick Ayres and William Miles, Royal Berkshire Regiment Territorials, and Pte E Price, reservist in the Grenadier Guards. Stanley Holbourn, who had been on the reporting staff for the previous twelve months, enlisted in June 1915 in the Inns of Court Officers' Training Corps, then stationed at Berkhamsted. He survived the war.

Pte Price was the first to join the Army fighting in Flanders, and he also survived the war. In December 1914, Pte Price, then serving with the 20th Infantry Brigade, wrote to friends in Windsor telling them of the rough weather encountered in the trenches, and the proximity of the German trenches:

> …It is just the width of the field that parts us – rather too close to be pleasant, but still we do not mind that much. They livened us up a bit on one or two nights, but we soon quietened them down when we started shooting. They are very good shots, too, some of them… There are several Guardsmen here from Windsor, and we are all hoping to get back together.

L/Cpl Jefferies sailed to Egypt in April 1915, after training in

Norfolk with the Berkshire Yeomanry. The regiment was employed on garrison duties for several months before taking part in the ill-conceived invasion of Gallipoli. Within days of landing at Suvla Bay on 18 August, the Berkshire Yeomanry was in action, as dismounted troops, against the Turkish army. At Scimitar Hill (Hill 70) on 21 August, when the Yeomanry attacked a heavily-defended enemy position, serious casualties

were sustained. Many men of 'A' Squadron Berkshire Yeomanry were killed in action, including L/ Cpl Jefferies. In the obituary to him on 11 September 1915, the *Windsor Express* noted:

Harold Jefferies was first of all at the Windsor British School and afterwards a member of the Eton College Choristers' School. He eventually became a solo boy in the Choir. He was a good all round athlete and was well-known both in the cricket and football fields. His last appearance in the cricket field at Windsor was in August 1914, when he played for the *Windsor Express* staff, against Messrs Oxley and Son's jobbing staff. He was an assistant reporter on the Express and was responsible for many excellent accounts of sporting events which have appeared in our columns… He had been a member of the Berks Yeomanry for some years and was a fine, well-set-up young fellow. His loss will be greatly deplored by a large circle of friends. He was the only surviving son of Mr and Mrs G Jefferies, of Queen's Road, Windsor.

Ptes Miles and Ayres had been members of the 4th (Territorial) Battalion Royal Berkshire Regiment (RBR). Although the Territorial Army was established primarily for home defence, such was the need for more men at the front that it was not long before territorial units went off to war. At the beginning of 1916 they were in trenches near Hebuterne in France. On 22 January 1916 the Battalion War Diaries recorded that the Germans shelled their trenches and during this bombardment one British soldier was killed, Pte William Miles. The *Windsor Express*, in an obituary to him dated 5 February, noted:

> ... He was the only son of Mr and Mrs T Miles, of 36 Duke Street, Windsor, and spent his 20th birthday in the trenches on January 12th. He came home on leave on January 4th and returned to the Front on January 10th. He was an apprentice at the *Express* office when the war broke out, and was called up with the Windsor Territorial Company of which he was a member... He was familiarly known as 'Smiler' among his companions, as he invariably had a smile on his face. He was an Assistant Scout Master before the war, and was a notable figure as trumpeter in the Windsor Children's Pageant a few years ago. He was a Battalion Scout in the 1/4th Berks for some time. He was very popular with his comrades, and was an efficient soldier. It was while doing a comrade a 'good turn' that he met his death. He was carrying some letters across shell-swept ground, when he was hit on the head by a piece of shell. He only lived a quarter of an hour after he was struck down and was unconscious from the first.

Pte William Thomas George Miles, 1/4th Royal Berkshire Regiment, died 22 January 1916, aged 20. He is buried at Hebuterne Military Cemetery, France.

On 12 August, under the heading 'Another Express Employee Falls', the newspaper reported the death of Pte Fred Ayres of 1/4th RBR, who was killed in action in 'the big advance' on 23 July. In its obituary to him in the same edition, the *Windsor Express* noted:

> After leaving school he became an apprentice in the office of the Windsor and Eton Express and was senior boy when he left on the outbreak of war.
> Prior to the war he had been a member of the Windsor Territorials, and had done sixteen months' foreign service

when he was killed. He was the son of Mr and Mrs Frank Ayres, of 29 William Street, Windsor, and was 20 years of age. Private Ayres was greatly respected and esteemed both by his employers and his fellow workmen. He was an excellent footballer and cricketer, and a thorough sportsman in all his actions. He is the third employee from this office to give his life for his country in the war.

Captain C A L Lewis, the officer commanding Ayres' Company wrote to his parents to express his regret:

The late FRED J. AYRES, 29, William Street, Windsor.—Killed in action. Aged 20.

On the 23rd we successfully attacked some German trenches, and later in the day, when we were holding the captured trenches, your son was killed instantaneously by a shell. Your son had been most brave, and it will be some consolation to you to know that he gave his life bravely, after doing his share in an important and successful advance. His many friends in the Company will miss him, and so shall I. He was one of those who have been with me some time, and I have always had special affection for the men of my old Windsor Company.

Pte Frederick Ayres, has no known grave, and is remembered on the Thiepval Memorial, France.

The fourth and final *Windsor Express* employee to die in the war was Harry Jeffries, who was married and lived with his wife at 14 Alexandra Road. He had worked at the newspaper until he joined the Army in December 1916. His battalion, 1/4th Hampshire Regiment, was sent to Mesopotamia (now Iraq) where British and Indian troops had been fighting the Turks since just after the beginning of the war. The heat and insanitary conditions there added to the casualties caused by enemy action. Pte Harry Jeffries died of enteritis, following typhus, at Basra on 8 June 1918, aged 31, and was buried at Tehran War Cemetery, Iran.

All *Windsor Express* employees who died during the war were mentioned, though not by name, in an editorial dated 28 December 1918:

> The war has deprived us, too, of the services of a number of young men of great promise who have laid down their lives for their country. We have lost no fewer than four from this office, who died nobly on the battlefield, while others have been wounded, and some are still on active service. We are naturally proud of these men, and their places have been difficult to fill...

In addition, two former apprentices who were working elsewhere when the war started, were killed during the Battle of the Somme. L/Cpl Arthur Lambert, 1/4th RBR, died on 14 August 1916, aged 24. After leaving Clewer St Stephen School he was apprenticed to Messrs Oxley and Son, publishers of the *Windsor Express*, and after completing his apprenticeship left to work for a firm of printers in Wexford. He returned home on the outbreak of war and enlisted in his local regiment. The family home was in Arthur Road, and his father had worked for Windsor Post Office for 28 years. L/Cpl Lambert is buried at Ovillers Military Cemetery.

Pte Ernest Ledgley, 1/7th Middlesex Regiment died on 26 August 1916, aged 25. He was the youngest son of Mr and Mrs Ledgley of Grove Road, and an old National School boy and chorister at Windsor Parish Church. On leaving school in 1906, he was apprenticed to the *Windsor Express* and at the end of his term he obtained employment with a firm at Willesden. He later joined the staff of the Electrical Law Press, by whom he was employed until he joined the Middlesex Regiment, in November 1915. Pte Ledgley is remembered on the Thiepval Memorial.

Military Tribunals

While *Windsor Express* employees were fighting abroad, the newspaper was fighting for its own survival at home. When conscription was introduced in 1916, Military Tribunals were established to hear claims from men, or their employers, who felt that their work was crucial to the war effort or other personal circumstances which would prevent them from serving.

In November 1916, George Reginald Pobjoy, a monotype operator, and Harry Jeffries, a printer's machine minder, both married men employed by Messrs Oxley and Son, came before the Windsor Tribunal in order that their cases might be reviewed. The Military Representative stated that he was of the opinion that one of these two men should serve. Mr Stanley Oxley said with regard to Pobjoy, who was in charge of the monotype installation, most of the production of the newspaper and a good deal of the general printing depended on him. Pobjoy was given an exemption until the end of the month and Jeffries was called up and sent to Mesopotamia, where he later died of enteritis.

At a further Tribunal held in March 1917, Mr Oxley pointed out the impossibility of obtaining monotype operators and that he was unable to revert to hand composition. Pobjoy was granted two months' exemption. Further successful appeals extended the exemption period to 31 December 1917. In 1918 the manpower shortage at the front was so serious that the call up age was increased to 50 and all existing exemptions from military service were reviewed. The newspaper, at a Tribunal in February 1918, again appealed to retain the services of George Pobjoy. Mr Oxley stated that in 1912 the firm abolished hand composition for the newspaper and bought one monotype keyboard and caster. The *Windsor Express* was being produced with a very small staff of six men, whose ages ranged from 51 to 67; Pobjoy and a young woman operated the keyboards and the caster attendant was unfit for military service. The members of the Tribunal considered the continued publication of the paper most important for the war effort and Pobjoy was granted three months' exemption. He was given conditional exemption in June 1918 and was still employed by the newspaper at the end of the war.

The Guildhall

From the start of the war, the recruiting office was in the Guildhall. The *Windsor Express* reported on 15 August 1914:

> Since Tuesday recruiting for the Regular Army and Lord Kitchener's Army of 100,000 men has been proceeding steadily at the Recruiting Office at the Guildhall. Up to Thursday night, nine men had been sent to join the Regular Service and 25 to help swell the ranks of Lord Kitchener's Army.

In October 1914, when the town was full of soldiers, the Corn Market was given over as recreation rooms for soldiers stationed in Windsor. In 1886 it had been enclosed and furnished, much like a lounge, and this area played an important part during the Great War. A committee headed by HRH Princess Alexander of Teck, furnished it with easy chairs and reading and writing materials.

The Guildhall became the meeting place for all sorts of groups, from the women's League of Honour to the place where the Mayor, Councillor William Carter, entertained troops for tea; exhibitions, concerts and fundraising events were all held there. From 1916 the Military Tribunal, which decided over applications for exemptions or postponement to serve, took place there each Thursday. In March 1916 a protest meeting at the Guildhall in response to a military proclamation summoning attested married men to the Colours, was crowded and lively. The Derby Scheme had pledged to call up 'single men first', but had not kept its promise.

Most of the soldiers who had come to Windsor in 1914 had left by 1916 and the lounge was under-used, therefore the committee dissolved itself and the room reverted to the Corporation. In November 1916 members of the Town Council petitioned for a pathway for the public through the Corn Market, which had been closed to them since 1914, but the Mayor had different ideas. At a special meeting called by him in January 1917 a resolution was carried unanimously that the Corn Market should be devoted for the remainder of the war to the use of wounded soldiers as a Municipal lounge, but any man in uniform could use it. An appeal went out for settees, easy chairs, bookcases, rugs, reading material and a piano. The lounge was officially opened in February 1917, with many of the wounded soldiers from King Edward VII Hospital in attendance. It was 'most comfortably and cosily fitted up'.

A photograph of the Windsor Squadron of the Berkshire Yeomanry taken in 1915 and published in the local newspaper, was presented to the Guildhall in April 1916, and hung in the Mayor's Parlour. It has now been replaced by a more recent photo of the Berkshire Yeomanry.

In September 1917 the Queen paid a visit to the Guildhall and inspected the Royal portraits, examining them all very carefully. A few days later the Mayor received the following letter:

Dear Mr Mayor,
I am commanded by the King and Queen to inform you that to commemorate the adoption by his Majesty of 'Windsor' as the name of the Royal House and Family, their Majesties desire to present their State Portraits to the inhabitants of the Royal Borough, to be placed in the collection of portraits of British Sovereigns in their Guildhall. LORD STAMFORDHAM [Private Secretary to the King] Windsor Castle, September 7th 1917.

It was noted that the Guildhall did not have a portrait of Queen Alexandra, this was going to be remedied and in April 1918 all three portraits were presented to the Guildhall. Each portrait had an oak frame decorated with oak-leaves, matching the frame of Edward VII's portrait.

The King and Queen, with Princess Mary and Prince George, visited the Town Hall on Monday 9 September 1918 to see their portraits and those of King Edward VII and Queen Alexandra. The Royal party walked from the Castle to the Guildhall where they were received by the Mayor, Cllr William Carter. They took an interest in the Food Control Office and the varied work of rationing, then returned to the Castle via some of the shops in the High Street.

In January 1918 a Windsor branch of the Comrades of the Great War was established in the Municipal Lounge at the Guildhall.

The Mayor's Prisoner of War Fund arranged a welcome home party for 50 men who had received parcels from the Mayor's fund during the war; a sumptuous tea was laid on for them in the Guildhall. Each man received a souvenir in the shape of a fully loaded cigarette case bearing the borough arms and the date January 1919. Drummer G Nicholls, who had been prisoner since 1914 gave a vote of thanks:

I can truthfully say that, without the goodness, the kindly actions, the unstinted charity of the people of Windsor, we should not be here at this gathering today.

Women

The editorial of the *Windsor Express* on 24 July 1915 stated that women were 'taking the place of men everywhere now.' They were working in the local banks and Post Offices and as ticket inspectors on the railway, even as chauffeurs 'and in nearly every calling they are finding their way'. Two Windsor women were licensed as taxi drivers in January 1915.

In April 1915 an appeal went out to 'strong and vigorous girls and women' to sign an agreement serve their country until the end of the war in the Women's Land Army as War Land Workers.

to

An advertisement in October invited women to join the Women's Army Auxiliary Corps. 5,000 women were needed every week for work with the forces at home and abroad. The Royal Flying Corps required good needlewomen to become sail makers, also needed were store keepers, engineers, cooks, clerks, waitresses, drivers and mechanics.

"I used to laugh at him a little."

MY husband has taken cocoa for years, and I used to laugh at him a little. He's a big, strong man, and I did not think he needed cocoa. It never struck me that the cocoa might have something to do with his good health. But when I went into the heavy hockey myself to feel the strain. "Take a cup," he said to me one day when I was making his cocoa, "it will do you a power of good." I did—and I felt a warm glow all over me. It put new life and strength into me.

I wasn't nearly so tired when I got to bed that night; and next day I started with another cup of cocoa; and the work seemed far lighter than before. I don't laugh at my husband any more—we have our cocoa regularly together.

a cup of
Rowntree's Elect Cocoa
makes a biscuit into a meal

The wealth of new opportunities meant that domestic service was no longer the main occupation for young women, and households found it difficult to get servants. There was a regular run on gas fires in Windsor, owing to their labour-saving capacities and the absence of servants, claimed the *Windsor Express*.

An increasing number of women drivers were placed in charge of tractors. It was worth reporting in the newspaper that some women had recently delivered their tractors by road at distances of 40 miles without mishaps.

Advertisements for women workers in a munitions factory in Middlesex started to appear in the press during 1916. An advertisement on 23 September 1916 called for 10,000 more women, who were needed urgently: the pay was good, the work clean and not difficult, and only a short period of training was needed.

Women Workers' Series.—No. 2.

Women had taken on the roles of men in an increasing way during the Great War. No fewer than 900,000 women were acting as substitutes for men, more than 500,000 were engaged in munitions works, and over 260,000 on the land, although farmers were hard to persuade at first to take them. However, by 1918, many farms were entirely run by women, and the land girls had formed a guild.

Many women joined up as nurses or auxiliary hospital workers and some were killed in the line of duty, but only two names appeared on a Roll of Honour. E A Barnham, Queen Mary's AAC, died on 28 November 1918 and is buried in Windsor Cemetery; she was described as a female worker, but there is no evidence she was a local woman. Sister O. Lundy, third daughter of Mr and Mrs

J W Lundy, 4 Dorset Road, died in hospital in Italy in November 1918, a victim of the Spanish Flu. No female is commemorated on a local War Memorial.

Women also filled men's roles in other ways.

Is this the first female minister?
Windsor Express 5 June 1915

Mrs George Kendall, wife of the minister of the Windsor Primitive Methodist Church, is carrying on his work during his absence as a chaplain at the front. She has already delivered sermons at Windsor, Slough, Chalvey and Sunningdale, and has just got through a bazaar at Slough. Mrs Kendal says she finds preaching easy. She speaks from a few notes only and her congregations are most attentive.

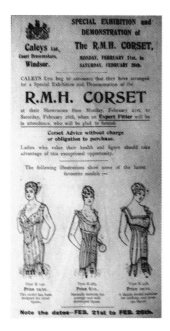

With elections approaching in the autumn of 1918, there was a talk in the Guildhall on 12 October 1918 on the women's vote. For the first time ever, women who were householders or wives of householders and over the age of 30, had the vote, and made sure to use it. The press reported that 'they outvoted' the men.

However some women, who had lost their husbands, faced very uncertain times especially if they had children to bring up. Many were left destitute due to the delay in getting widows pensions from the War Office. The Board of Guardians could only offer a place in the workhouse. The Forces Help Society and Soldiers' and Sailors' Families Association (SSFA) established in 1885 was able to give assistance in cases like these. In 1919 they became SSAFA, with the addition of the Royal Air Force, and also became a registered charity.

Charitable Funds and Fundraising

Windsor people dug deep into their pockets to support a large number of charities and funds to support the war effort. The Mayor immediately set up two funds, one to support the less well off citizens of Windsor and those adversely affected by the war, and one for Belgian Refugees. At the start of 1915 the fund for local purposes stood at £583 1s 5d, his fund for the Relief of Belgian Refugees amounted to £591 11s 7d.

There was also the Windsor Branch of the Prince of Wales' National Relief Fund into which Windsor people had paid £1,004 12s 3d within one month of it opening.

'ARF A MO' KAISER!

Our Soldiers are giving their lives; you are asked to give them something to smoke.

A fund that might be frowned upon today was the Royal Berkshire Regiment Tobacco, Pipe and Cigarette Fund, however it was extremely well supported and stood at £725 3s 8d by the end of October 1914, and in January 1915 it rose to £1,116 10s 1d. Subscribers were listed each week by name, together with the sum given. Soldiers at the front were grateful for the donation for tobacco goods, and many letters of thanks were published in the local newspapers.

Appeals for a fund for local prisoners of war, started by the Mayor, appeared in the newspaper for the first time in June 1915. It received £5 8d in early July and £29 13s by the end of November, but as well as money, articles of clothing and similar items were also received. On 6 November it was reported that weekly parcels containing 'comforts of many and varied kinds' had been sent to prisoners of war, 'carefully packed by a dozen or so lady helpers'; that week the parcels contained warm clothing. Since the fund started, every Windsor man who was a prisoner of war, and who was not being regularly looked after by his regiment, had a parcel sent to him.

On 17 July 1915, Windsorians were asked to give money to the French Relief Fund on French Flag Day. It was very successful, despite the rather inclement weather, and over twenty-thousand miniature flags were sold. A total of £240 was raised, which went towards buying ambulances for France. In October it became known that the ship that had taken 50 fully-equipped motor ambulances across the Channel had been sunk by a German sub-marine. The Mayors who had helped with the appeal were urged to open special subscription lists in their respective towns to buy more ambulances.

During the same month a special appeal was started 'towards paying off the debt upon King Edward's Hospital' which amounted to £3,000. Mr Elliman had given the sum of £1,450 on 7 June, and the rest was raised by subscriptions. The debt was cleared by the end of July.

Another flag day called 'Our Day' on 21 October 1915, raised £255 for the British Red Cross and the Order of St John. In answer to an appeal from the Mayor, the streets were 'gaily beflagged,' and a 'large number of energetic ladies sold button-hole flags'. At the end of November, Windsorians were again asked to open their purses for the Serbian Relief Fund. Another subscription list was set up, but nothing further about the fund appeared in the local newspaper, perhaps people had grown weary of fundraising. However, a 'white elephant' exchange opened by Princess Alexander of Teck in the Guildhall in December, raised

£60 towards the Windsor War Hospital Supply Depot. Some of the articles for disposal had been 'made in Germany' and thus considered to be real 'white elephants.'

By 1916 the Royal Berkshire Prisoner of War Relief Fund had regular despatches of clothing and food. There were 124 prisoners on the book, two more had died, and two who had been sent home disabled told stories of hardship and shortages. The Mayor appealed for gifts in money or in kind, so that a continuous supply of parcels might be kept up: 'the Germans evidently do not believe in giving our soldiers enough food to properly exist on', he said. In return the Mayor received a number of letters from prisoners who had received parcels. 'Everything sent is of remarkable value to us; there is no doubt the whole parcel is really too good for words…' wrote one prisoner. The fund had received £41 19s 10d since May 1915 and £20 1s 4d from the St George's Day Fund.

In November the Mayor's fund had to fall in with the Government's requirements and give up their local organisation to the Central Committee which looked after all prisoners. Henceforth all donations both in money and in kind would be sent to London once a month. The Mayor expressed concern that 'under the new system, local interest in the matter may wane'. It was found that under the old system some prisoners received several parcels while others had none. A letter written to the Mayor from Private C Fordham of the Royal Berks Regiment, who was now a prisoner of war in Germany, followed an article about the changes:

> It is with the greatest pleasure I write these few lines to thank you for the many parcels I have received from you. I am very pleased to say I get them regularly, and they arrive in good condition. I can assure you they are of great value here. It is very good of you all in the old country to think of us, and it is good to know we are not forgotten… We shall soon have Christmas, but I suppose we shall have to make the best of it here, as I don't expect we shall be home for it…

Windsor's Prisoners of War Fund continued to raise funds regularly until the end of the war. Between £10 and £25 came in each month but a minimum of £14 was needed to send the monthly parcels. The money was spent on despatching the goods, all the work was done by volunteers, and the goods were donated.

The Royal Berkshire Regiment Tobacco Pipe and Cigarette Fund seemed to be the most successful; it had raised £2,603 19s 6d by the end of 1916.

A 'Roll of Honour Day' was held on 7 November 1916. There was a bazaar in the Corn Market under the Guildhall. The King sent fruit and vegetables from the Royal gardens, and flags were sold to the strains of the drums and fifes of the Coldstream Guards and the band of the 2nd Life Guards. The sum of £240 was realised despite the heavy downpours. The money was divided between the Lord Kitchener National Memorial Fund and the fund for the benefit of the widows, children and dependants of men of the Royal Navy.

The Government raised extra money for the war effort through War Savings. In an advertisement by the newly established Windsor & District War Savings Committee in November 1916, people were asked to help the country by becoming subscribers for War Savings Certificates. They were promised that 'in five years time you will receive £1 for every 15s 6d you subscribe'. The Association accepted weekly instalments from as little as sixpence, or any number of sixpences, towards buying war loan certificates worth 15s 6d, thus everyone could take part and buy just a small share, or as many as they could afford.

Christmas always brought appeals for presents for soldiers at the front. In December 1916 Mrs Clarke, the mother of the Commanding Officer, 1/4th Royal Berks Regiment, and Colonel A F Ewen appealed for donations towards a fund of £200 for providing Christmas gifts for the men of the regiment. They had been with the British Expeditionary Force since March 1915.

Each year there were 'Flag Days' and 'Our Days' which raised money for the Red Cross or other worthy causes, but the most money raised in one week by the people of Windsor was for the war itself. War Weapons Week from 8 to 13 July 1918 aimed to raise £20,000 in Windsor and Eton – a sum recently raised by Wokingham. The amount actually raised, through the sale of National War Bonds and National Savings Certificates, was a staggering £75,000.

Entertainment

Cinema

The cinema had become very popular by 1914; however when war broke out there was only one picture house in Peascod Street, the Windsor Cinema. The film industry immediately responded to the war situation, although all films at the time were silent. The films on offer during the first weeks of August 1914 were *Crucible of Fate, Britain's Might* and *Dangers of the Veld*, but locals were also soon able to see actual footage of the war. In September the cinema featured *Whirlpool of War* and promised that all war pictures obtainable would continue to be

shown. In October, *Belgium at Bay* featured 'many scenes of desolation in that unfortunate land', including footage of 'the Germans entering Brussels', taken at 'considerable risk'. Later that month, *True Irish Hearts* was followed by *In the Wake of the Huns*. Footage of the evacuation of Ghent and Ostend was shown in November, and *Fighting around Dixmude* in December, together with the films *Who shall Judge, The Brute* and *Indian Troops in England*. There was also a weekly cartoon called *Bully Boys*.

Patriotic and military films, many shot at the front, continued to be popular during 1915 such as that of *King George at Ypres*. A drama called *For the Honour of Belgium*, and the naval drama *England's Menace* were on offer in January. There was also a mock harlequinade called *The Clowns of Europe*, in which the Kaiser and

Crown Prince played leading roles. The patriotic trend continued with *The Heroine of Mons*, which was much acclaimed.

As a result of a DORA regulation, the Windsor Magistrates decided in February 1915 that there would be no further film shows on Sundays. The decision generated a lot of debate, with many people pointing out that if the soldiers billeted locally could not go to the cinema on a Sunday evening they would spend the time in the public houses instead.

Footage from the front such as *Bombardment of the Dardanelles, War in Africa* showing British troops in that continent, or *Skirmishing Party in Flanders*, remained popular viewing. They were combined with cartoons like *John Bull's Scrap Book,* military dramas such as *In the Ranks* and regular feature films like *The Prisoner of Zenda*, or *Atar of the North*. Charlie Chaplin was always popular with *His New Profession*, or *Charlie's Knight Out*, and of course *The Tramp*.

During 1916 the Windsor Cinema continued to show a variety of films, from the patriotic and military to dramas and comedies. The war films tried to keep the public abreast of what was going on not only at the fighting end with *The Russian Campaign, From Trench to Trench,* and *Destruction of a German Blockhouse,* but also the home front with titles like *Manufacture of Huge Shells*. Of course there were always *John Bull's War Cartoons*.

Some of the regular features included *The Eternal City, The Girl Who Might Have Been, The Mill on the Floss,* and *Peer Gynt*.

A new picture theatre was opened in May in the Royal Albert Institute, which aimed 'to show only wholesome pictures'. The newspaper reported that there had been an

…outcry against picture theatres owing to the bad effect a certain class of films had on the minds of boys, there are few things so bad for a child's mind than to see gruesome and blood-curling pictures.

The cinema opened with *Flanders my Country* and *Two little Vagabonds*. The theatre also put on the pantomime *Cinderella* with a company of 30 children. Another cinema, the Windsor Empire in Peascod Street, opened in June 1916 with titles like *The Fallen Idol* and *The Hun's Daughter*. In October the greatest of First World War films came to the Windsor Empire; *The Battle of the Somme* was shown in five reels from Monday 30 October. It was the war picture everybody was talking about and an advertisement in the *Windsor Express* claimed that the film 'presents and brings home to everybody what our Gallant Lads have got to do to defeat the Prussian War Lord'. Mr Lloyd George, after seeing the film exclaimed: 'If the exhibition of this picture all over the world does not end the war, God help civilisation!' A film critic declared:

It is not only a great war picture, but it is really the finest peace picture the world has seen, for whosoever sees it should, once and for all, condemn the pretensions of those who too long have claimed the right to doom their fellow creatures to suffering and destruction for the gratification of their mad ambitions'.

The cinema recorded full houses the week the film was shown, and it has remained the most watched film in the history of the British film industry.

At the beginning of 1917 the Empire started with a special star variety programme as well as films like *Answer the Call*. The films of the month were the French official war films, which dealt with the heavy artillery, 'from the manufacture of the guns to their work on the field of action'.

The Windsor Cinema started the year with the *Spirit of France* and *Lady Windermere's Fan*. *The Battle of the Ancre and the Advance of the Tanks*, were shown both at the Windsor Cinema and

WINDSOR EMPIRE,

PEASCOD-STREET, WINDSOR.

MONDAY, TUESDAY AND WEDNESDAY,

FRENCH OFFICIAL WAR OFFICE FILMS,

Guns and Munitions, Official Pictures ; and an English Drama in 3 parts,

"J.M THE SCORPION."

THURSDAY, FRIDAY AND SATURDAY,

"THE MOTTO ON THE WALL,"

"I shall pass through this world but once ; any good therefore that I can do, or any kindness that I can show to any human being, let me do it now. Let me not defer or neglect it for I shall not pass this way again."

Admission and Hours as usual.

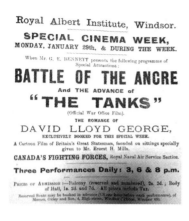

the Royal Albert Institute Cinema. The film had attracted huge crowds in London and there was great public interest in the new tank.

The Empire Theatre closed in February, and the Royal Albert Institute obtained the exclusive rights of all the latest Chaplin films like *Charlie Shanghaied* and *The Vagabond*. At the Windsor Cinema Mary Pickford made her appearance in *Madame Butterfly*, and later in the comedy *Hulda from Holland*. Other notable films of 1917 were *The Nation's Peril*, a tale of German espionage, *The Picture of Dorian Grey*, and *The Vicar of Wakefield* with Sir John Hare as Dr Primrose. *The Birth of a Nation* about the American Civil War, was acclaimed as the 'most wonderful film that had been seen at Windsor'. There was less war footage in 1917 than in previous years, however, films with a military content but which were also entertaining like *Tommy Atkins, The Boys of the Old Brigade* or *The Girl who loved a Soldier* were ever popular. There was also more comedy; people had become war weary and wanted to be entertained.

During 1918 Windsor cinemas continued to show a mixture of drama and comedy, but war-related films had become less popular. Only the *History of the War*, shown at the beginning of the year, drew the crowds. The main films *Rebecca of Sunny Brook Farm* starring Mary Pickford, *Merry Miss Madcap*, 'the story of a fascinating young Miss who would manage her own love affairs in her own ways', *Nanette of the Wilds* featuring Pauline Frederick, and *What Every Woman Knows*, all reflected an increased interest in the role of women. There was also Fatty Arbuckle in *A Rough House* or *Fatty at Coney Island* and the ever-popular Charlie Chaplin films. On Armistice Day the Cinema was showing *The Splendid Coward*, starring Houghton Townley.

Theatre

The Theatre Royal in Windsor closed in June 1914 for the

season; it was expected to re-open in the autumn, but there was no explanation why it did not do so. Certainly the staff had responded enthusiastically to the call of duty, which may have left the theatre short staffed.

On 5 December a letter appeared in the *Windsor Express*:

> May I suggest that the present would be an opportune time to re-open the Windsor Theatre Royal? The town has loyally responded to the strain of providing accommodation for several thousand soldiers, but it must be confessed that there is a very limited number of recreations open to them in their spare time. There can be no question that the Theatre would be well-filled every night…

It finally re-opened on Boxing Day 1914 with *A Pair of Silk Stockings*. For the New Year there was some much needed light entertainment in the form of vaudeville. There were two pantomimes: *Aladdin* in January and *Dick Whittington* in February. Plays like *Charley's Aunt, Two Little Drummer Boys* and *Grumpy*, also promised light entertainment and laughter. In March 1915, the musical comedy *The Quaker Girl* was followed by another revue *To-day and Tomorrow*. On 24 April the stirring military play *The Second in Command*, was preceded each evening by *The Call of Duty*. *Gypsy Love* and *A Trip to Chicago* were staged in May, as well as the musical play *The Marriage Market*. Tickets cost from 6½d to 3s.

After the summer closure, the theatre reopened at the end of September with a programme that included the musical comedy *All the*

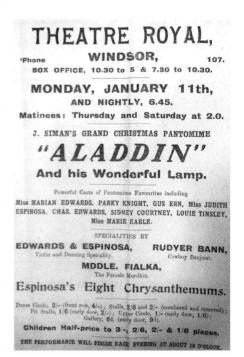

THEATRE ROYAL,
WINDSOR,   107.
'Phone
BOX OFFICE, 10.30 to 5 & 7.30 to 10.30.

MONDAY, JANUARY 11th,
AND NIGHTLY, 6.45.
Matinees: Thursday and Saturday at 2.0.

J. SIMAN'S GRAND CHRISTMAS PANTOMIME

"*ALADDIN*"
And his Wonderful Lamp.

Powerful Caste of Pantomime Favourites including
Miss MARIAN EDWARDS, PARKY KNIGHT, GUS ERN, Miss JUDITH
ESPINOSA, CHAS. EDWARDS, SIDNEY COURTNEY, LOUIE TINSLEY,
Miss MARIE EARLE.

SPECIALITIES BY

EDWARDS & ESPINOSA,   RUDYER BANN,
Violin and Dancing Speciality.   Cowboy Banjoist.

MDDLE. FIALKA,
The Female Mordkin.

Espinosa's Eight Chrysanthemums.

Dress Circle, 3/- (front row, 4/-); Stalls, 2/6 and 2/- (numbered and reserved);
Pit Stalls, 1/6 (early door, 2/-); Upper Circle, 1/- (early door, 1/6);
Gallery, 6d. (early door, 9d.).

Children Half-price to 3/-, 2/6, 2/- & 1/6 places.

THE PERFORMANCE WILL FINISH EACH EVENING AT ABOUT 10 O'CLOCK.

Nice Girls, and ended with the pantomime *Robinson Crusoe*.

The 1916 season started with an increase in the price of the cheapest seats, which were now 9d. The extensive programme ran from January to 6 March, and included comedies of which *The Glad Eye* was hailed as the funniest farce within memory. The pantomime *Little Jack Horner* concluded the season. The theatre remained closed until 1 October 1917; this may have been because many theatre staff and actors had been called up. The new season started with *When Knight Were Bold*, the funniest farce of the century. 'In these days of anxiety… nothing is more beneficial than the tonic of laughter', reported the *Windsor Express*. There was more comedy in *Nobody's Daughter* and *A Game for Two*, but *Damaged Goods* was a play that dealt with social evil.

In 1918, the Theatre Royal started the year with *Cinderella* and *Dick Whittington*, as well as *Three Weeks*, 'an epoch-making love drama', followed in February with the play *A Better 'Ole*, which looked at the war from a less serious angle. It was based on the characters Old Bill, Alf and Bert, created by Captain Bruce Bairnsfather.

March offered *The Love Chase*, a musical comedy in three acts, and more seriously in May *A Butterfly on the Wheel*, the great Divorce Court play. *The Fatal Wedding* was staged in April, 'A play of New York life that is drawing all London to the Haymarket Theatre'.

The Theatre Royal closed for the summer vacation and re-opened on 26 August with *My Lady Frayle* a musical comedy, followed in September by *Peg 'O My Heart*, a comedy of youth, and in October *The Balkan Princess* another musical comedy. Another farcical comedy, *Monty's Flapper,* was staged in November.

On Armistice Day the Theatre was performing *The Misleading*

Lady, a comedy. The *Windsor Express* reported that:

> A spirit of jollity engendered by the peace news, as well as a good audience, invaded the Theatre and had its effects on both sides of the footlights.

Although there was a shortage of food, there was plenty of money about. Not just in Windsor, but up and down the country places of amusement were filled nightly, theatres and picture houses were doing good business. The Theatre Royal Windsor was filled to capacity when it was open, and The Royal Albert Institute sold out for all performances of its pantomime *Cinderella*, in addition the large hall was packed for Saturday concerts.

Two weekly concerts and two lantern lectures at the YMCA Hut on Bachelors' Acre were always well attended.

Talks, shows, exhibitions and concerts

Many or these were associated with fund raising, and were generally well attended. Only after a concert of the Windsor and Eton Choral Society in December 1914 was it felt that 'the attendance still leaves something to be desired'. Perhaps soldiers were looking for less serious entertainment. There is no record of Music Hall in Windsor until soldiers created their own in the YMCA Hut on the Acre. Military music was well received, like the free concert put on for soldiers in December at the Baldwin Institute in Eton, or a concert in aid of the Mayor's Poor Box, held at the Conservative Club, where the drums and fifes of the Coldstream Guards played.

The Royal Albert Institute provided entertainment for troops in the form of variety shows, concerts, lectures, and exhibitions. In October 1914 there was an exhibition of flowers, fruit and vegetables on behalf of the Mayor's local relief fund. A lecture on the German composer Robert Schumann, with musical illustration of orchestral works and songs, was well attended in November, but it was stressed that Schumann's Germany was very different, then it was a country of 'learning and music'. A lantern-slide talk *The Sister Ireland* was also well attended, so was a Hilaire Belloc lecture on 10 May 1915, on the latest developments of the war, in which he said there was good ground for optimism for the victory of the Allies. Tickets ranged from one to four shillings, but there were always concessions for soldiers. The Windsor and Eton Choral Society's performance of the *Messiah* and *May Queen* at the Albert Institute was more successful than their earlier concert.

The Guildhall was another venue for concerts for the troops. The Duchess of Albany and Princess Alexander of Teck 'helped to raise the moral among the troops billeted in the Borough' by their attendance at a concert on 23 February 1915.

The 5th East Surrey Regiment enjoyed weekly evening concerts at the Trinity Parish Rooms while they were billeted in Windsor during 1915, mostly organised by the soldiers themselves with talents drawn from among the troops. In charge was Private Field, helped by soldiers of the Life Guards, and they always included a hearty sing-along and comic sketches.

Once the YMCA Hut on Bachelors' Acre was up and running in early 1915, it became the venue for a variety of entertainments, including homespun concerts like those put on by the East Surreys. There was an entertainment committee, which made sure everybody was catered for. The *Windsor Express* reported on 9 December 1916:

Passers along Victoria Street, Windsor, little think that the beehive Hut in the acre is the hive of activity that it is. Open every day from 2.30pm it is a boon to hundreds of our Tommies daily. Between 6 and 7pm sixty or seventy men may often be counted writing letters. Two good concerts are provided weekly and billiards and games at any time. On Sunday evenings a short service is held after the usual Church hours, at which ministers of all denominations do their part. There is a Post Office and a counter where refreshments are provided at popular prices...

There were concerts at Victoria Barracks when 'the large dining hall was filled with soldiers and families'. Band concerts, which were free of charge, were also held at Holy Trinity Church. In November 1917 a competition concert was held at the Parish Room, where soldiers could show off their talents. More serious

Sunday lectures were regularly held at the Windsor Reformed Church in their 'Empire Theatre' with titles such as: *A Message from the Front, Germany and the Next War, The Harvest of Souls* but also *When the Men Come Back, What do they Need?* Talks were often given by visiting vicars and there was band music before and after the talk, probably to get people in, but admission was free.

Dances

There were very few dances advertised in the local newspapers during the war. Only Oakley Hall invited members of the forces to dances, with tickets costing 1s or 1s 6d for doubles. Once the war was over, everybody seemed to be dancing; Victory balls were held in both barracks. There were balls at the Castle Hotel with a jazz band playing from 9pm to 2am, 10s 6d included refreshments. The Royal Albert Institute held dances each Saturday from 25 Jan 1919 with a Fancy Dress Ball held on Monday 3 February; tickets cost 2s.

There was also a new cinema in Eton in 1919, which opened with *In the Days of Trafalgar* with Charles Hawtrey.

Sport

Local newspapers did not carry the sports pages expected today. There was little reporting on national football or cricket, only the occasional local fixture. Sporting events tended to centre on the soldiers in the town, with inter-regimental matches dominating the fixtures. A cricket match played at Victoria Barracks in July 1917 between the Coldstream Guards and the Royal Flying Corps, resulted in a win for the Coldstream Guards. During the winter months there were football matches.

Boxing was very popular. A forces boxing competition at the Theatre Royal was reviewed in depth in the local paper on 3 April 1915. 'One of the finest displays of boxing ever given at Windsor', enthused the reporter. On 12 May a 'Boxing Entertainment' was held at the Conservative Club Hall, with the proceeds going to King Edward VII Hospital. The only competitors were soldiers.

Horse racing was the other spectator sport that featured regularly. Steeplechases took place at the Royal Windsor Racecourse on 14 and 15 August 1914, and they continued with regular meetings throughout the war. Advertisements in the newspaper offered outings to other racecourses; motor charabancs left for Newbury from the White Hart Hotel at a cost of 7s 6d; with the price of tickets for the enclosure at 30s, this was not for the low or even average earner.

Ascot racecourse remained closed throughout the war. However, the 'five shilling stands' were used as a reception centre for wounded soldiers sent to the new military hospital that was being built across the road, (now Heatherwood Hospital)

Trade And Rationing

Windsor traders 'jumped on the bandwagon' of war fever without delay. A week into the war, Herbert's Supply Stores Ltd of Eton sold 'The Daily Mail War Map of Europe' for 6d, or on cloth at 2s, and flags and pins at 6d a dozen. Caleys Ltd advertised hospital requisites, army flannels, rugs and blankets, on page one, and Creak's advertised similar goods on page four of the *Windsor Express*. In October, Herbert's Supply Stores announced their stock of 'Special Hampers for Soldiers', and E V Tull, confectioners of Thames Street sold 'a highly nutritious form of plain chocolate specially suited for the use of our soldiers on Active Service'. Wills & Son of Eton and Thames Street, offered to convert ordinary cars to ambulances, at low cost. One trader put a humorous notice in the Observer claiming, 'Business as usual During Alterations to the Map of Europe'. Did he know how true his words were going to be?

Many advertisements soon took on a military flavour, especially those for soap. Lifebuoy, Pears', Lux, Rinso, and Sunlight were all vying with each other as to which could keep the soldiers cleanest. Lifebuoy soap enlisted a soldier to 'counter-attack upon the germs and microbes of disease'. Pears' soap used the slogan: 'Links in Britain's Chain of War'. Sunlight soap declared that the British Tommy was the cleanest fighter.

Christmas goods were advertised from early December 1914 with the emphasis on warm clothing for 'Troops serving at home and abroad', and at Creak's Christmas Bazaar 'British-made goods for British people', could be purchased.

Wood's Pharmacy at 50 High Street had 'Welcome Gifts for the Troops' which included meat lozenges, corn remedies, elastic knee-caps, waterproof pillows at 7s 6d, field service body belts at 2s 6d, vacuum flasks at 4s 6d, or Auto-strop razors and Gillette razors at one guinea. A C Caffyn of High Street offered useful presents for the men in Khaki and Blue, which included thick woollen underwear. There was no shortage of vine fruit for plum puddings at Christmas.

With the threat of Zeppelin raids in 1915, F Radford, Castle Hill Stores, came up with a really clever idea to entice customers into his shop. In case of Zeppelin or Aeroplane raid, 'we shall be pleased to permit a limited number of citizens into our capacious cellars, where they will be interested in a very large stock of fine wines and spirits.'

During 1915, the shops were well stocked despite shortages, and a lack of male staff. Only goods 'made in Germany' were missing, which gave a boost to British manufacturing.

In June 1915 a proposal to close shops earlier was put forward to the Borough Council by the Windsor Earlier Closing Committee. A number of smaller tradesmen protested, claiming that most of their customers shopped after they had finished work, and many letters on this controversial subject appeared in the correspondence columns of the *Windsor Express*. Major tradesmen agreed

272

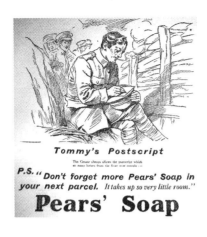

Tommy's Postscript

The Censor always allows the postscript which
so many letters from the front now contain :—

P.S. "*Don't forget more Pears' Soap in
your next parcel. It takes up so very little room.*"

Pears' Soap

to close their establishments at 7pm Mondays to Thursdays, at 8pm on Fridays and 10pm on Saturdays. Although the Borough Council did not see fit to make this compulsory, thirty of the principal traders and most grocers and butchers of the town voluntarily started to close earlier in the evening from the end of October 1915. It was not until 1916 that DORA passed legislation on closing times.

Windsor publicans, however, were restricted in selling alcohol under the new DORA Regulations. From 21 August 1915, no alcohol could be sold to soldiers between the hours of 12 noon and 2.30pm and between 6pm and 8pm – this was extended to 9pm in September. These restrictions, of course, soon became the norm for everyone, and continued, with some small changes for many years. The November and December issues of the *Windsor Express* hotly debated the evils and otherwise of alcohol, but also the demise of the licensed victuallers whose trade was hard hit. Two of the oldest public houses in Windsor closed, the New Inn in Park Street shut in January 1918, and the Red Lion in Thames Street was not able to renew its licence 'on the grounds of redundancy'.

Banks had to reduce their opening hours in December 1915 due to 'the great depletion of their respective staffs in consequence of the war'. Barclays, and the London County & Westminster Bank (now NatWest) gave notice that they would in future open their local branches from 10am to 3pm on weekdays and 9.30am to 12.30pm on Saturdays.

Although the huge shipping losses had created severe food shortages, goods from around the world were still on offer at Windsor shops; coffee from Mexico, cheese from Holland, Canada and New Zealand, and bacon from Denmark.

The price of foodstuff started to go up during 1915. In September the price of milk rose from 4d to 5d a quart. In November, Creak's

Christmas Bazaar urged people to shop early for Christmas, before the rush began.

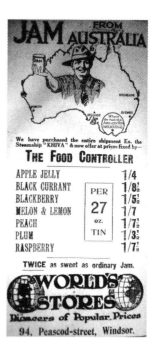

The summer of 1916 did not bring the usual return of visitors to Windsor. Pleasure boat owners on the Thames were experiencing a difficult time and there were fewer notices in the local newspapers advertising boat trips than in previous years. The stores continued to advertise goods for servicemen, from clothes to chocolates, and Oxley & Son sold large sheets of waterproof brown paper at 6d a sheet for sending parcels to soldiers on active service.

Bread prices went up again in 1916. In January 1914 a 4lb loaf cost 5½d, by January 1916 it had risen to 9d, and in April of that year the price of beer rose by 1d per pint. The price of milk went up to 6d per quart in November. At the same time a newspaper feature claimed that although some articles of food had become dearer, others were cheaper, and the average increase in retail prices was less than one per cent, however, the buying power of a sovereign had gone down since the start of the war, to around 13s 4d. Only the rates had actually become cheaper as there had been a reduction by 8 ½d in the pound in April 1916.

The Trading with the Enemy (Amendment) Bill came into force in February 1916. German toys had already been singled out, although some goods still entered via America. German made pianos were targeted now, they could no longer be tuned by German companies. Dyson & Sons emphasised in advertisements that they employed only British subjects as tuners.

The shortage of staff also took its toll on trade. In October 1916, Messrs Aldridge and Son, old established bakers of Peascod Street, 'closed their business owing to their staff being taken for military purposes'. Mr Aldridge recalled his great-grandfather telling him that he stood at the shop door watching the Royal Horse Guards go by on their way to Waterloo.

The shortage of eggs pushed the price of cooking eggs up to 3d, and new laid to 4d, just before Christmas 1916. Fears were expressed that the cost of making a Christmas pudding would be too high for many poor families.

The New Lodge Estate owned by the Van de Weyer family was broken up in 1916 and sold at the Town Hall Windsor. There were 70 lots, including Monkey Island Hotel and Water Oakley Farm; only seven remained unsold including New Lodge itself. The sale realised over £90,000.

The *Windsor Express* increased its price from 1d to 1½d from 24 March 1917, railway fares went up by fifty per cent, and the General District Rate increased from 2s 4d to 2d 8d. In April 1917 the price of beer went up again, bitter went from 6d a pint to 10d.

Waste paper became the new commodity; it had been sold at £1 per ton, but in early 1917 was worth between £4 and £5 per ton. Everyone was encouraged by the Council to collect waste paper.

In August 1917, the Board of Agriculture and Fisheries made an Order authorising the killing and eating of a number of migratory wild birds from 1 August to the next close season, with a view to increase the food supply. Curlew, Knot, Whimbrel, Golden Plover, Red Shank, Godwit, Snipe, Woodcock, Teal, Widgeon, Mallard, Shoveler, Pochard, Pintail, Brent Goose, Barnacle Goose, Pink-Footed Goose, White-fronted Goose and Grey-Leg Goose could be killed and eaten.

In September 1917, the Board of Education encouraged children to collect horse chestnuts, which could replace the grain used in certain industrial processes essential to the war, thus releasing more grain for human consumption.

With Christmas 1917 approaching, Windsor shops started once more to advertise presents for 'our soldiers'. Khaki gloves at 2s 6d, socks, woollen shirts and khaki handkerchiefs were on offer at W Creak Ltd. The Secretary of the War

Office stated that soldiers at the front would get half a pound of Christmas pudding each, although many people at home would have to go without that year.

With meat, butter and margarine all in short supply, people ate more potatoes; luckily they were plentiful in 1917 due to a good harvest, although they had been in short supply earlier in the year.

Herbert's Supply Stores offered 'Special Bargains for your boys in khaki' such as coffee, sardines, biscuits and cigarettes. Parcels were packed free of charge, but carriage cost 10s 6d. They advised that their jams (marmalade was not available) should be 'dispatched at once' in the Christmas parcel for 'your friends serving in distant parts'.

Another problem was the scarcity of meat. At one Slough meat market in 1918, for instance, there were only two heifers and a sow for slaughter, whereas the previous year there had been twenty-four bullocks, four heifers and four cows. Many Windsor butchers closed during most of the day because they had nothing to sell, only rabbits were available and in great demand. To help the meat shortage, pig breeding was encouraged. Windsor shops like Darville & Son offered meat substitutes in the form of pulses.

Another commodity in short supply was coal, as many miners were at the front. This affected gas and electricity output, thus coal had to be rationed eventually. Anyone wanting coal had to register with a coal merchant.

Windsor Council Rates, which had been kept low throughout the war, and had even decreased by 1d, went up by 3d and Poor Rates by 2d in 1918.

The Post Office also had to tighten its belt, it closed from 1pm to 2pm, excepting for urgent telegrams, and collections from town letter boxes were reduced to five times daily on weekdays. Letters posted in time for the second collection, at 10.30 am, would still be delivered in London on the same day.

Many basic food items became too expensive for many people, eggs could cost up to 4d each and butter 2s 2d per pound; Darville & Son offered eggs from 1½d to 3½d each, and butter from 1s 10d to 2s. People were encouraged to eat margarine, 'Darville's Royal Margarine in Perfection' cost 1s, (it went up by 2d in May 1918) but 'Milk & Nut' margarine cost just 8d.

At the start of 1918 the Windsor Borough Food Control Committee introduced a temporary and voluntary scheme of food rationing to a guaranteed minimum of one ounce of tea and two ounces of butter, margarine or other fat per week. The Committee hoped that everyone would 'make the scheme a success by the exercise of self-restraint and consideration for the needs of others'. They also wanted to avoid issuing ration cards, but the scheme was not very successful. Hoarding food became a criminal offence, but anyone who was caught could avoid being prosecuted by offering up their stock to King Edward VII Hospital.

A system of rationing came into force on 13 July 1918. Ration cards were introduced for sugar, fats and meat. The sale of tea was regulated, it could not be sold for less than 2s 8d per lb. This was to stop customers transferring their custom from shop to shop.

Householders had to apply for a sugar card, and name the grocer they wished to supply them. One Windsor grocer took the opportunity to advertise: 'Who is to be the Grocer? This is the question and how can it be better answered than by selecting the well-known firm of Darville & Son'.

There were some concessions for jam makers, who could apply for extra sugar at the Control Office at the Town Hall. What jam there was had to be secured for the Army. Dr E Lyttelton, former headmaster of Eton College wrote to The Times: 'The prospective scarcity of jam is not pleasant, but how is it that German prisoners are said to be enjoying plenty?'

Some traders inevitably fell foul of the food laws. Food

Controllers had fixed the maximum prices of meat, butter, cheese, fish and bread, which aimed to stop profiteering. In August 1918, Richard Hughes, fishmonger of Peascod Street was fined £1 for selling herrings at 8d a pound when the Food Office had set the price at 7d.

Another untapped source of food supply was fresh-water fish. The King gave permission to net the lakes in Windsor Great Park, and the Royal Albert Institute gave a demonstration of cooking fresh-water fish in June 1918. (The Germans were said to make great use of fresh-water fish). The following week, 1,300lb of fish were taken from Windsor Great Park and sold, with the proceeds going to the British Red Cross Society. Much of the fish was cooked and served at the communal kitchen.

Food shortages encouraged allotment holders to grow more and more vegetables, in particular potatoes. During 1917 allotment holders of the country grew over a million tons of vegetables. About 200,000 new allotments had been created under the Cultivation of Lands Orders, and it was estimated that there were about one million allotments in England and Wales in 1918.

Another 100 plots had been made available in Clewer ready for the spring cultivation of 1917, and seeds that had been ordered were despatched on 9 March. A plot in Bolton Road, the 'Windsor Fair Ground', was divided into 79 ten-pole plots and in Old Windsor 2½ acres of glebe land in Church Road were staked out and instantly let. The tenants were already working on them before the deeds were signed.

There were 1,163 allotment holders in Windsor, Clewer and Eton. As all fit young men were fighting at the front, allotments were managed by older men and women, all doing their bit in the production of food. Women who held allotments could get help from schoolboys to dig their plots. Even the King was said to have been planting potatoes at Frogmore.

Pilfering from allotments became a problem during the summer of 1918 when food shortages were at their most severe, but as much of the pilfering was done by children, magistrates were advised to resort to corporal punishment, rather than fining the parents.

Crime

Crime reporting at the outbreak of war had changed little since the early days of the *Windsor Express*, except that children were no longer judged in an adult court. The most commonly reported offences were still drunkenness, disorderly behaviour and assault. Even swearing in public places would be punished. Typical examples are:

Ernest Davis, aged 90, was summoned for being drunk, and assaulting George Goodchild at the Why Not public house in Oxford Road on 8 August 1914. Later that month Sillas Groves, licensee of the Duke's Head and barmaid Mrs Tindall, were charged with assaulting Sophia Snook; she had been calling Mr Groves 'a dirty rotter'. Morby Hutton and his wife were charged with being drunk and disorderly in Peascod Street in October. Hutton had 63 previous convictions against him, 38 of which were for drunkenness. William Pearson of Clewer Fields was fined 2s 6d for swearing in the street in 1917.

A fine of a few shillings was the usual punishment, or a few days in prison if the fine could not be paid. For more serious offences, the culprit was committed for trial at the Quarter Sessions or Assizes.

War changed the crime scene as DORA created a new list of criminal offences, the guardians of which were the new Special Constables. 'The work of the Special Constables in Windsor could not be too highly rated', said HM Inspector of Constabulary for England and Wales. They patrolled the roads, and kept observation on suspects for the purpose of preventing and detecting crime and offences against the Defence of the Realm Act. The most common were motoring offences, such as showing too much light, or having no rear light. Mrs Minnie Miles of Victor Road was charged on 11 September 1914 'that she did unlawfully exhibit a bright light without the same being effectually shaded and obscured'. This was the first summons of its kind in Windsor and was dismissed under the First Offenders Act.

On 12 April 1915, a new bye-law made it imperative that a red light should be fixed at the rear of a bicycle. The *Windsor Express*, in its editorial of 25 September 1915, noted that:

> On Monday morning last, there were no fewer than nine defendants charged at Windsor Police Court with riding bicycles without red rear lamps to their machines, and in practically every case the defence was that 'they did not know of the Order'.

George Meadows of Old Windsor was summoned for failing to have his number plates properly illuminated, and Lt Symondson was fined 10s for 'driving a motor-car with lights of greater brightness than necessary,' at Clewer on 18 July 1915.

The problem became more complicated as new regulations came into force. George Evens was the first to be charged and fined 5s in 1917 under a new order, which made it obligatory to display two white lights at the front of the vehicle. There were weekly reports of persons failing to show the correct lights on their bikes or cars, the fines were usually 5s, although the maximum penalty could be £100.

With the first Zeppelin raids in January 1915, came the black-out regulations, called the Lighting Order. Again this was one order many people fell foul of, like Joseph Mercer of 50 Thames Street who was fined £1 for failing to shade the inside light of his shop, as was Edward Taylor of the Windsor Steam Laundry in Peascod Street. The editorial of the *Windsor Express* on 4 March 1916 warned the people of Windsor:

> A number of lighting prosecutions were heard again this week in the Windsor Police Court, and fines of varied amounts inflicted by the Magistrates. It will thus be seen that the authorities are determined to carry out the orders vigorously. We would impress on all the residents the necessity for lowering their lights as much as possible, and thus assist the authorities

in the protection of the town from air raids. With the arrival of better weather, the Germans are expected to make a number of air expeditions to this country, and we must do our best to make it most difficult for them to 'find' Windsor!

Yet each week there were several convictions reported in the newspaper. Even Caleys department store was summoned for showing lights at the back of the store in Acre Passage, reported by someone living in Clewer. The Mayor, as Chief Magistrate, said he could impose a fine of £100, but would let them off lightly and inflicted a fine of £1. No one was exempt from prosecution and in March 1916, the Vicar of Windsor, the Rev E M Blackie, was fined 5s for unlawfully showing a light at the Parish Room at Grove Road School.

On the night of a Zeppelin raid, 3 September 1916, William Elsbury of Clewer failed to obscure his light; he was further summoned for using obscene language and was fined 15s for the two offences.

On 14 October, the editorial tackled the inconsistencies of fining by different magistrates for these offences; a case from Eton College was dismissed with a caution by Slough Magistrates, whereas a Windsor war widow with four children was fined 10s by the Windsor County Justices, which she could ill afford. 'Surely some uniformity of action is needed'. The following week there were ten Lighting Order offences heard by the Windsor Magistrates, which resulted in higher fines for everyone. The editor stated: 'It has been clearly proved that many towns have escaped the attentions of Zeppelins by carrying out the Lighting Order strictly'. As nights got darker, Lighting Order offences increased, there were twelve convictions in the first week of November 1916.

Being in possession of torches was another new criminal offence. Lennox Bywater was summoned on 22 May 1915 for being in possession of a searchlight in Datchet without lawful authority. The lamp was confiscated and he was fined £10. Philip Lane was fined 5s for using a flare light in the Windsor Market in August 1915. The Chairman of the Magistrates pointed out that the full penalty for such an offence was £100 or six months' imprisonment.

A letter from the Home Office was read at the Windsor County Bench in November 1917, in which people were reminded that it was an offence under Regulation 21A of DORA to shoot carrier and homing pigeons, as they often carried important messages. A number of pigeons had recently been shot, possibly for food. Hannah L Pickstone was charged with failing to hand over a homing pigeon she had found in Windsor, but was fined just 5s, because her husband was in the Army.

In January 1917, it became law that all employers had to display the names of persons of military age in their offices, and a copy had to be sent to the recruiting office. Failure to comply with these regulations could result in fines of £100 or six months in prison. The first person to fall foul of this Act was charged just 5s, as the man in question had only been employed for a few days.

Food regulations were stringently enforced during the war. In June 1915, several Windsor bakers were summoned on charges of selling bread 'otherwise than by weight'. According to the Bread Act of 1836 a quartern loaf should be 4 lb and must be weighed in front of the customer. Some of the bakers summoned had sold 2lb loaves between one and two ounces short. They were fined between 5s and 10s.

Being a foreigner could also land someone in gaol under the Aliens Registration Act 1914. A stranger with a camera taking pictures of the Castle was liable to be arrested. Tourist Edward Newman from Australia was remanded for such a 'crime' and questioned, but eventually discharged. Hans Georg von Chorus was arrested for being in possession of a motor-cycle without permission. He claimed to be an American, but photographs of the Kaiser and letters from Berlin were found on him, and he was sentenced to six months imprisonment in September 1914.

On 27 March 1915, the Windsor Magistrates charged a German national, Gustav Kuhl, with being an alien enemy travelling over five miles from his place of residence without a permit. He was registered to live in London but was discovered in Windsor. Kuhl had previously lived and worked in Windsor and wanted to visit his sick wife, who lived there with her mother, but did not have a travel permit. The Magistrates decided to deal leniently with

Kuhl; he had been interned at the beginning of the war before being released on parole, he was fined £5.

There were also a number of foreign subjects who failed to report. Julie Joran of King's Road, a French subject, failed to furnish the registration officer with particulars of her address, and she was fined 5s.

The large numbers of soldiers in town created other problems. First reported in the newspaper were three wounded soldiers who had been sent home from the front to recover at Victoria Barracks; they were caught stealing a box of figs value one shilling, but were handed over to the military authorities.

Pte Alec F H Small, 6th East Surrey Regiment, was charged with stealing a bicycle in March 1915. He was remanded for seven days. In April 1915 three soldiers of the Queen's West Surrey Regiment stole three billiard balls from the Royal Albert Institute. 'After all the kindness the Albert Institute had shown the soldiers it was a poor return for them to steal the Institute property,' said the Magistrate, but decided to deal leniently with them and bound them over in the sum of £5 for three months.

In May, Pte John W Palmer appeared before the Magistrates for stealing soldiers' letters and parcels, many written to soldiers at the front. He had been in trouble previously for taking other soldiers' property, and was sent to prison for six months. Henry Bartle, a private in the Coldstream Guards, was fined 'only' 13s for stealing a cigarette case and cigarettes at Victoria Barracks, because his senior officer gave him a good character. The constable said that the question of robberies at Victoria Barracks was a serious one. Re-enlisted man George A Hyde was charged in June with being drunk, using foul language and breaking 14 panes of glass at the police station. As he had similar previous convictions he was sent to prison for five months.

In July, a 15-year-old drummer boy in the Coldstream Guards, who had joined the Army from a reformatory school, was charged with stealing a pair of rubber heel-pads value 6d. He pleaded guilty and had confessed to the Police that 'his only trouble was that he could not keep his hands from stealing'. The Magistrates told him that he was 'rather an incorrigible young man and he would receive six strokes with the birch rod.'

In August 1915, a serious charge of assault with intent to do grievous bodily harm to Emily Smith was brought against Pte Henry Lemon, Royal Berkshire Regiment, living in Clewer. Pte Lemon denied the charge and volunteered for the front.

Another soldier who was charged with assault was Pte James Allagan, Reserve Battalion Coldstream Guards. On 14 August 1915, Allagan assaulted three people: Police Constable Tamlin – 'he kicked him and forced his fingers into his nostrils' – Pte Frederick Stone – 'he put his fingers into his eye, causing him great pain', and Joseph Fellowes. He was sentenced to six months' hard labour.

Cpl L Barnett, Coldstream Guards, who had distinguished himself in the field by being awarded the DCM, was charged with stealing a number of postal orders with a total value of 9s 6d, and a parcel containing socks, cigarettes and soap. He was sentenced to eighteen weeks in prison with hard labour. In January 1916, a soldier was charged with using obscene language, and he was fined 10s, another soldier who was charged with obtaining 2s by false pretences was bound over for £5.

A Court Martial at Victoria Barracks was reported in depth on 4 March 1916. Pte Ernest W Glithero, Coldstream Guards, was charged with stealing half a leg of mutton. He was an ex-soldier, who had re-enlisted as soon as war broke out. As he was very popular with his comrades who thought he had been 'stitched up', they raised money for a defence lawyer with the result that he was acquitted of the charge. He was, however, convicted of being in improper possession of public property, but this was quashed by a higher military authority.

On 18 May 1918, two black Canadian soldiers, Charlie Some and George Albert, serving with the Construction Battalion, were charged with being drunk and disorderly in Peascod Street,. They were fined 2s each. More serious was a charge of attempted murder; on 24 May 1919 Sgt Thomas Le Blanc, Canadian Forestry Corps, Windsor Great Park, was charged with attempting to murder Joseph Killen, the case was referred to the Sessions. On 12 July 1919, two soldiers from the Canadian camp, were charged with passing a counterfeit £5 note.

There were also crimes which may not have happened but for the soldiers.

On 17 April 1916, Mabel Kelsey was charged with murdering her new-born child. She lived at 7 Dunboyne Villas, Elm Road, Clewer, the home of her mother-in-law; her husband had been away on active service with the Royal Garrison Artillery for two years. Mabel Kelsey told the police: 'I had the child in my bedroom; I did not know what to do with it and I went and threw it on the garden'. She was charged with wilful murder and sent to the Berkshire Assizes. The Jury threw out the bill for murder and charged her with manslaughter, to which she pleaded guilty. The defence lawyer said 'the case arose out of the war. Soldiers were billeted in the district, and her husband having been away for a long time, she yielded to temptation.' The Judge said he did not 'look upon the case as a very serious one' and passed sentence of six month's imprisonment.

Martha Louisa Grantham, a servant girl, summoned Pte John Vincent, Coldstream Guards in respect to the maintenance of her illegitimate child. Pte Vincent protested that he was married and blamed the girl for her condition. He was ordered to pay 4s a week till the child was 16 years old. There is no record of whether the girl received any money, as the soldier was soon back at the front. John Vincent is not on any casualty list.

Another person tempted by the war to commit fraud was Edith Hill, landlady of the Sebastopol beer-house, Clewer. She was charged on 5 February 1916 with making a false declaration with an application for Army Separation Pay with a view of defrauding the Government. She was fined £2 or 25 days in prison.

The Problem with Drunkenness.

In 1911 Windsor had a population 12,081, and at that time there was one public house to every 160 inhabitants. One problem DORA tried to grapple with was drunkenness; it was the associated disorderly conduct and bad language, which the authorities aimed to curb, but the main drive, was for a sober workforce especially in munitions factories. The first measure was cutting opening hours of public houses.

Samuel John Walklett, a turner of Albany Road, and recently employed by a local munitions manufacturer, was charged with being drunk at the Stag and Hounds on 25 April 1916, for which he was fined 5s. He was also charged under the Defence of the Realm Regulations for 'unlawfully impeding the production of certain war materials' and 'for delaying the production of certain war materials on 25 April' because he was drunk. For this more serious charge he was committed to prison for one month with hard labour.

It is astonishing how many women were charged with drunkenness; Martha Sheppard was charged with being drunk and disorderly in Surly Hall Road on 26 June 1915. Amy Wilson was charged with being found drunk in charge of a child, and was bound over to the sum of £5. Rose Greenslade, 38, of no fixed abode, was charged in November 1915 with being drunk and disorderly on High Street. She had eight previous convictions of a similar kind against her. In 1916 Ellen Smart, a pedlar, was remanded in custody for being drunk and disorderly in Oxford Road. Alice Ward was detained in the police cells for four days for being drunk and disorderly in Peascod Street on 5 April 1917. There was a perceived increase of drinking amongst women, which was blamed on the war.

By 1918, the Chief Constable noted a marked improvement: 'with reference to drunkenness, I am pleased to report a decrease of 28 – down from 56 – in the number of persons proceeded against'.

The Magistrates continued to deal with all other crime. Theft was mostly petty, two examples from 1915 are typical: William Airston was charged with stealing a loaf of bread, value 4½d and was remanded and later fined. In July, Charles W Hudson of Temple Road was charged with stealing a lady's umbrella worth £1 1s. He was refused bail and remanded for a week.

Embezzlement was a serious crime. Albert Edward Pratt of Oxford Road was sent to prison for six months in 1917 for embezzling £1 4s 11d from his employer Mr E Taylor of the Windsor Steam Laundry, stealing a sheet, two pillow cases, five collars, a towel and a table cloth. He managed to escape from police custody as he was taken from Windsor to Wandsworth Prison, but was recaptured at Camberwell by detectives from Windsor and Scotland Yard.

There were regular convictions for failing to send children to school. Antonio Sacco was fined 2s 6d for failing to send his two girls to school regularly, three similar cases were heard at the same session in March 1917.

The oldest trade was also flourishing in a town full of soldiers. Ann Williams and Caroline Grace, both well over 40, were charged with using 13 Goswell Cottages as a brothel. They received prison sentences of three months each.

The Chief Constable's 1916 annual report on the Royal Borough, stated that crime had increased during 1915. There were 104 persons who had been proceeded against, which was an increase of 36 on the 1914 figures, but he said, 'it is worth noticing that of the 123 persons apprehended for various offences, only 49 were residents of the Borough', the others were 'strangers'.

Suicide was still a chargeable offence. Ethel Rhodes, aged 17, was charged with trying to commit suicide in May 1917; she had let a disreputable life consorting with soldiers and was possibly pregnant.

A Children's Court had been established in Windsor for young offenders as part of the Children's Act of 1908, but justice was still harsh. Throughout the war, child crime increased. The main reason given was that fathers and older brothers, away at the front could not exercise control over their children, and many mothers were working during the day, but also scoutmasters, school-teachers and club leaders were not there to guide the young. The Home Secretary, Herbert Samuel, was of the opinion that the war had encouraged what was euphemistically termed 'the spirit of adventure' among boys, but also unsuitable films shown at the cinema 'contribute to a spirit of lawlessness among boys'. He proposed to establish a central censorship of all films.

Older children were often absorbed into the forces after committing a crime, or they were sent to reformatory schools. Fourteen-year-old Richard Carter of Clewer was charged with stealing a watch and chain; he was sent to join the training ship *Cornwall*.

In May 1915, a little girl was remanded at Windsor with the view to be sent to a home; she had stolen 2s. Four 'Bad Boys of Clewer', a gang of boys aged from seven to nine, who had been birched on a number of occasions for minor pilfering, were remanded to the Workhouse in December, with a view to sending them away to Industrial Schools. Two sons (aged nine and eleven) of Ernest William White, Acre Passage, were sent to an Industrial School until they were sixteen for repeated theft, the father was ordered to pay 4s 6d a week for each child. Two fourteen-year-old boys who had absconded from the Workhouse boys' home in 1918 were sent to an Industrial Home in London.

Much child crime was born out of hunger and want. Three little boys appeared before the Magistrates in November 1915 for pulling up cabbages and eating the hearts out of them. Their parents were fined 1s each. A ten-year-old lad was charged with stealing 1½ pints of milk from a doorway in June 1915. He was fined 5s, or in default to spend four days in prison. In May two brothers aged eight and ten were charged with stealing a half pint can of milk. The boys had no mother, and the father gave them a few pence for food before he left for work in the morning. Two older brothers had already been sent away, one to a reformatory school and the other to Borstal. As the lads had already been birched for an earlier theft, the father was fined 5s for each boy, or in default committed to 14 days hard labour.

Other child crime seems to have been born out of boredom. Four lads were summoned for gambling on Bachelors' Acre, and fined between £2 and £5. Another boy of 14 was fined 2s 6d for throwing stones in Osborne Road. In May 1918, several boys were charged with playing football in the highway at Bridgewater Terrace, and breaking a window at the home of Mrs Frost. The boys were fined 1s each and the parents promised to pay 5s for the broken window.

Wilful damage, especially to allotments, was seen as very serious. The Chief Constable reported in 1918 that such crime was on the increase. He stated that he had ten lots of boys at the Windsor

Children's Court in just one week for this crime. Two brothers aged twelve and nine were charged with breaking 100 earthenware pots at the Windsor Cemetery on 11 March 1917. Their parents were bound over to the sum of £5 for the good behaviour of the boys. In March 1917, two boys aged fourteen were caught throwing stones at a man. They had also broken a window in the Mayor's house and were each fined 5s.

Common theft was also a serious matter. On 17 February 1915, two boys aged thirteen were caught stealing from the sweet dispenser at the SW Railway station, by putting in metal disks instead of 2d coins. They both received six strokes of the birch rod. In February 1917 two boys aged 12 and 10 received six strokes of the birch after stealing chocolate from shops.

There was the case of seven youths from Clewer who were fined 5s each for 'disorderly bathing' in the Thames in August 1917, and using indecent language.

Some cases, however, bordered on farce. William Pearson of Clewer Fields, pleaded guilty to using obscene language in Grosvenor Place on 27 October 1917. He denied the particular words attributed to him, but admitted using language equally bad. He said as he and some friends came out of the Theatre on Saturday night, they saw some little pies in a window marked 2½d and started swearing at them on account of their size. They then left the pie shop and went to Mrs Dunn's sausage shop in Oxford Road. Sgt Baughan then came up and told him he would be summoned for using bad language. Chief Constable Carter: 'Did you swear at the sausages?' Defendant: 'No, Sir'. Asked what his occupation and wages were he said he was a labourer, sometimes he earned 5s a day and sometimes nothing at all… The magistrates warned him against using bad language in the streets. Swearing at pies would not increase their size. As there was no previous conviction against him the charges were dismissed under the Probation of First Offenders' Act upon the defendant paying 2s 6d costs.

Public Health, The Workhouse, and Spanish Flu

The twice-monthly Report of the Board of Guardians and Medical Officer of Health was a regularly feature of the *Windsor Express*, and included the Inspector of Nuisances' reports on public health and infectious diseases, as well as the state of the drains.

Windsor had a relatively new hospital and temporary isolation hospital for infectious diseases, built in Old Windsor during the last smallpox epidemic in 1893; more permanent isolation hospitals were in Maidenhead and Slough. There was a workhouse located in Old Windsor, which also had its own hospital.

The biggest killer of adults and children alike was tuberculosis; it had been responsible for 50,298 deaths in England and Wales in 1914, equal to 9.7 per cent of mortality from all causes. Smallpox was still a dreaded disease, although there was an effective vaccine. The Medical Officer of Health lamented the fact that vaccination against smallpox and inoculation against typhoid were not made compulsory, as popular opinion was against such measures, but he made one positive comment in his report in June 1915:

> The most remarkable fact of all the remarkable facts of this wonderful war is the almost total absence of enteric – the scourge of armies. Never have armies lived and fought under more dangers of this disease than those in Flanders, and yet the mortality from it is practically negligible.

Venereal disease was another cause for concern. It was estimated, according to a feature in the local newspaper on 2 December 1916, that about one per cent of the population was infected and brought to the notice of medical practitioners, but this was just the tip of the iceberg. Financing laboratory research cost 5s a case, but money was not forthcoming. From 1917 newspapers carried announcements by the Berkshire County Council, that

Venereal Diseases would be treated free under 'conditions of strict SECRECY' at the Berkshire Hospital in Reading.

It was infant mortality that came up for regular discussion; scarlet fever, diphtheria and measles were still killing large numbers of children. Measles, 'the great waste of child life', killed about 2,000 infants every week under the age of one and 3,000 a week under five.

An outbreak of measles in 1915 among the boys at the Old Windsor Workhouse caused eleven boys to be isolated and classes cancelled during June. The Inspector of Nuisances stated in November that there had been 12,414 deaths due to measles for the first half of that year in England and Wales, mostly in children under five, adding, 'these figures are simply enormous'.

During an outbreak of German measles in March 1917, 33 cases were reported in Windsor. In April 1917 a more serious outbreak of measles resulted in the death of 12 children, and a total of 131 local people were reported sick. Some schools closed during the measles outbreak and parents were advised not to send their children to school if there was measles in the home. Even the soldiers in Windsor barracks did not escape these child ailments; fourteen soldiers had German measles and two had scarlet fever in the spring of 1917. Something had to be done.

To counter the high infant mortality, an advice centre was set up for mothers and babies at the Boveney Institution where all were welcomed and babies were examined free of charge. To raise awareness of the need to save infant life and promote the welfare of mothers and children, a National Baby Week was held in July 1917. A special service on Sunday, 1st July, attended by Princess Christian, was followed by a baby show at the Guildhall.

National Baby Week was repeated in July 1918. The *Windsor Express* reported:

The welfare of the babies of the Empire becomes more important every year, and now that this Great War has taken thousands of our best men, it is most necessary that the little ones are looked after as they never were before. The object of Baby Week is to help to secure to every child born in the United Kingdom a birth right of mental and bodily health.

The second Baby Week at Windsor was opened with a sermon at Windsor Parish Church on Sunday morning by the Vicar. There followed a public meeting at Holy Trinity Parish Room on Tuesday afternoon. Then on Wednesday afternoon there was a baby show and pram parade in Alexandra Gardens, at which Lady May Cambridge presented prizes.

Windsor had always seen itself at the forefront of child care; forty years earlier the first Infant Nursery had been established, and in 1912 the Infant Welfare Centre was opened on Bachelors' Acre, free for mothers and babies. Of concern to the Windsor authorities were the 'large number of ill-clad and badly-shod children in our town'. One reporter wrote:

> On bitterly cold days lately we have seen youngsters about the town and playing in the Acre, who had barely clothes enough to cover them. Their poor little white faces told a tale of poverty and neglect.

Often they were in charge of tiny infants. The NSPCC investigated thirteen cases of child neglect involving thirty-one children in Windsor during February 1918. There were 2,750 cases nationwide.

The Workhouse

The Union Workhouse at Old Windsor also had a regular write-up in the local paper. It held between 200 and 300 men, women and children throughout the year, and 70 to 90 in the infirmary. Between 50 and 60 inmates died each year. A former inmate, then a lance corporal in the Welsh Regiment, and wounded at Neuve Chapelle, visited his mother at the workhouse in 1915. This was probably the only home he knew; he was given permission to stay for a few days.

At Christmas 1915, the *Windsor Express* reported that the 293 inmates of the workhouse thanked the Guardians for the 'good things provided for them during the Christmas season', and on Monday after the festivities a large number of them took advantage of the 'usual leave'. 'They all returned quite orderly, and gave no trouble'. As this was considered worth mentioning, there must have been trouble in the past.

Not all inmates were old and infirm or young and vulnerable. Although the average age was 69 for women and 64 for men, there were some men fit and able to serve. In May 1915 two men of military age were sent to the recruiting officer for enlistment.

As food became scarce and restrictions came into force in April 1917, two pauper inmates, William Taylor and John Mahoney objected to the war rations and refused to work until they were given more bread. They were sentenced by the local magistrates to seven days imprisonment for their rebellion.

Spanish Flu

In 1918 a new and devastating form of influenza struck the world. It had first emerged in the spring of that year and more deadly strains appeared in August and November 1918 and lasted until the following spring. Although commonly named 'Spanish flu', its true origin was unknown. The flu virus struck servicemen and civilians alike; young adults were particularly vulnerable. The extremely high infection rate caused death on a colossal scale, and it is estimated that at least fifty million people died worldwide – considerably more than the number of victims of the Great War. The first reference to the new influenza epidemic reaching the

Windsor area was reported in the *Windsor Express* on 6 July:

> The influenza epidemic has claimed a number of victims in
> this district, and reports from all parts of the country indicate
> a considerable extension of the epidemic. It is also said that
> the German Army is suffering in the same way, and that is
> why the expected great offensive is held up. The symptoms of
> the present scourge are in practically all cases the same at the
> outset – violent headache with renal pains and rapid rise of
> temperature, many persons being in a high fever before they
> can reach home. The malady attacks both sexes of all ages, and
> local doctors are very much overworked as a consequence. The
> present visitation is chiefly remarkable for the suddenness of
> the attack, persons who feel perfectly well and are able to go
> about their business at 9 o'clock in the morning being prostate
> at noon. To go to bed at once is said to be the safest course to
> pursue…

The Windsor district did not escape the ravages of the new
influenza epidemic. The children attending Windsor schools
suffered considerably. On one day alone there were a hundred boys
away from the Royal Free School. The School Nurse, too, became
a sufferer, and was compelled to be away from duty for about a
week. The Windsor Secondary School was closed owing to several
of the staff and nearly 40 of the boys being laid up with flu.

The recommended treatment for the illness – going to bed
– proved ineffectual and the epidemic continued claiming lives.
The viral cause of the disease was unknown at the time, making
prevention and treatment impossible.

The first known victim who died locally was Cpl Geoffrey
William Stevens, Coldstream Guards, who died at King Edward
VII Hospital from acute pneumonia following an attack of Spanish
Flu. Cpl Stevens, who was acting as an instructor at Windsor, had
been in France for about two years. The *Windsor Express* reported
on 6 July 1918: 'The funeral took place with military honours at
Uxbridge on Monday last'.

Four local flu victims, not on any local War Memorial, appeared
in the newspaper's Rolls of Honour. Driver E J Kidd, 70 Oxford

Road, Royal Engineers, died of influenza on 16 October 1918 in Salonika, aged 22. Driver F G Kidd is on the Windsor War Memorial, but there is no F G Kidd listed in records, this could be a case of incorrect initials. Driver William Russell, 5 St George's Place, Dedworth, died in hospital in Salonika, suffering from fever and influenza.

CSM W Woodley, 1st Royal Berks Regiment, who was severely wounded in both legs and gassed in France in April 1918, was waiting for his discharge when he contracted influenza, and being weak from the effects of gas died in a few days at Warneford General Hospital, Leamington Spa. He lived at York Place, Windsor, had 21 years continuous service with the 1st Royal Berks, and obtained the Long Service and Good Conduct Medal. He had served in India and Ireland in pre-war days.

Pte W J Squelch, eldest son of Mr and Mrs Squelch, Surly Hall Road, Clewer, serving with the Wiltshire Regiment, died of pneumonia following influenza, on 1 November in Stevens Hospital, Dublin, aged 18.

On 2 November, the *Windsor Express* reported that 'hundreds are down with the flu' and that Windsor County Boys' School, the Royal Free Boys' School, the Infants School, and the Clewer St Stephen Intermediate Boys, Girls and Infant Schools had all closed. At the Imperial Services College, 87 boys were reported to be suffering from flu. Because of the number of funerals, the resources of Mr Sargeant, the local undertaker, were so heavily taxed that he had to requisition the assistance of soldiers to dig the graves.

The following week the editorial was more optimistic, claiming that 'there are indications that the outbreak is abating', and that some schools had re-opened, but on 16 November the death was reported of a husband and wife, Thomas and Emily Edith Joyce of Surly Hall Road, who died within a week of each other.

The *Windsor Express* editorial on 30 November read: 'These are dull days, and although the war is over Death has been very busy in our midst of late, which adds to the gloom of this dreary month of November'. The last reported death in 1918 was on 14 December, taking Edith Ladd, aged 28, of 44 Price Consort Cottages. However, the flu continued to claim lives. The last in the Windsor area were two sisters, aged 22 and 20, of Crown Cottage near Queen Anne's Gate who died in March 1919. The parents of the two girls, who had lost one son Frederick Charles Giles, MM in April 1917 were also ill, but survived. Another son George Albert had been wounded in the neck, but was home.

A series of advertisements in the *Windsor Express* in December 1918 used the flu epidemic to advertise Bovril:

There is a simple way of helping others during the present influenza epidemic. It is to refrain from buying Bovril if you have a stock in the house, which will carry you on for a month. In this way you will leave the available Bovril in the shops for those who have illness at home. Bovril Ltd recognising that those who are deprived of the body-building power of Bovril may more easily fall victims to the epidemic are doing their utmost to increase the supply. But the lack of bottles seriously hampers their efforts, and it is hoped that men will soon be released for the bottle factories so that there may be, once again, Bovril for all.

The Habgood Family

During the war details of patriotic families, who had a number of sons serving their country were regularly featured in local newspapers. On 4 December 1915, the *Windsor Express* published the first of two articles about the Habgood family under the heading 'A Patriotic Family':

> Mr A Habgood, of 86 Bexley Street, Windsor, who has now rejoined the Metropolitan Police Force, has three sons and a son-in-law serving with the colours, viz, Leading Seaman F Habgood HMS *Midge*; Machine Gunner E Habgood, 1st Royal Berks Regiment; Private G Habgood, West York Regiment, and Cpl W Drew, Royal Engineers. He has also a younger son who is employed in Munitions' Works.

Two more sons enlisted later in the war, when they were old enough, and the *Windsor Express* mentioned the Habgood family again in its edition of 12 January 1918, under the heading 'Five Patriotic Sons':

> Bernard M Habgood, of 86 Bexley Street, Windsor, is the last of five sons of Mrs Habgood to join His Majesty's forces. His eldest brother, Leading Signaller F A Habgood, is on a submarine; George E Habgood, West York Regiment, died of wounds on July 5th 1916; Ernest V Habgood, 1st Royal Berks Regiment, is one of the 'old Contemptibles' who fought at Mons; Victor St C Habgood is in the RFA; and Bernard M Habgood is in the RNVR (Wireless Section).

In addition to the five sons, there was also a daughter Ada. Their father, Albert Habgood, was a Metropolitan Police pensioner and at one time was attached to the Metropolitan Police at Windsor

Castle. He rejoined the police force at the outbreak of war, but his health broke down; after a long illness he died at his home in Bexley Street on 16 February 1917. His widow, Mary Habgood, survived him by many years.

Their third son, Ernest Victor Habgood, was mentioned in the local newspaper on many occasions. He was born in Windsor in 1896, and after leaving St Edward's School, where all his siblings were educated, found employment locally. In 1911, aged 15, he was an errand boy for a chemist but when the First World War started three years later he enlisted immediately. His Army service records did not survive the Blitz, but other sources show that he joined the 1st Battalion Royal Berkshire Regiment on 13 August 1914. (At some stage he also served in the Royal Army Service Corps {RASC}, but the dates of this service are not recorded.) Pte Ernest Habgood fought at Mons in 1914, making him one of the 'Old Contemptibles', and received the 1914 Star with 'Mons' clasp. Later in the war he was attached to the 2nd RBR as a machine gunner, before returning to 1st RBR.

On 25 December 1915 the *Windsor Express* published a report of a football match, played on 4 December in France, between the machine gunners of 2nd and 5th Battalions Royal Berkshire Regiment. Ernest was in goal for the 2nd RBR: 'Habgood, in goal, being stuck in the mud and unable to move, the ball went into the corner of the goal…' Later, when the action was at the other end of the pitch: 'Habgood, in our goal, by this time was nearly frozen as he had nothing to do', but despite letting in three goals, he helped them win the match.

He wrote to the *Windsor Express* describing how the 2nd Berkshires spent Christmas Day 1915 (which was a quiet time in billets behind the front line):

I am writing this letter on behalf of the machine gunners, to thank you for publishing the account of our football match with our 5th Battalion. Being a native of Windsor myself, I am very pleased to see the Windsor paper show itself amongst us every week, so that we can always see how the old place is getting on. Christmas Day has come and gone. I expect you all at home wonder how we spent it out here. Well, I must say that it was a great success, of course as far as circumstances would permit… After breakfast nothing much doing, a proposal was made for a sing-song… Pte Gigg, who before the war was a star turn at the Palace, London, immediately came forward, and in his soft, sweet voice gave us that good old song, Down in Baffin land where the fishes are cheap, Pte Hart supplying the music…

This continued until lunch, when we partook of three courses, viz, first course, baked potatoes and cauliflower, supplied by a neighbouring farm, and chicken… second course, Christmas pudding (kindly supplied by somebody in England); and the third course was chocolate…[After which Habgood and his comrades enjoyed another impromptu concert.]

On 22 March 1916, Ernest was wounded and sent back to England for treatment at the Northern General Hospital in Leicester. In a letter to the *Windsor Express*, published on 2 December 1916, he mentioned that he 'had a decent spell in England, after being hit again' and that he was on his way to join his old regiment at a place 'somewhere in the East'. It is not clear what he meant by this as both 1st and 2nd Battalions RBR spent the entire war on the Western Front. It is possible that after being wounded twice he was temporarily attached to the RASC, which served on every front, pending his return to 1st RBR. His letter continued:

I have got a few local men with me, so we are enjoying ourselves as far as circumstances will permit. We went to see the sights of [*censored*] on Sunday, the 12th November, and everything went A1 until it was time to go home, which the boys didn't like. I must say the sights around here are the best to be seen anywhere, but I would sooner be in the Long Walk or on the Terrace. Still we must put up with all little troubles now-a-days; only we all hope that the Windsor paper will find itself amongst us before long, as I myself have not seen one for three weeks now. All the boys send their best wishes and live in hopes of seeing the old place once more... Of course as the Censor is so strict, I cannot tell you what I would like to.

Ernest Habgood survived the war and returned to Windsor, where he worked in an aircraft factory in Slough, and later became a school caretaker. His son, Bill Habgood (*seen left*), now proudly owns his campaign medals. Eighty-seven-year old Bill, like his father, is a lifelong resident of Windsor; he grew up in the family home in Bexley Street (which is still owned by them) and served in the Royal Army Ordnance Corps in 1946-47, before becoming a heating engineer.

The Habgood's eldest son was Frederick Albert. He was born in Windsor in 1892 and served in the Royal Navy during the war. Leading Signaller Habgood served on submarines, his last posting being HMS *Victory*. After surviving at sea almost to the end of the war, he died of Spanish Flu at the Royal Naval Barracks, Portsmouth on 22 October 1918, aged 25. He is buried at Haslar Royal Naval Cemetery, Gosport.

George Edward Habgood, the second eldest, was born in Windsor in 1895, and after leaving school became an errand boy for a local chemist. When war was declared he enlisted in the Army and was posted to 10th (Service) Battalion West Yorkshire Regiment (Prince of Wales's Own). This was a

Kitchener Battalion (K2), formed in September 1914, and served on the Western Front. Pte George Habgood's battalion took part in the Battle of the Somme in July 1916 and was involved in the capture of Fricourt on 2 July. He was wounded in battle and died on 5 July 1916, aged 21. He is buried at Abbeville Communal Cemetery, France. Both are remembered on the Clewer War Memorial.

The two younger sons, Victor and Bernard, also served but survived the war. Victor St Clare Habgood was born in Windsor in 1898 and was too young to enlist when the war started. He worked in a local munitions factory until he was old enough and then joined the Royal Field Artillery as a gunner. Bernard Montague Habgood was born in Windsor in 1899 and because of his age was the last to join the services. The *Windsor Express* report of 12 January 1918 stated that he was in the Wireless Section of the Royal Navy Volunteer Reserve.

Bill lost another relative in the Second World War. His cousin Victor, aged 22, was on board the Norwegian submarine *Ured* when it was sunk by a mine in February 1943. In 1988 Bill was invited to Norway to a ceremony over the wreck of the *Ured*, which had only recently been discovered.

Lance Corporal Arthur Frederick Stevens

Arthur Frederick Stevens was born in Clewer in 1897. His father, also Arthur, was a painter and decorator with Goddards, the builders in Eton, and his great grandfather had been a miller in Clewer village. Arthur grew up with five sisters, at 8 Sudan Terrace, Duke Street, he was the only son, and attended St Edward's and St Stephen's schools, he also played the bugle at Holy Trinity Church. When he left school he worked as a telegraph boy in Slough, and when war came he and his work colleagues joined the territorials; the Buckinghamshire Battalion of the Oxford and Bucks Light Infantry rather than the Berkshires, as Slough was then part of Buckinghamshire.

In July 1916, the Ox and Bucks together with the 5th Division Australian Imperial Force and the British 61st (South Midland) Division held the line west of Pheasant Wood near Fromelles, from 'Bond Street' to 'Picantin Avenue', opposite the German salient known as the 'Sugar Loaf'. Arthur sent this field postcard to his sister Eugenie, most probably from Fromelles, just 11 days before he was killed.

They were to attack a well-defended German line, to divert enemy forces away from the Somme battle, raging some 50 miles to the south. The bombardment of enemy trenches started at 11am on 19 July; at 6pm the order was given to assault the German lines. As the men left the trenches they were mowed down by machine-gun fire from the high point of the 'Sugar Loaf'.

Lance/Corporal Arthur Frederick Stevens (*on right of photo*) was seen getting into the German lines, but he did not return. He was reported wounded and it was thought that he died as a prisoner of war, but his body was never found. He became one of the battalion's 89 missing. His death was reported in the local newspaper.

The attack was a disaster, creating over 7,000 casualties; most of the dead were never recovered. In fact they were buried in mass graves by the Germans, but the site remained undisturbed until the Australian Government carried out a survey in 2008. They were looking for 337 Australian soldiers known to have been killed during the Battle of Fromelles, (it was known as the Battle of Fleurbaix at the time). Very soon the remains of 250 bodies and personal effects were discovered in six pits. Of these, 137 were Australians and 75 have since been identified by DNA.

Family members of British soldiers who fought at Fromelles were contacted to give DNA samples, including the descendants of Arthur's family. A male descendant of his sister Norah was chosen, but there has been no positive identification as yet. The children, grandchildren, great-grandchildren and great-great-grandchildren of Arthur's sisters still live in Windsor.

A new cemetery with a museum was built at Fromelles, not far from the original burial pits, called Pheasant Wood Military

Cemetery. Members of Arthur's family were invited to the formal opening on 19 July 2010, the 94th anniversary of the Battle of Fromelles.

A restored First World War general service wagon, drawn by horses from the King's Troop RHA, carried the coffin of the last (unknown) soldier to be interred, from the mass-grave site to the new cemetery. They were accompanied by British and Australian soldiers.

Arthur is commemorated on the Loos Memorial, Dud Corner, in France and on the Clewer War Memorial.

Based on research by Mary Skelly, great niece of Arthur F Stevens.

Thomas (Tom) Luff
and His Brothers

My father Tom Luff was born in 1894 above the family shop in Windsor, but I do not know if it was the shop in St Leonard's Road or in Thames Street (now the site of McDonald's burger bar). As a young man he rowed with the Eton Excelsior Rowing Club.

He and his younger brother Henry joined the Berkshire Yeomanry on 17 December 1912, and when war broke out they were among the first to volunteer for service abroad. He is in the

photo of 'A' Squadron of the Berkshire Yeomanry, published in the *Windsor Express* on 21 November 1914 (*Tom Luff second from the right, next to Cyril Dyson who is on the far right.*)

Another brother Edmund, returned from Canada as soon as war broke out, to join the Berkshire Yeomanry; he was mentioned on the Roll of Honour on 3 October 1914. In April 1915 all three went out with the regiment to Egypt, and in August they set sail for Turkey.

Tom's baptism of fire came in Gallipoli, where he fought alongside his brothers Edmund and Henry at Suvla Bay. Miraculously they all survived a fierce battle for Hill 70; the photograph (*on page 307*) shows them after the battle in their dugout, together with a close family friend, Freddie McNeil.

A letter from Edmund to their father Cllr Thomas Edmund Luff was published in the *Windsor Express* on 18 September 1915:

Have at last got the time, although hardly the energy to write a few lines. Our surmise before we left Egypt that we were in for a stiff time has been fully justified by recent events. We landed under shell fire, which happily did no damage to the Berkshires. Our first job was to dig ourselves in, as we were still within range of the enemy's artillery. Later in the evening we moved further up the hillside to a less exposed position, where we stayed three days. We then, under cover of the darkness, moved a mile or two further on, where we rested until the next afternoon. As we were near water, we were able to indulge in a bathe as do the sailors before they go into action. All this was preparatory to our next move, which gave us our first real experience of active service. For some considerable distance we had to advance in open country under very heavy shell fire, when, though many fell, there was never a waiver. It was just like being in a hailstorm, so heavy was the shower of lead. How far we advanced I do not know, but it seemed as if we went miles. After covering the open country, we had to climb a hill, and then down through a valley where vegetation had all been burnt up, having been ignited by the shell fire. Still on and on and higher and higher, we had to go through burnt and burning shrub and undergrowth, till we reached the enemy's trenches. What was done there is for others to tell when the time comes. At present it seems to us like a bad nightmare, and I am thankful that we came through without wounds.

Another letter, written by Tom, then a corporal, to a friend in Windsor about the fighting on 21 August, was published on 16 October:

I will do my best to give you a few details I know of my lost comrade, L/ Cpl H G Jefferies, known to us all as 'Jeff'. We were in different troops in the charge, and how I came across 'Jeff' was like this. Evening had fallen, and all who were left of our little band were busy digging themselves in etc. Well I managed to slip away, and going to one of the poor dead fellows, took his water bottle off. Next I found four fellows very near each other all out of No 2 Troop. The four were 'Jeff' and Wheeler,

Pearce and Smith. The first two were about a dozen yards from the last two. I managed to give all four a good long drink. 'Jeff' recognised me, for he said 'Is that you Tommy?' I can't say for certain but I think his wound was in the leg somewhere for he would not let me touch him there. 'Jeff' fell within thirty yards of the Turkish trench. This was the last I saw of my late Pal. But the most extraordinary thing is that morning found Jefferies near Chocolate Hill. How he got there I cannot say, for from where I left him to Chocolate Hill is well over two miles. I fancy he must have got to the first aid dressing trench, and I expect he must have died while he was being taken to the base. I fancy Sgt [J] Ottery and Private [L] Howard (Scouts) were near by at his end, but I cannot say for certain.

He was buried on the Western side of Chocolate Hill. Pearce was out for three nights and two days before he got to the first dressing station, it being impossible for the RAMC to get up there.

I see by the press that they talk of the 'CHARGE UP CHOCOLATE HILL' this is not so. The hill was already in our hands when we started our advance over the SALT LAKE. I should think we had every gun trained on us, so as to take the Turks attention off the fellows who were advancing from the trenches up HILL 70.

Now the point that does not seem clear it that it was only our Brigade that made the charge up Hill 70. Why reinforcements were not given I cannot say.

Tom Luff (left) in the dug-out at Suvla Bay
August 1915

Lord Longford was in charge of our Brigade. I am sorry to hear about Fred Blane. I thought he was going on well, and I am surprised to hear of his death!

It shows how lucky they were to survive; but Henry was invalided out to Malta with dysentery on 4 October[1], and Tom was injured and spent some time in hospital back in England, before returning to Alexandria to join the Imperial Camel Corps in Palestine. In September 1918 he was transferred to the Worcestershire Yeomanry and I believe he served at the Battle of Damascus with Lawrence of Arabia. He was demobbed on 26 December 1919, over seven years after he joined the Yeomanry. The war left Tom with malaria and, although he didn't know it, with hepatitis. The disease was triggered in 1963 by another infection and he died that year; his ashes are spread near Bishopsgate in Windsor Great Park. He married twice, and I am his son with his second wife Joyce Mills.

My grandfather Cllr T E Luff had been Mayor of Windsor in 1912 and served on the Council throughout most of the war. However, in 1918 he 'had to vacate his position – a position which he valued with a force few could feel – because of the state of the war and the country'[2]. What he was called upon to do is a mystery to me; I have heard speculation that he could have been on a War Office or Red Cross committee examining conditions in France or Germany, but there is no mention of this in his obituaries. In April 1919 he was welcomed back to the Council Chamber, and was allowed to take his old place at the Council table. He expressed his joy and relief that his three sons returned safely from the war. A week later he chaired the National Federation of Discharged Soldiers in the Guildhall.

Sir Peter Luff, MP for Mid Worcestershire

1. WO 372/12 from Berkshire Yeomanry Museum
2. Windsor Express 12 April 1919

Private Edward Frederick Johnson

When the Windsor War Memorial was unveiled on 7 November 1920, there were many names missing from it. It is not known if these omissions were due to poor record keeping or the relatives of the dead servicemen failing to supply information in time. No-one questioned authority then; it was just accepted and many thought that if a relative's name was not on the memorial he must have done something wrong to warrant being omitted. (Some of the missing names were added subsequently.) Pte Edward Frederick Johnson, 5th Battalion Royal Berkshire Regiment, was one of the local men not on the Windsor War Memorial. He was the subject of much speculation and it was even thought by some that he had been shot at dawn.

Privates
B. G. L. BRANT
P. BREADMORE
W. BROWN
T. F. BUCKLAND
F. COLLETT
E. J. COLMAN
F. W. A. COLMAN
W. COLMAN
H. E. COOPER
J. COOPER
H. G. COSTA
G. E. DAVIES
W. H. DAVIES
H. A. DAY
G. R. DICKINSON
F. W. DISBURY
F. E. DRAYCOTT
C. A. DRYE
S. DRYE
E. V. ELKINS
A. FERRIS
J. R. FOLKER
S. GODDARD
W. GODDARD
F. W. GRAY
W. G. GREEN
G. GROVES
W. GUNDRY
G. HALE

Lifelong Windsor resident Lynda King was told, as a child, about her great uncle Fred and vowed that one day she would find out why his name was not on the war memorial and try to get it added. With the help of a local historian she established the truth about her long-forgotten relative.

Edward Frederick Johnson (always known as Fred) was born at

8 Keppel Street, on 1 April 1890, the son of Richard Johnson, a general labourer, and Mary Johnson, née Cole. He was the fourth of their six children and after leaving school he worked as a general labourer. Around 1904, the Johnson family moved to 8 Goswell Place. In 1911, aged 21, he was the eldest of the three children still living at home with their widowed mother, their father had died a few years earlier.

After Britain declared war on Germany in August 1914, Fred Johnson decided to volunteer for service in the Army. He enlisted at the recruiting office in the Guildhall on 1 February 1915 and joined the 5th (Service) Battalion Royal Berkshire Regiment. His service number was 16892. After training in England, the battalion left for France and disembarked at Boulogne on 31 May 1915. Pte Johnson's medal record indicates that he joined his battalion in France several weeks later on 23 June 1915; the reason for this is not known. When the battalion reached France it joined 35th Brigade, which was part of 12th Division.

Although Johnson's service records were destroyed in the Blitz, it has been possible to piece together his military career from other sources. His battalion was at Ploegsteert Wood, in Belgium, during the summer of 1915 before moving to Loos, to take part in the new offensive in October 1915. During an attack near Hulluch he was wounded in the head and face, but was soon back in action. His wounds were reported in the casualty list in the *Windsor Express* in November 1915.

In early 1916 5th RBR was in a relatively quiet sector of the front near Béthune, France, where there had been no major action for some time. There followed periods of rest in Lillers and training in 'back areas'. On the last day of March, the Germans exploded a mine, killing three men and injuring twenty. By mid-April the battalion was at Sailly Labourse and there were British casualties every day. Although not on an active front, the battalion lived with the constant danger of snipers and enemy shelling.

On Sunday, 16 April 1916 Pte Johnson, then aged 26, was struck by an enemy shell and killed instantly. That day the battalion War Diaries noted 'Casualties – Other ranks, 1 killed 1 wounded'. The *Windsor Express* recorded his death in its casualty list on 6 May 1916, under the sub-heading 'Killed Action'. He is buried in Vermelles British Cemetery, near where died.

Following the research into Fred Johnson's background and war record, the Royal Borough of Windsor Maidenhead agreed that should be remembered on Windsor War Memorial and Pte E F Johnson was added, without ceremony, in June 2007.

Privates
B.G.L. BRANT
P. BREADMORE
W. BROWN
T. F. BUCKLAND
F. COLLETT
E. J. COLMAN
F. W. A. COLMAN
W. COLMAN
H. E. COOPER
J. COOPER
H. G. COSTA
G. E. DAVIES
W. H. DAVIES
H. A. DAY
G. R. DICKINSON
F. W. DISBURY
F. E. DRAYCOTT
C. A. DRYE
S. DRYE
E. V. ELKINS
A. FERRIS
J. R. FOLKER
S. GODDARD
W. GODDARD
F. W. GRAY
W. G. GREEN
G. GROVES
W. GUNDRY
G. HALE
E. F. JOHNSON

Private Harry Frederick Sharp

My uncle Harry was born in Ealing, but the family lived at 1 Garfield Place, Windsor. When war broke out he joined the Royal Army Medical Corps, 109th Field Ambulance, and went to France on 21 February 1915. In 1916 he sent a beautiful embroidered silk card to his sister May for her 10th birthday with a greeting written in French. He signed it with his nickname Sonnie. He also purchased another card, which reflected the pride in his regiment, the RAMC. These cards were very popular during the Great War, and were usually sent in envelopes, as even then they were quite pricey, and of course delicate.

Harry married Olive Stock of Romford on 17 January 1917, without his family's knowledge and had a son called William, who was born in March 1916. Harry died of wounds on 14 September 1918 and is buried in Terlincthun Cemetery Wimille, France.

Lynda Cottrill

The Tank on Bachelors' Acre

On Saturday, 29 May 1920, a tank arrived at the Great Western Station goods yard; it was driven by four men of the Tank Corps and travelled under the viaduct in Goswell Road, into Arthur Road, Alma Road, Clarence Road and on to Victoria Street. The crew, which had stayed at the Bull Inn, allowed the landlord's daughter Mary Lovejoy, and older sisters Betty and Mercia to travel in the tank with them to Bachelors' Acre. Their excitement was somewhat marred when they were told off for getting their spotless summer dresses covered in oil and dust.

A concrete stand had been prepared for the tank, and among

the large crowd assembled was the Windsor County Boys' School Cadet Corps with their drum and bugle band, the drums and fifes of the 1st Battalion Scots Guards and contingents of Boy Scouts and Girl Guides.

The tank had been given to the Royal Borough in recognition of the very generous aid raised by the people of Windsor towards the expenses of the war. The Mayor, Cllr W Fairbank, and five members of the reception party climbed on top of the tank for the handing over ceremony by the Army. The Mayor revealed that £1.3 million had been collected over the four years of conflict. He was sure that the people of Windsor would always prize this emblem of the Great War; he hoped they would always look on it, not only with respect but with reverence, because it was a means of saving their country.

The tank was number 6039, type Mark IV and female (because it was armed with machine guns in barbettes on each side – male tanks had a gun); some 1,200 of this type, weighing 27 tons each were built. She had seen service in France, possibly at the Battle of Bourlon Wood in November 1917, and wore her battle-scars with

pride; with numerous bullet marks and two missiles still embedded. Stripes on the front indicated that she had never been captured and used against the Allies.

Not everybody gave the tank the respect she deserved. Children soon climbed all over, and threw stones at her. The council sold the engine for £50 to Mr Farrow, manager of the Windsor Electricity works in Acre Passage, but after some angry letters in the local paper, the engine was returned, but dumped on the chassis, not bolted down. The machine guns and final drive tracks were removed by the Army – ostensibly so that Irish terrorists could not commandeer her. Some people called for her to be removed as she was an eyesore and eventually a fence was erected around her to stop vandalism.

Finally in 1940, she was sold as scrap metal for making munitions for another war. It is said that the tank, together with Windsor railings, gates and other metal scraps were loaded onto a ship at the London docks. On the way out to sea, the ship was bombed by the German air force and sank into the mud of the Thames estuary.

Taken from The Bachelors' Acre Tank, by Gordon Cullingham, published in Windlesora 13, and information from: theroyalwindsorwebsite.com

A Soldier In The Kaiser's Army
My Father Adolf Breitenstein

Both authors had relatives fighting in the Great War. Derek Hunt's grandfather, Charles Hunt, fought for King and Country in The Buffs, the Royal East Kent Regiment. He survived the war. Brigitte Mitchell's father fought with the German Infantry for the Kaiser. This is his story.

'We have known that which cannot be told'[1], wrote a French veteran of Verdun. My father would endorse these words. Verdun was for French and German soldiers what the Somme was for the British. My father was there, both at Verdun and the Somme.

Adolf Breitenstein was born in Düsseldorf in September 1895, the youngest son of a large family, his father was a wealthy property developer. He was at school when war broke out, working towards

his final exams, and in the spring of 1915, together with his classmates, he joined the Kaiser's army straight from school, in the way that the group of schoolfriends did in *All Quiet on the Western Front*. They were all promised places at university as soon as the war was over.

It was sometime during the 1950s that my father asked me to watch a film on television with him, as he did not want to watch it on his own. I was the only one of his four children interested in his stories about history, and who would listen to the occasional account of the Great War, but not daring to ask for more.

1. Malcolm Brown, Verdun1916 (1999), p.161

The film was *All Quiet on the Western Front*. It had been banned by the Nazis. I remember being deeply moved and horrified to think that my own father had fought and suffered in this terrible war. After a few moments of profound silence at the end of the film, I asked my father, 'Was it really this bad?'

'No' he said 'it was much worse', and then after another pause, 'but there were no butterflies'.

Those who have seen the original film will recall that Paul, the last survivor of the group of pals, was in a ruined building with his rifle through a gap in the wall, when he spotted a butterfly land on the end of the rifle. As he reached out to touch the butterfly, a French sniper spotted him...

It was only much later that I understood what my father was telling me, this war was devoid of any beauty, any hope.

He only told me snippets of his war, of how he was invalided out at Verdun and the Somme, how he was captured on the Aisne and taken prisoner, and how he had escaped, but it was not until years after his death, when I found his war records, that I was able to research his story.

After three months training with the 39th Regiment in the spring of 1915, Adolf was sent to the Chemin des Dames, where his war was to end two years later. German author Ernst Jünger, whose first experience of the war was in the same sector, wrote about his arrival at the nearby station:

> The train stopped at Bazancourt, a small town in Champagne, and we got out. Full of awe and incredulity, we listened to the slow grinding pulse of the front...'[2]

In December 1915 Adolf's division was sent to Damvillers near Verdun in preparation for something big.

The attack on Verdun, planned by General von Falkenhayn was to break the stalemate of trench warfare, and was due to start on 12 February 1916.

On the 11th three army corps with 62 battalions, 221 batteries, 850 guns, 40 pioneer corps, 8 flame thrower companies, 18 mortar companies, and 3 artillery companies went into position to the

2. E.Jünger, *Storm of Steel (2003), p.5*

east side of the river Meuse, but the attack was delayed because of bad weather with snow, rain and poor visibility. Adolf was with the 7th army corps, nearest the river Meuse. The soldiers had to remain in freezing, rain-soaked trenches for nine days, their clothes did not get dry, and their boots rotted on their feet. Finally, on 20 February, the weather changed and the attack was scheduled for the following day.

The delay had given the French time to rush in reinforcements, thus a bitter six-day struggle ensued over a heavily wooded and hilly terrain until the Germans were finally halted just out of reach of Verdun.

As the French had also fired into the flanks of the Germans from the other side of the river Meuse, another attack was called to stop them. Adolf's division was among those sent over the river. During a huge artillery battle on a hill called Morte Homme, along with dozens of other soldiers, Adolf suffered burst ear drums[3], and was invalided out.

After a few months at Freiburg University hospital, Adolf, now a corporal, was sent to join the 91st Reserve Infantry Regiment at Gommecourt, where a British offensive was expected. The main attack on 1 July 1916 came further south than anticipated by the Germans. Fighting at Gommecourt was bitter, but it was over by 2pm, and for a few days they had a fairly quiet war.

On 10 May the orders came to move south and retake Mametz Wood, which had been lost to the British in a bitter fight. A German memo stated that 'the evacuation of Mametz Wood had not been authorised and it had to be retaken forthwith'! [4] The attack which started on 12 May was a disaster. The men of the 91st soon found themselves surrounded by British troops, they had food but no water and they soon ran out of ammunition and hand-grenades. The Regiment lost fifty per cent of its strength, three company commanders were killed[5] but Adolf was evacuated to Bapaume on 16 May with just a broken arm.

His arm in plaster and healing, he worked at Staff Office in

3. *Hospital Records, Berlin*
4. *Official German History of WWI ,Weltkrieg' vol. 10*
5. *Adolf Kümmel, Reserve Infantry Regiment 91 im Weltkrieg 1914-1918 (Berlin, 1926), IWM Archives.*

Bapaume where he was given the Iron Cross, offered to go on an officer's course, which he declined, and on orders of his Commanding Officer, threw an application by another corporal who wanted to become an officer, into the bin He remembered this only because the other corporal happened to share same first name. However, this didn't deter the other corporal from getting above himself!

In November 1916, he was sent to join the 73rd Reserve Infantry Regiment on the Chemin des Dames, where the French were planning their big breakthrough. This came to be known as the Battle of the Aisne. The Germans knew that the French attack was planned for early April.

Adolf's regiment went into line on 1 March, the French bombardment started on 11 April. The 16 April was bitterly cold with driving sleet, but at 7am the 10th Colonial Division from Senegal stormed up the hill and overran the forward position of the 73rd. Adolf and his comrades did not have a chance to get out of their dug out, but found themselves surrounded. A black face with gleaming white teeth, and a hand-grenade ready to release, looked in on the startled German soldiers. Adolf engaged the face in the most bizarre conversation given the circumstances, and, so he told me, asked after his family, his home, his children, in broken French, and would they both not rather be at home than in this God forsaken place. He persuaded the Senegalese soldiers to take them prisoner rather than kill them, which was their usual practice. They preferred to send their enemies' ears home to the family.

Adolf spent two years as prisoner of war in Caen, Normandy. He

318

gained a position of trust and as French speaker was sent on errands, once the war was over. One day in April 1919 he had to go to a nearby village, but decided to carry on walking east-south-east, in the hope of reaching the river Rhine, where it formed a border with Germany. He walked at night, and slept under hedges, in barns or woods during the day. He stole clothes off clothes' lines, eggs from hen houses and vegetables from gardens and fields. Sometimes he managed to sit on the back of a goods train, which rattled eastwards. In one month he had reached the Rhine north of Strasbourg and swam across it at night. Back in Germany he reported himself to the police, but was promptly arrested, as he had no papers. He was detained in a camp in Giesssen on 7 May, until his family could vouch for him.[6]

In September 1919, he entered the University of Freiburg, not sadly to study history, his life long passion, but political economy, one of only four subjects available to students after the war. In just five years he gained a PhD, and joined his father's business.

In August 1939, Adolf narrowly avoided being called up into the Wehrmacht, by asking an old friend and Verdun comrade who was in charge of the fire service, if he would take him on as a fireman. It was not an easy option, but he survived another war, which left him more of a broken man than the first one had.

Brigitte Mitchell (nee Breitenstein)

---

6. *Hospital Records, Berlin*

Appendices

Appendix I
Gallantry Awards to Windsor Men

Appendix II
Local men on the Windsor War Memorial

Appendix III
Local men on the Clewer War Memorial

Appendix IV
Other War Memorials, Old Windsor, Royal
Chapel War Memorial, Eton, Eton Excelsior
Rowing Club, Eton Wick,

Appendix V
'A' Squadron, Berkshire Yeomanry War Memorial

Appendix VI
Not On Any War Memorial

Appendix VII
Imperial Services College

Appendix I

Gallantry Awards to Windsor Men

Name	Rank	Regiment	Awards
Allen, A	Stretcher-Bearer	Royal Berks Regt	MM
Allen, F	Gunner	Royal Garrison Artillery	MM
Allen, J T	Sgt	Royal Horse Artillery	MM
Allhusen, F H	Major	9th Lancers	DSO
Aspey, W	CSM	4th Rifle Brigade	DCM
Balchin, Fred	Sapper	Royal Engineers	MM
Banin, E J	Cpl	Royal Engineers	MM
Bennington, J S	Pte	Royal Defence Corps	DCM
Best, H C	Sgt	Royal Engineers	MID
Blake, Sidney J	Stretcher-Bearer	The Queen's Surrey Regt	MM
Boswell, F W	L/Cpl	Berks Yeomanry	DCM
Botting, R	Cpl	Royal Fusiliers	DCM
Bowley, Tom	CSM	Royal Engineers	DCM MM
Brooks, Ernest	Lt	British Expeditionary Force	Croix de Guerre
Boyles, S	Captain	1/4 Royal Berkshire	MC
Butler, Edward	QMS	Royal Garrison Artillery	MM
Caley, F G	Captain	RAMC	MID
Caley, Hugh W	Captain	RASC	MC
Cawley, J W	CSM	Royal Berks Regt	MM MC
Clarke, A	Pte	Royal Berks Regt	MM
Couldrey, V H	Captain	Royal Sussex	MC
Cousins, W	Pte	Royal Berks Regt	MM
Dainty, A J	Lt	Royal Field Artillery	MC
Davis, F		Lincolnshire Regt	MID
Dent, A C	Cpl	Royal Engineers	MM
Dowsett, E A	Sgt	King's Royal Rifle Corps	MM

Duggan, T	CQMS	Coldstream Guards	MID
Fairbanks, CAH	Lt	Royal Field Artillery	MC
Fairbanks, H N	Captain	Royal Field Artillery	MC
Fennell, Harold	Pte	Royal Berks Regt	RMStG
File, Charles E	Pte	Seaforth Highlanders	MM
Forbes, L H	Sgt	Royal Engineers	MID
Foster, George	Signaller		DCM
Fox, Charles E	CSM	Coldstream Gds	Croix de la Guerre DCM MM
Fuzzens, Fred	Cpl	Royal Engineers	MM, Bar MID
Fuzzens, Henry	Pte		DCM
Giles, Fredrick C	Sgt	1/4 Royal Berkshire	MM
Goding, F J	Sgt	Machine Gun Corps	DCM
Goodford, J H	Lt	Hampshire Regt	MID MC
Haines,	Sgt Major	Berks Yeomanry	DCM
Hawtree, Albert	Pioneer	Royal Engineers	DCM
Hester, G	Pte	Royal Berks Regt	MM
Higgs, G	Sgt	Hussars	MM
Hogg, Ralph	Pte	Royal Berks Regt	MM
Hollis, C H	Captain	East Surrey Regt	MC, Bar
Hughes, C	Driver	Royal Engineers	Cmdn
James, A	Pte	Royal Berks Regt	MM
Kadwill, George	Sgt	Canadian Forces	MM
Kemp, C M	Major	Manchester Regt	DSO
Kirk,	Trooper	Berks Yeomanry	DCM MID
Knibbs, K	Sgt	The Queen's Surrey Regt	DCM
Liddle	Sgt Major	Berks Yeomanry	MID
Lloyd, J H	L/Cpl	Oxon Bucks L I	MM
Lovejoy, F	Cpl		MM

MacCarthy, F	L/Cpl	Machine Gun Corps	MM
MacKray, W H	Sgt	Army Service Corps	DCM
Majoram, J E	Sgt	Royal Berks Regt	MM
Mason, F	Sgt	Royal Engineers	MSM
Meade, A E C	Gunner	Royal Field Artillery	MM
Meredith, A C	Lt	Machine Gun Corps	MC, Bar
Miles, E V	CQMS	Middlesex Regt	DCM
Morrow, F	Lt	Royal Engineers	MC
Orsgood, J	CSM	Royal Berks Regt	MM
Parking, G	Pte	Royal Berks Regt	MM
Parson, L E	Lt	Royal Berks Regt	MC
Pearce, James		RE	MM
Procter, J W	Gunner	Royal Garrison Artillery	MM
Ricketts, F T	Sgt	Royal Engineers	MM
Robertson, A	Captain	RAMC	MC
Sanders, Jack	Lt	Royal Fusiliers	MM
Short, G W	Sgt	2 Dragoon Gds	MM MID
Skinner, G G	Sgt Major	Royal Berks Regt	MM
Skinner, H G	Pte	Army Service Corps	MM
Smith, A G	Sgt	The Rifle Brigade	MM
Smith, J H	L/Cpl	Middlesex Regt	MM
Taylor, C H	Sapper	Royal Engineers	DCM
Taylor, O J	Major	Army Ordnance Dept	MID 3 times
Tedder, G	Sgt	Coldstream Gds	MM
Tedder, G M	Drill Sgt	Coldstream Gds	MM
Thomas, J	Sgt	Grenadier Guards	DCM, MM
Tindall, W J	Sgt	12th Boys Brigade KRRC	MM
Trinder, W J	Sgt	Royal Berks Regt	DCM
Tuston, T	Driver	Army Service Corps	MM

Varnham, W	L/Cpl		DCM
Vickers, A	Sgt	The Rifle Brigade	MM
Watson, W S	CSM	Coldstream Guards	MM
Way, S F	Gunner	Tank Corps	MM
Wellbelove, A W	CSM	Army Service Corps	MM
Wells, H T	Sgt	Royal Berks Regt	MM
Wood, Alfred	Pte	Royal Berks Regt	MM

DSO	Distinguished Service Order
DCM	Distinguished Conduct Medal
MC	Military Cross
MM	Military Medal
MSM	Meritorious Service Medal
MID	Mention in Despatches
Cmdn	Commendation
RMStG	Russian Medal of St George

Appendix II
Local Men on Windsor War Memorial

Anderson, J G Private
Anstey, W H Sergeant
Archer, T. Private
Archer, William Albert. Rifleman
Ash, F G. Private
Atkins, Michael Glover. Private
Attride, George James. Corporal
Axton, William Thomas. Private
Ayres, Frederick John. Private
Balchin, Arthur B. Private
Barry, William T Henry. Sergeant
Bates, Bernard E Petty Officer RN
Battye, Cyril Winyard. Lieutenant
Baverstock, Harold. Private
Belcher, H F. Private
Benyon, Godfrey B J. Lt Cdr R N
Biggs, A E. Corporal
Birrell, A A. Private
Birrell, W E. Private
Blackburn, W. Private
Blackford, William, Private
Blane, Alfred. Trooper
Bosher, George Jesse. Private
Bowcott, H. Private
Brant, B G L. Private
Breadmore, P. Private
Brennan, W. Rifleman
Brennan, William. Private
Brown, Alexander. Private
Brown, William Frederick. Private
Buckland, Henry John. L/Cpl
Buckland, Thomas Frank. Private
Bush, E F. Sergeant
Butler, G E. Private

Butler, Harry. Corporal
Butler, W R. Private
Caley, Hugh William. Captain
Caron, William George. Corporal
Chapman, Arthur Horace. Sergeant
Clark, Henry. Drummer
Clarke, William. Corporal
Coleman, W. Private
Collett, F. Private
Collins, Francis Winslow. L/Cpl
Colman, E. Private
Colman, F W A. Private
Compton, William G Trooper
Cook, George. Air Mechanic
Cooper, H E. Private
Cooper, J. Private
Cooper, Robert A. Gunner
Cornabie, Arthur E Corporal
Costa, H G. Private
Darby, John Sprake. Captain
Darville, Harold George. Sergeant
Davenport, Lancelot R Corporal
Davies, H G E. Private
Davies, W H. Private
Day, Alec. Lance Corporal
Day, H A. Private
Dean, Charles Edward. 2nd Lt
Dickinson, Henry George. Private
Digby, J H. Sergeant
Disbury, F W. Private
Dolby, Arthur Reginald. Officer's Steward RN
Dowsett, Ernest Arthur. Sergeant

Dowswell, Charles Victor. 2nd Lt
Draycott, Edward Arthur. Gunner
Draycott, Frederick E Private
Drye, Charles A. Private
Drye, Sidney John. Private
Dunford, Charles C Corporal
Durant, Noel Henry C F Lt
Eldridge, C. RSM
Eldridge, Walter. Private
Elkins, C V. Private
Elkins, John Bertram. L/Cpl
Elmer, F. Sergeant
Emony, W R. Rifleman
Evans, Fred V. Lance Corporal
Fennell, H T. Private
Ferris, Albert. Private
Finch, William M Corporal
Fleet, Ernest J. Sergeant
Folker, John Robert. Private
Fox, Charles Edward. CSM
Gaze, Jesse. Sergeant
Gilbert, P N. Private
Giles, Frederick C. Sergeant
Goddard, Stephen. Private
Goddard, William. Private
Goodchild, Albert George. L/Cpl
Goodford, Charles James H Lt
Goodman, C. Sergeant
Gray, Edward. Lance Corporal
Gray, F W. Private
Gray, W G. Rifleman
Green, W G. Private
Green, William Wesley. 2nd Lt
Groves, Fred. Private
Groves, George G. Private
Groves, George. Private
Groves, L G. Driver

Gundry, William. Private
Gunn, Norman. Lance Corporal
Hale, George Charles. Private
Harding, Albert Harry. Corporal
Harding. L F. CSM
Harnack, Frederick C Private
Hartwell, Ernest L Corporal
Haverly, Frederick Robinson. Able
Seaman RN
Hayward, Edgar Albert. Private
Hearn. Charles Bertie. Private
Heather, A E. Rifleman
Hedley, Gerald M Captain
Hessey, George. Private
Hester, James William. Private
Higgs, Alfred William. Private
Hiley, Herbert Henry. Trooper
Hillyer, Horace H. Private
Hines, Claude H. Rifleman
Holderness, S. Bombardier
Holloway, A T. Private
Holloway, R. Drum Corporal
Holton F V. Private
Holton, Frederick. Private
Holton, Thomas. Lance Corporal
Horton, F. Private
Humphreys, David Virgil. 2nd Lt
Iremonger, Alfred T Sergeant
James, John Henry. Private
Jefferies, Harold George. L/Cpl
Jeffries, Harry. Private
Jeffries, Thomas Henry. Private
Johnson, Edward F Private
Johnson, J H. Sergeant Cook
Johnstone, John. Captain
Johnstone, R M. Captain
Jones, Albert Edward. Private

Jones, P W F. Rifleman

Keeble, A V E. Private

Kelsey, James G Lance Sergeant

Kemp, Charles Matthew. Major

Kendall, A. Private

Kidd, F G. Driver

Kidd, W E. Lance Corporal

King, William Robert. Corporal

Kyte, John William. Bombardier

Larkin, W J. 2nd Lieutenant

Leader, A. Private

Leader, J. Lance Corporal

Ledgley, Ernest. Private

Ledgley, J P. Sapper

Leveson-Gower, William G G Lt.

Lewin, Frank H. Sergeant Major

Lewin, William. Private

Liddiard, George. Private

Lines, Samuel Arthur. Private

Long, Dennis. Private

MacMillan, William M. Private

Marsh, R J F. Corporal of Horse

Marten, Frederick L. Sergeant

Martin, Arthur Thomas. Private

Martin, W J B. Trooper

Mason, T. Drummer

May, George Henry. Private

McGrath, John. Private

Melvin, R A. Private

Melvin, R G. Private

Michie, J G. Corporal

Moody, L F. Private

Nicholls, H T. Private

Nott, E B. Private

Nott, W J. Private

Ottaway, William James. Private

Ottrey, J A. Private

Palfrey, Phillip Alexander. Private

Parsonage, Albert. Trooper

Parsonage, Edward. Stoker RN

Pert, James Edward. Private

Pert, W. Private

Petley, Thomas Harry. Private

Picking, R. Rifleman

Poole, Hugh Edward A 2nd Lt

Powers, Robert William. Private

Richards, William. Bombardier

Roberts, T. Private

Roebuck, A C. Private

Russell, Reginald Charles. Gunner

Sanders, J F. 2nd Lieutenant

Scarlett, Frederick George. Private

Scarlett, J. Private

Shanks, H J. Private

Sharman, Alfred W. Private

Sharp, Harry Frederick. Private

Short, George William. Sergeant

Shrimpton, Alfred. Sapper

Shurley, G F. Private

Skittles, E W. Private

Smith, A G. Sergeant

Smith, A L. Corporal

Smith, A. Gunner

Smith, F T. Rifleman

Smith, Henry James. L/Cpl

Smith, William Charles, Private

Somner, E. Private

Stevens, Arthur F Corporal

Stevenson, F A. Private

Stone, Ellis Robert Cunliffe, Lt

Stratton, Archer. Rifleman

Swain, Alfred. Private

Tame, Alfred. Lance Corporal

Tame, J. Private

Tame, W G. Corporal

Tamlin, T A. Private

Tanner, L A. Gunner

Taylor, A. Private

Thomas, James. Sergeant

Thorne, W T. Lance Corporal

Tindall, Walter John. Sergeant

Tracy, F E. Lance Corporal

Tracy, Hubert. Private

Tracy, J B. Bombardier

Trotter, Arthur Francis. Captain

Uglow, George H. Private

Venner, Walter. Lance Corporal

Vicary, Leonard James. Private

Vicary, Lionel. Sergeant

Vickers, James. Private

Vickers, R. Private

Wadeson, A R. WO1

Waite, George Douglas. Lt

Waite, John Henry. Corporal

Watson, W S. CSM

Weeks, Ernest Samuel. Private

Wellbelove, John V L/Bombardier

Wells, A W. Sapper

White, Arthur William. Private

White, G F. Private

White, Robert Edward.L/Cpl

Wickham, Henry O W Private

Wilkins, F. Lance Corporal

Wilkinson, Arthur Benjamin. Lt

Wilson, C. Gunner

Wilson, J. RSM

Wilson, R G. Corporal

Wilson, Robert. Trooper

Winckworth, A C. Private

Witney, Edward Alfred. Private

Wood, R H. Lieutenant

Woods, Alfred. Private

Woyen, A. Sergeant

Appendix III

Clewer War Memorial

Adey, Edward A. Rifleman
Ansell, William. Private
Anstiss, Percy R. Private
Ash, Frederick James. Private
Attride, George James. Corporal
Austin, Roland William. Private
Barnett, Horace John. Private
Bartlett, Frank. Private
Bedford, Walter Ernest. Driver
Beesley, Charles Victor. Corporal
Beesley, Harry James. Private
Belcher, H. Driver
Belcher, Walter William. Sergeant
Bennington, J S. Private
Betteridge, Frederick A J Private
Biggs, A E. Corporal
Biggs, Herbert Frederick. Private
Blackford, W R. Private
Blake, Sydney John. Private
Blake, William Henry. Corporal
Bosher, A. Driver
Bowcott, H. Private
Bowley, Luke. Lance Corporal
Bright, Alfred John. Private
Brown, Frederick William. Private
Buckel, Charles. Private
Bush, E F. Sergeant
Buttress, William Hilliam. Private
Butler, William Richard. Private
Carter, Albert Henry. Private
Carter, A H.
Church, Alfred Ernest. Rifleman
Church, Frank Reginald. Lance Corporal

Clarke, Alfred. Lance Corporal
Clarke, Edmund W Corporal
Clarke, H.
Cocking, Edward George. Private
Cocking, John H A Corporal
Colman, W. Private
Cooper, Charles Thomas. Private
Cooper, Ernest Walter. Private
Cooper, Harry. Private
Cornish, C P.
Coventry, W J. Private
Cox, Frederick. Private
Culvert, A E.
Darby, John Sprake. Captain
Deller, Frederick Ernest. Sapper
Deller, Harold William. Private
Dentry, L.
Denyer, Harold G Corporal
Dibbs, Frank. Private
Dunn, F J. Private
Eades, Frederick. Private
Eames, W A. Gunner
Elkes, John Henry. Able Seaman
Essen, R M.
Field, Maurice Alfred. Private
Finch, Joseph F C. Corporal
Fountain, Harold E Corporal
Francis, C E. Rifleman
Freeman, C.
Freston, Hugh Reginald. 2nd Lt
Fuller, Ernest Alfred. Marine
Fuller, George. Private
Garland, Frederick. L/Cpl
Garwood, Arthur L Bombardier

Goatley, Arthur. Private
Goddard, Stephen. Private
Goldswain, Francis W Private
Goodchild, Charles John. L/Cpl
Gower, Victor Alexander. Private
Groves, A W. Sergeant
Groves, John Isaac. Private
Habgood, Frederick Albert.
Leading Seaman
Habgood, George Edward. Private
Ham, R F. Sergeant
Harman, Percy Edwin. Private
Harper, Ernest Victor. Private
Hatch, John. Private
Hawthorn, Harold. Private
Haynes, Frederick George. Private
Hearn, Charles Bertie. Private
Hensley, William. Private
Herne, Alfred. Lance Corporal
Hester, James William. Private
Hibbert, Henry Walter. L/Cpl
Hiley, Herbert Henry. Private
Hill, F W. Corporal
Holt, Thomas. Lance Corporal
Horan, P G. Private
Horton, F. Private
Hughes, Herbert. Corporal
Ive, Edward. Gunner
Ive, George Robert. Private
Ives, William Henry. Sergeant
Jackson, Arthur. Private
Jillians, Alfred Edward. Private
Jordan, James Clark. Sergeant
Kershaw, Henry H Corporal
Knight, Burckham A S/Sergeant
Knight, William Thomas. L/Cpl
Lambert, Arthur John. L/Cpl

Lambert, William G Rifleman
Lawes, A C.
Laws, Herbert Victor. Stoker
Liddell, J.
Liddiard, George. Private
Lloyd, James Ambrose. Private
Long, W C D. Private
Lovegrove, Charles F Sapper
Marjoram, J E. Sergeant
Martin, Frederick Charles. Sapper
Maslin, J D B.
Mead, A E C.
Merkett, J. Rifleman
Miles, William T George. Private
Morgan, A.
Morgan, Thomas Charles. L/Cpl
Mott, Ernest B. Sapper
Mott, W J. Private
Nash, J H. Private
Newell, Anthony. Lance Corporal
Nixon, John. Private
Orsegood, William T Private
Pardoe, Horace. Private
Payne, Sidney. Corporal
Peaty, Frederick. CPO
Pegg, J W.
Perkins, E H R. Lance Corporal
Pert, James Edward. Private
Plumridge, Frederick. Private
Pomfret, F T. Driver
Ponting, Reginald Arthur. Private
Prime, John Charles. Private
Pusey, James Edward. Private
Quarterman, James E Private
Quarterman, John Arthur. Private
Quarterman, Thomas R L/Cpl
Rains, A J. Private

Roebuck, A C. Private
Rogers, C.
Russell, Joseph Barnes. Private
Russell, Reginald Charles
Bertram. Gunner
Scothern, James. Trooper
Scouse, J. Sergeant
Shurley, G F. Private
Shuttle, G H. Private
Simmonds, L E. Sapper
Slade, W A. Gunner
Smith, Henry James. Private
Squelch W J. Private
Stevens, Arthur F Corporal
Stevens, C A. Driver
Sumner, E. Private
Tame, Alfred. Lance Corporal
Tame, W G. Corporal
Taylor, G W. Driver
Taylor, H.
Taylor, William A H. Rifleman
Tegg, Arthur. Private
Tegg, C E. Private
Tegg, James Frederick. Private
Tinson, H. Gunner
Treadwell, A E.
Treadwell, J J. Private
Uglow, George H. Private
Vickers, James. Private
Vine, William Lewis. Private
Wake, W.
Wallace, A.
Wallace, George William. Private
Wallace, Henry Edward. Private
Ward, A.
Ward, John. Lance Corporal
Webb, Sidney Ernest. L/Cpl

Wells, Harry T. Sergeant
Welsh, John Henry. Able Seaman
Wetherall, W H.
Wicks, E J. Gunner
Wilkins, Alfred. Bugler
Wilkins, Ernest David. Private
Wilkins, Frederick. L/Cpl
Wilkins, William. Private
Wilkinson, William. Corporal
Williams, Francis. Private
Willings, T W. Private
Woolhouse, Charles E Private
Wren, Christopher G Private
Young, G A.

Appendix IV
Other War Memorials

Windsor Post Office War Memorial

Cordery, Edwin
Pierce, J H

Old Windsor War Memorial

Bagot, Edward, Lieutenant
Banner, Frank
Beesley, Dick Harry
Bogot, Edward. Lieutenant
Bowen, Charles
Branscombe, Harry
Branscombe, James
Branscombe, William
Carpenter, Harold Albert
Carter, William
Coltins, Alfred
Cordery, Edwin
Curtis, Thomas
Elliott, Charles
Giles, Robert
Haines, Albert
Hall, George
Heymer, Benjamin
Jacobs, Ernest Reginald
Knibbs, William James
Madden, Gerald Hugh James
Lt Col
Meshur, George
Middleton, William
Miles, James
Pimm, George
Pullein, William

Rennie, Guy. Captain
Rose, Horace
Simmons, Herbert Arthur
Spelling, John
Varnham, William
Vaughan Williams, Wyinn
Wood, Maurice

King Edward VII Hospital War Memorial

Surgeon Captain Angus McNab FRCS, London Scottish,

Lieutenant David G Watson, MBBC, RAMC,

Captain Archibald Cowe, MD, RAMC,

Eton Excelsior Rowing Club

White R E
Starling, L B
Mertz, W S
Jackson, C S
Hiley, H H
Le Grove, W
Blane, A
Bennett, S W J
Harnack, C

Royal Chapel War Memorial

Benn, Charlie. Sgt
Bowyer, Charles John. Pte
Canfer, R
Dibble, Robert John. Pte
Dixon, J
Edwards, W H
Folker, John Robert. Pte
Gibbons, L
Giles, Frederick Charles. Sgt
Gunn, N
Green, F J
Hartley, C P
Hewitt, F B
Holley, A
Horton, A W
Jones, F
Knight, William George Tpr
Lambdin, John Reginald
Llynch-Keogh,
J MacMillan, William
Pusey, Frederick W L/Cpl
Rogers, E R
Smith, P
Sirrett, G
Snatchfold, Graham
Spurrell, E J
Tanner, George
Walkinshaw, J
Warner, A E
Wrixon, A

Eton War Memorial

Ashman, Cyril
Ashman, Douglas
Baldwin, Peter
Batt, George
Beesley, John
Bolton, George
Buckland, Fred
Bunce, Arthur
Brown, Ernest
Browne, Alfred
Bruce, Angus
Bryant, Thomas
Caesar, Albert
Church, Frank
Clark, Jack
Clements, Albert
Clements, Charles
Colbourne, Fred
Cowley, James
Deacon, William
Delaperrelle, Alfred
Dobson, Horace
Dolan, Frank
Dolan, Frederick
Durnford, Richard
Edwards, Arthur
Fletcher, George
Fidler, Harry
Godwin, Charles
Groves, Ernest
Groves, Leonard
Hammerton, Charles
Hart, Percival
Hill, Henry
Hill, James

Hobrough, Robert
Holloway, Thomas
Holtum, Percy
Hutson, Frederick
Ironmonger, Alfred
Jackson, Cyril
Jones, William
Jordan, Ernest
Knight, Leo
Lipscoombe, David
Long, Ernest
Lyford, George
McPeak, Lemuel
Maguire, Albert
Marshall, Richard
Mead, William
Middleton, George
Miles, Charles
Mitchell, Herbert
Morgan, Fred
Moseley, Edward
Moss, Henry
Munday, Arthur
New, Herbert
Newell, James
Newell, Joseph
Newman, George
Oldham, Wilford
Page, Stanley
Pardoe, Henry
Parker, George
Payne, Walter
Percy, George
Pithers, Herbert
Plaistowe, Frederic
Prior, Edward Foss
Richards, Arthur

Ridgwell, James
Rowland, Frank
Rowland William
Sable, Henry
Sayer, Harry
Sellers, George
Somerville, Martin
Stallwood, Albert
Stroud, Maurice
Springford, Isaac
Springford, Joseph
Sutton, William
Thoday, Walter
Turner, George
Underwood, William
Warre-Cornish, Gerald
Wilson, George

Eton Wick and Boveney

Ashman, Cyril A
Ashman, Henry D
Baldwin, George P
Bolton, George E
Brown, Alfred
Brown, Ernest
Bruce, Angus
Buckland, Frederick T
Bunce, Arthur
Bryant, Thomas
Caesar, Albert
Church, Frank R
Clark, John C
Colbourne, Fred
Dobson, Horace C
Godwin, Charles F

Hammerton, Charles W
Hill, Henry C
Hoborough, Robert T
Iremonger, Arthur T
Jordan, Ernest
Knight, Peter
Miles, Charles
Quarterman, Harry
Moss, Henry
Newell, James J
Newell, Joseph
Payne, Walter W
Percy, George F
Pithers, Herbert
Richards, Arthur
Springford, Isaac
Springford, Joseph
Stallwood, Albert H

Appendix V
'A' Squadron, Berkshire Yeomanry War Memorial

Officers
Major E Gooch
Captain A Headington
Lt W V R Sutton
Lt R Hewer

NCOs
CGP Andrews
WE Baldwin
WTH Barry
H Batten
H D Champion
L R Davenport
A Else
E A Excell
J Fielder
F Gale
L M Hawes
A E Hilman
H G Jefferies
J Liddle
C J D Martin
W McNeil
J Scouse
H Waller

Privates
H D Ashman
H Barford
H Biggs
A Blane
P Bowyer
J Budd
W R Butler

W C Collins
C H P Courtney
W Durrant
W Eldridge
S H Ewins
E T Engell
F H Ford
A Freeman
W Goldswain
C F C Harnack
H H Hiley
R J Legg
F J Martin
W J B Martin
A Parsonage
A H Price
J Proctor
H Thorpe
F Webber
P J Wheeler
G Wooldridge

Appendix VI
Not On Any War Memorial

Name	Rank	Regt	Cemetery
Barnes, F A	Pte	East Surrey	Windsor
Bell, J C A	Capt	Royal Field Artillery	Pozieres
Bennet, E	Marine	RMLI	Arras
Bird, EL	Cpl	Somerset LI	
Blane, MGS	Lt	Cameron Highlaners	Loos
Brown, W T	Tpr	Life Guards	Windsor
Clancy, J A	S/Sgt	Coldstreams Guards	Windsor
Cunningham,EJC	Pte	Green Howards	
Davis, T H	Sgt	Royal Berks	Meaulte
Edwards, P V	Pte	Coldstream Guards	Windsor
Elder, J	L/Sgt	Coldstream Guards	St Pierre
Groves, P	Colonel	Inniskilling Fusiliers	Windsor
Grubb, T W	Bdr	Royal Garrison Artillery	Windsor
Hasley, A J	Pte	Bedforshire	
Hunt, C F	S/Sgt	Royal Garrison Artillery	Staglieno, Genoa, Italy
Jackson, C	Tpr	Berks Yeomanry	
James, J	Pte	Royal Sussex	Thiepval
Kidd, E J	Driver	Royal Engineers	Salonika
Lessimore, J	Pte	Scottish Rifles	Arras
Lewin, J A	Pte	Royal Berks	Tyne Cot
Lovelock, C	L/Cpl	Berks Yeomanry	Palestine
Luker, G H	L/Cpl	Royal Berks	Cambrai
Lundy, O	Sister		Italy
Mead, E C		Royal Field artillery	Windsor
Murphy, J	Sapper	Royal Engineers	Windsor
Nash, J H	Pte	Devonshire	Beaurevoire
Parker, A D	Cpl	Life Guards	Windsor
Pearman, J	Pte	Royal Fusiliers	Kemmel Chateau
Pendry, H J	Pte	Royal Berks	Etaples
Philips, A	Tpr	Life Guards	Windsor

Sellers, G A	Bdr	Royal Field Artillery	Hooge Crater
Shelton, W E	Pte	Coldstream Guards	Windsor
Singer, E	Rifleman	Rifle Brigade	Ploegsteert
Smith, J G	L/Cpl	London Irish Rifles	Arras
Squelch, W J	Pte	Wiltshire	Dublin
Symons,	L/Bdr	Royal Garrison Artillery	Windsor
Tack, R T	L/Cpl	Ox & Bucks	Tyne Cot
Taylor, F E	Pte	Coldstream Guards	Windsor
Thorn, W T	L/Cpl	Ox & Bucks	Tyne Cot
Tubb, E	Sgt	Royal Berks	
Warner, W G	Pte	Leicestershire	Sever
Webb, S E	Ptc	Royal Berks	Tyne Cot
Wender, W C	Sgt	Royal Berks	Oxford Rd Belgium
Wetherall, H J	Pte	Coldstream Guards	Duhallow
White, G E	Pte	Canadian Infantry	Bandhoek
Wilson, J	Cpl	London Scottish	Warlincourt Halte
Woodey, W	CSM	Royal Berks	Clewer

Appendix VII

Imperial Services College
Roll of Honour
1914-1918

Private John Grant Anderson (Camperdown, 1910-12)
City of Winnipeg Regiment Royal Canadian Contingent D: 13.10.15
Son of Lt. Col J S Anderson Military Knight, Windsor Castle

Lieutenant S. Armstrong (Lawrence, 1913-15)
Royal Artillery (attached Royal Flying Corps) D: 17.2.18

Second Lieutenant Arthur R D Bacon (Camperdown, 1912-14)
West Yorkshire Regiment/Royal Berks D: 25.4.17

Lieutenant Philip Burnet Bass (Camperdown, 1909-13*)
London Cheshire Regiment D: 1.7.16

Lieutenant T. A. Bidgood (Cambridge, 1910-14*)
Royal Garrison Artillery D: 28.10.17

Second Lieutenant Keith Ford Bishop (Cambridge, 1909-13*)
London Royal Garrison Artillery D:8.8.16

Lieutenant Edward Bulmer Whicher Boileau, (Lawrence, 1912-15)
London Dorset Regiment D: 3.10.18

Lieutenant Arthur Vivian Burlton, (Lawrence, 1912-13)
Royal Flying Corps D: 30.8.17

Second Lieutenant N. L. Collins, (Lawrence, 1912-12)
Royal Artillery/Royal Sussex Regiment D: 15.8.16

Lieutenant Charles Rollo Cooch, (Cambridge, 1908-13*)
Border Regiment D: 17.12.14

Corporal Lancelot Reginald Davenport, (Camperdown, 1905-12*)
Berkshire Yeomanry Turkey D: 21.8.15

Second Lieutenant R. Davis, (Camperdown, 1914-15)
Indian Infantry Iraq D: 10.1.17

Second Lieutenant L C. Findlay, (Lawrence, 1912-14)
Yorkshire & Lancashire Regiment   No record found

Captain C. C. Ford, (Camperdown, 1908-12*)
Somerset Light Infantry   D: 2.7.16

Lieutenant Arthur Hugh C Galbraith, (Cambridge, 1911-15*)
Royal Artillery   D: 9.9.18
Son of Sir William, K C B

Captain John Hartley Growse, (Camperdown, 1909-12*)
Northern Regiment/Northamptonshire Regiment   D: 1.4.18
Was awarded sword of honour at Sandhurst

Lieutenant P. R. Hale, (Lawrence, 1912-15)
Royal Naval Air Service   D: 16.10.18

Lieutenant John Dampier Hallifax, (Camperdown, 1909-13*)
Green Howards   D: 17.5.15

Second Lieutenant Arthur A S Hamilton, (Camperdown, 1908-12*)
Royal Berkshire Regiment   D: 24.11.16

Captain Howard Jack Hamilton-Cox, (Cambridge, 1910-12*)
Royal Marines Artillery   D: 22.10.17

Second Lieutenant C. F. B. Hodgins, (Camperdown, 1908-12*)
Wiltshire Regiment   D: 25.9.25
M I Despatches

Lieutenant Arthur Henry Augustus Jacob, (Lawrence, 1912-13)
Royal Fusiliers London Regiment   D: 16.7.16

Lieutenant Jasper Moore Mayne, (Lawrence, 1911-13*)
Royal Fleet Auxiliary   D: 9.5.15
Brother of:

Lieutenant Victor Charles Moore Mayne, (Lawrence, 1911-13*)
South Wales Borderers   D: 19.2.16

Second Lieutenant R. C. Paske, (Camperdown, 1913-14)
Royal Flying Corps   D: 22.3.18

Lieutenant Henry Drummond Payne, (Lawrence, 1912-14)
East Yorkshire Regiment   D: 20.3.15

Private Gerald Ferguson Peacocke, (Lawrence, 1913-15)
The Buffs   D: 9.8.17

Captain Walter Hamilton Riach, (Lawrence, 1912-14)
London Cameron Highlanders   D: 5.5.18

Captain Percy Richard Oliver Trench, (Lawrence, 1912-12)
The Queen's Regiment   D: 25.1.17
M I Desp.

Lieutenant Geoffrey Bernard Vores, (Camperdown, 1908-12*)
Lancashire Fusiliers   D: 4.6.15

Lieutenant L. D. Wand, (Lawrence, 1912-12)
East Lancashire Regiment   No record found

Captain N. West, MC, (Lawrence, 1912-12)
Royal Berkshire Regiment   D: 17.2.17

Lieutenant Amor Lowry Corray Wintle MC, (Lawrence, 1912-13)
Royal Inniskilling Fusiliers   D: 22.8.17
Father Indian Army, retired.

* Also at United Services College

The above named gave their lives in The Great War and were pupils at Imperial Service College, Windsor, in the preceding years.

The list above has been compiled by an OCR process from the ISC's own records. In addition the abbreviations used have been expanded to their full equivalents. Whilst every care has been taken, we ask that any apparent errors be reported to the editor.
Source: The Imperial Service College Register, 1956.

Bibliography and Sources

Books

Austin, E H and Gammon S, *The History of Windsor County Boys' School 1908-1929,* published by Luff & Son, 1929.

Begent, Peter J and Chesshyre, Hubert, *The Most Noble Order of the Garter 650 Years,* Spink, 1999.

Blanch, John, *Gowrie VC,* Barbara Blanch, 1998.

Bond, Frank, *Their Names Shall Be Carved In Stone,* Amadeus Press, 2000.

Cull, Ian, *The 2nd Battalion Royal Berkshire Regiment in World War One,* Tempus Publishing, 2005.

Gliddon, Gerald, *Somme 1916: A Battlefield Companion,* Sutton Publishing Ltd, 2006 .

Haythornthwaite, Philip J, *The World War One Source Book,* Brockhampton Press, 1998.

Hedges, Beryl, *Windsor in old Photographs,* Alan Sutton Publishing Ltd, 1988.

Hedges, Beryl, *Around Windsor in old Photographs,* Alan Sutton Publishing Ltd, 1992.

Hunt, Derek, *Windsor Victoria Cross Exhibition Programme,* published by author, 1998

Hunt, Derek, *Valour Beyond All Praise: Harry Greenwood VC,* published by author, 2003.

James, Brigadier E A, *British Regiments 1914-1918,* Naval & Military Press Ltd reprint.

McAuley, J E, *The Hospital at Windsor,* Oxley & Son, 1960.

Marson, Pamela and Mitchell, Brigitte, *Windsor Guildhall: History and Tour,* Friends of the Windsor & Royal Borough Museum, 2011.

Petrie, F Loraine, *The Royal Berkshire Regiment (Princess Charlotte of Wales's) 1914-1918,* Naval & Military Press Ltd reprint.

Rose, Kenneth, *King George V*, Weidenfeld & Nicolson, 1983.

Verey, Anthony; Sampson, Stuart; French, Andrew; and Frost, Simon, *The Berkshire Yeomanry: 200 Years of Yeoman Service*, Alan Sutton Publishing Ltd, 1994 .

Windsor Local History Group (WLHG), *Windsor: A Thousand Years*, WLHG, 2001.

Newspapers and periodicals

Windsor, Eton & Slough Express
Slough Observer
The Times
Windlesora

Other Sources

Census Returns for 1901 and 1911
The Ken Shepherd Archive, RBWM
Mitchell. Brigitte, *Problems of a Garrison Town, Windsor 1815-1855*, unpublished Ph.D.
Royal Windsor Website
Commonwealth War Graves Commission
Forces War Records
Anestry.com.uk

Index

Barracks: See Combermere Barracks; Victoria Barracks;

Bates, Bernard Emile 49

Beaurevoire 335

Belgium 15, 16, 22, 41, 50, 63, 84, 109, 114, 116, 123, 128, 139, 162, 197, 219, 220, 225, 228, 231, 259, 308, 336

Berkshire Yeomanry 4, 5, 7, 11, 16, 19, 35, 36, 48, 50, 62, 74, 75, 84, 102, 103, 104, 115, 124, 125, 129, 130, 165, 168, 219, 222, 223, 237, 241, 242, 248, 303, 306, 318, 334, 337, 341

Birrell, A A 48

Birrell, W E 48

Boxing 156, 267

Brandhoek 50

Branscombe, Harry 34

Branscombe, James 34

Branscombe, William Frederick 33

Brie 224

British Red Cross 58, 72, 213, 214, 215, 216, 255, 276

Brooks, Oliver 187, 188, 192, 193, 194, 195, 196

Browning, Charles Hunter 24, 233

Bucquoy 227

Burnett, Leslie 219

Businesses: See A C Caffyn; Aldridge and Son; Caleys; Castle Hill Stores; Creaks; Darville & Son; Dyson & Son; E V Tull; Goddards; Herberts Supply Stores; International Stores; Oxley & Son; Russell and Co; White Hart Hotel; Wills & Son; Windsor Steam Laundry; Windsor Motor Coaches; W J Daniel & Co; Wood's Pharmacy;

C

Cairo 132

Caleys 18, 51, 76, 87, 269, 279

Cambrai 73, 152, 335

Camm, F J 53

Camm, Sydney 53

Canada 18, 36, 43, 50, 84, 216, 271, 303

Canadian Red Cross Hospital 91

Carnoy 184

Carter, Councillor William 20, 29, 46, 58, 78, 247, 249

Castle Hill Stores 270

Cave, Reg 48

Cemeteries and Memorials: See Abbeville; Arras; Aubigny; Beaurevoire; Brandhoek; Brie; Bucquoy; Cambrai; Carnoy; Chatham Naval Memorial; Clewer War Memorial; Crucifix Corner; Datchet War Memorial; Doullens; Etaples; Eton War Memorial; Faubourg D'Amiens; Gezaincourt; Grandcourt Road; Haslar Royal Naval Cemetery; Hebuterne; Helles; Jerusalem Memorial: Karasouli; Kemmel Chateau; Kut-el-Amara; La Clytte; Le Touret; Loos; Maroilles; Mendingham; Menin Gate; Mont Huon; Old Windsor War Memorial; Pheasant Wood; Ploegsteert; Portsmouth Naval Memorial; Pozieres Memorial; Putney Vale; Queant Road; Staglieno; St Pierre; Strand; Struma; St Vaast Post; Tehran; Terlincthun; Thiepval; Tyne Cot; Varennes; Vermelles; Villers-Bretonneux; Windsor Cemetery; Windsor War Memorial;

Charities: See British Red Cross; Order of St John; Royal Berkshire Regiment Tobacco Pipe and Cigarette Fund; Serbian Relief Fund;

Chatham Naval Memorial 63

Churches: See All Saints' Church, Dedworth; Holy Trinity Church; Royal Chapel; Windsor Parish Church

Cinema. See Windsor Cinema; Windsor Empire

Clarence Road 28, 214, 311

Clewer 4, 18, 20, 27, 33, 48, 49, 52, 61, 63, 64, 65, 70, 73, 74, 75, 82, 83, 95, 106, 110, 128, 134, 139, 145, 150, 153, 154, 184, 196, 197, 214, 221, 223, 245, 276, 277, 278, 279, 282, 283, 285, 286, 287, 293, 299, 300, 302, 318, 327, 336

Clewer Horticultural Society 20

Clewer St Stephen Intermediate 293

Clewer War Memorial 4, 64, 83, 223, 299, 302, 318, 327

Coldstream Guards 7, 17, 26, 30, 31, 32, 35, 39, 43, 50, 54, 60, 72, 106, 107, 108, 119, 120, 133, 187, 193, 194, 195, 196, 236, 257, 265, 267, 281, 282, 283, 292, 320, 322, 335, 336

Combermere Barracks 5, 7, 12, 30, 39, 54, 106, 108

Commendation 61, 259

Conscription 32, 200, 201, 205, 245

Cranbourne 30

Creaks 9, 269, 270, 271

Great Western Railway 15, 17, 41, 46, 72, 91, 222
Greece 34, 35, 45, 64, 142
Greenwood, Harry 7, 188, 191, 192, 340
Grenadier Guards 49, 83, 115, 131, 135, 189, 194, 241, 321
Grenfell, Francis O 233
Grenfell, Gerald W 233
Grenfell, Julian 232, 233
Grenfell, Riversdale N 25, 233
Grenfell, William Henry, Lord Desborough 232
Guildhall 3, 8, 16, 18, 20, 21, 29, 43, 45, 54, 58, 67, 68, 72, 78, 80,
    91, 198, 200, 202, 214, 247, 248, 249, 253, 255, 257, 266, 289,
    306, 308, 340

H

Habgood, Albert 295
Habgood, Bernard 295
Habgood, Ernest 295
Habgood, Frederick 295
Habgood, George 298
Habgood, Victor 299
Hainaut 128
Haslar Royal Naval Cemetery 298
Hawes, Len 35
Hebuterne 243
Helles 84, 103, 223
Herberts Supply Stores 269, 274
Hiley, Herbert Henry 8, 84, 103,223
Hindenburg 152, 159, 167, 190, 224
HMS *Agamemnon* 178
HMS *Brilliant* 19
HMS *Cornwallis* 35
HMS *Fearless* 110
HMS *Hampshire* 42, 49
HMS *Implacable* 33
HMS *King Edward VII* 178
HMS *Midge* 295
HMS *Recruit* 63
HMS *Superb* 35

HMS *Tara* 169
HMS *Tipperary*, 142
HMS *Victory* 19, 298
HMS *Wrestler* 179
Hobbs, Charlotte 51
Holbourn, Stanley 241
Holland 168, 171, 172, 173, 262, 271
Holy Trinity Church 37, 80, 217, 267, 300
Home Park 41, 57, 82
Hore-Ruthven, Alexander 188, 196
Hospitals. See Ascot Hospital; Canadian Red Cross Hospital; Queensmead VAD Hospital; King Edward VII Hospital; Princess Christians British Red Cross Hospital; Princess Christiams Hospital and District Nursing and Maternity Home; Queen Mary's Hospital; St Andrews Hospital; Windsor War Hospital Supply Depot;
Household Cavalry 5, 7, 11, 12, 17, 106, 108, 113

I

Iceland 179
Imperial Camel Corps 169, 174, 175, 306
Imperial Service College 81, 83, 339
India 7, 15, 34, 49, 101, 121, 133, 147, 179, 213, 221, 233, 293
International Stores 8
Iraq 115, 132, 244, 337
Irish Guards 221

J

Jefferies, H G 8, 35, 103, 241, 242
Jeffries, Harold 202, 244
Jerusalem Memorial 141
Johnson, Edward Frederick 307
Jutland 14, 142

K

Karasouli 64
Kemmel Chateau 84
Kemp, Charles Matthew 234
Kendall, Mrs G 252, 325

Kidd, F G 35
Kidd, W E 35
King's Own Yorkshire Light Infantry 189
King's Royal Rifle Corps 159, 189, 319
King Edward VII Hospital 3, 8, 57, 73, 90, 95, 99, 100, 207, 208, 211, 213, 238, 248, 268, 292, 330
King George V 6, 11, 22, 67, 77, 89, 90, 97, 191, 192, 210, 238, 341
Kirkee 221
Kitchener, Lord 7, 17, 18, 42, 90, 134, 183, 200, 227, 247, 257, 298
Knibbs, H G 19
Knibbs, James 19
Knibbs, William J 19
Kut-el-Amara 121

L

La Clytte 220
Lambert, Arthur 245
League of Honour 20, 247
Le Cateau 17, 109, 111, 234
Ledgley, Ernest 245
Le Touret 34
Life Guards 5, 6, 7, 17, 18, 28, 29, 30, 35, 41, 43, 45, 65, 66, 72, 80, 81, 83, 106, 108, 211, 257, 266, 335
Loos 75, 115, 189, 192, 194, 195, 302, 308, 335
Luff, Councillor Thomas Edmund 303
Luff, Edmund 303
Luff, Henry 303
Luff, Thomas (Tom) 4, 9, 303, 305
Lundy, Sister O 252, 335

M

Maroilles 24
Mendingham 63
Menin Gate 114, 149, 225
Mentioned in Despatches 196, 220
Meritorious Service Medal 322
Mesopotamia 14, 115, 121, 136, 141, 146, 147, 152, 165, 178, 202, 221, 236, 244, 246

HMS *Tara*; HMS *Tipperary*; HMS *Victory;* HMS *Wrestler;*

Slim, James 32

Slough, Eton and *Windsor Observer* 15, 16

Smith's Lawn 45, 92, 96

Smith, J H 48, 50

Somme 3, 6, 7, 34, 41, 42, 45, 49, 74, 84, 94, 136, 143, 146, 150, 155, 162, 163, 178, 181, 182, 183, 184, 185, 187, 190, 195, 209, 220, 225, 228, 245, 261, 299, 301, 313, 314, 340

Spanish Flu 4, 213, 291+,

Sport. See Ascot Racecourse; Boxing; Cricket; Eton Excelsior Rowing Club; Football; Royal Windsor Racecourse; Swimming; Windsor and Eton Football Club

Stag and Hounds 284

Staglieno 335

St Andrews Hospital 214

St Edward RC School 49

Stevens, Arthur Frederick 4, 9, 300, 301

St Nazaire 112

St Pierre 335

Strand 228

Streets

  Alma Road 32, 40, 65, 205, 234, 311

  Clarence Road 28, 214, 311

  Denmark Street 21

  Goswell Road 35, 311

  High Street 41, 76, 104, 168, 198, 227, 249, 270, 284

  Osborne Road 22, 76, 198, 286

  Peascod Street 5, 15, 22, 41, 48, 71, 75, 79, 81, 87, 88, 123, 160, 165, 202, 211, 259, 261, 272, 276, 277, 278, 282, 284

  River Street 24, 34, 79, 97, 110, 144

  Sheet Street 51, 105, 139

  South Place 35

  St Leonard's Road 35, 50, 63, 88, 106, 135, 207, 214, 225, 303

  Sun Passage 34, 164

  York Road 35, 84

St Vaast Post 228

Sumner, Alfred George 35

Sumner, Frank 35

W